"HE HAS KICKED UP A CREATIVE STORM IN THE AD WORLD
. . . AND MADE A MAJOR IMPACT ON THE BUYING HABITS
OF THE NATION."   —*Wall Street Journal*

Terrific advertising is what this book is about. The theory and
the practice. How to come up with the Big Idea and how to
sell it first to the business executive who has to buy it and then
to the public that represents the bottom line. Nobody in America
today is better qualified than George Lois to write a book like
this. Nobody could be more outrageously iconoclastic and fear-
lessly frank in writing it. And no one in the advertising trade or
the business world can afford not to read it and profit from
it—not to mention enjoying it every wonderfully entertaining
page of the way.

"George Lois may be nearly as great a genius of mass communications as he acclaims himself to be."   —*New York Times*

"This arrogant maverick . . . has done as much as anyone to
change modern advertising."   —*Louisville Courier-Journal*

"Lois is an original. He seems crazy enough and tough enough
to shake up an entire system."   —*Chicago Tribune*

"He is plugged into the American dream and nightmare. He
knows what he wants, therefore he knows what people want."
—*Los Angeles Times*

GEORGE LOIS is America's premier art director, a member of both
the Art Directors Hall of Fame and the Creative Hall of Fame. The son
of a Greek immigrant florist, raised in the Bronx, Lois is chairman
and creative director of the Lois/GGK ad agency in New York, Chicago,
and sixteen cities around the world. He is the author of *The Art of
Advertising*, which has been praised as the bible of mass communications.

BILL PITTS has co-authored several books with Lois on advertising
and communications.

What's the Big

How to Win with Outrageous Ideas (That Sell!)

George Lois
with Bill Pitts

A PLUME BOOK

PLUME
Published by the Penguin Group
Penguin Books USA Inc., 375 Hudson Street, New York, New York 10014, U.S.A.
Penguin Books Ltd, 27 Wrights Lane, London W8 5TZ, England
Penguin Books Australia Ltd, Ringwood, Victoria, Australia
Penguin Books Canada Ltd, 10 Alcorn Avenue, Toronto, Ontario, Canada M4V 3B2
Penguin Books (N.Z.) Ltd, 182-190 Wairau Road, Auckland 10, New Zealand

Penguin Books Ltd, Registered Offices: Harmondsworth, Middlesex, England

Published by Plume, an imprint of New American Library, a division of
Penguin Books USA Inc. This is an authorized reprint of a hardcover edition published by
Doubleday, a division of Bantam Doubleday Dell Publishing Group, Inc.

First Plume Printing, January, 1993
10 9 8 7 6 5 4 3 2 1

REGISTERED TRADEMARK—MARCA REGISTRADA

LIBRARY OF CONGRESS CATALOGING-IN-PUBLICATION DATA
Lois, George.
    What's the big idea? / George Lois with Bill Pitts.
        p.   cm.
    Includes index.
    ISBN 0-452-26938-5
    1. Advertising. 2. Marketing. I. Pitts, Bill. II. Title.
HF5823.L745   1993
659.1—dc20   92-21351
                                                          CIP

Original hardcover design by Richard Oriolo

Printed in the United States of America

BOOKS ARE AVAILABLE AT QUANTITY DISCOUNTS WHEN USED TO PROMOTE PRODUCTS OR SERVICES.
FOR INFORMATION PLEASE WRITE TO PREMIUM MARKETING DIVISION, PENGUIN BOOKS USA INC.,
375 HUDSON STREET, NEW YORK, NEW YORK 10014.

To the sweet memory
of my son Harry Joseph Lois
1958–1978

Section One
Create the Big Idea

Section Two
Nourish the Big Idea

Section Three
Execute the Big Idea

Section One

Create the Big Idea

Will he go for
the $64,000 question?

THINKING
OF
GOING
TO
LOS ANGELES?

FLY AMERICAN AIRLINES

AIRCOACH

1

A Thoughtful
Definition
of Our Subject

Advertising is poison gas

Some time ago I appeared as a panelist on a television talk show to discuss advertising along with two moguls in our business. In his customary investigatory style, the program's host, David Susskind, got to the heart of the matter. He looked each of us in the eye and asked, "Gentlemen, what is advertising?"

My colleagues on the panel were pillars of the advertising establishment, the head honchos of two enormous advertising agencies—big-name shops with awesome hierarchies, precise divisions of labor—plus an ethic and an attitude about our profession that was entirely different from mine, one which clearly defined their structured enterprises as "marketing agencies."

One of my fellow panelists tackled the question with an extraordinarily detailed answer. Sounding very much like an emeritus professor in a college course on advertising, he traced the odyssey of a typical product from its original concept to the supermarket shelf. He took us through the classic marketing steps—defining the product, profiling the consumer, research procedures, competitive analyses, category precedents, media strategy—but said almost nothing about *advertising*. In fact, he concluded his "definition" by explaining that when all these steps had been taken, his agency would then create the advertising, which would say, in effect: "Here is our product—please buy it!" The second expert witness, clearly impressed, complimented his colleague, praising his summary as a succinct explanation of advertising.

As I listened to these two good ol' Establishment boys, I sank steadily into my chair and my eyes rolled in dismay. Susskind may have thought I was ill (and indeed I was). "Why are you making those faces, George?" he asked. "Don't you *agree* with these gentlemen?"

I leaned forward to the edge of my chair and said, "I think these guys and me are in a different business."

Susskind was titillated by my assuming the role of provocateur. With relish he asked me, "Well, what do *you* think advertising is?"

"Advertising," I replied, "is poison gas. It should bring tears to your eyes. It should unhinge your nervous system. It should knock you out!"

I meant those words as an expression of hubris that would set me apart instantly from the Establishment. I had my persona to preserve—as the bad boy of Madison Avenue, as its most incorrigible enfant terrible, as the industry's personification of advertising temerity—and I had succeeded, almost extravagantly. My zinger, picked up by the wire services, was promptly printed in major newspapers across the nation. "Adman Says Advertising Is Poison Gas," they headlined, accurately. I suppose the phrase *poison gas* is probably excessive and may be a harsh image, but I regard it as forgivable hyperbole because it certainly describes the powerful *possibilities* of advertising. Great advertising should have the impact of a punch in the mouth. And great advertising should never kneel or genuflect or plead for the sale. It should ask, without literally asking, "Do you get the message?" And the viewer should answer, without literally answering, "Yeah, I got it!" All this can be accomplished with The Big Idea that packs the power of a large explosive—but none of this can result from a *scientific* process.

Obviously, all great advertising must be part of an intricate mosaic that includes extensive research, market planning, media analysis, and all the building blocks of marketing. But these disciplines are worthless if the advertising sucks.

Plato and Spinoza may have been able to describe the *reasoning* process that should lead to great advertising, but they could never have created poison gas—or great advertising that bowls you over.

About a year ago, I recounted this story to two executives from Doubleday, who suggested to me over lunch that their company would like to publish a "how-to" book on advertising—one that might unravel its mysteries for the growing numbers of students and practitioners of advertising, communications and marketing, as well as for the vast general public that "consumes" advertising every day. The poison gas story didn't deter them. I decided to do this book when they explained to me they wanted a fresh point of view that would offer a distinct break-away from the David Ogilvy "school" of advertising with its well-behaved words, benign imagery, and rigid do's and dont's.

What's the Big Idea is the result of that beguiling proposal, although I must caution you at the outset: this is a "how-to" book with a lot of *what* and *why*. The lessons to be learned here can lead to new insights into the mystique of advertising—but these are lessons that derive from the wide variety of experiences that have shaped my own life as an advertising professional. They are not the lessons of a dispassionate scholar. Many of these experiences spring from a passionate "calling" I have felt since my childhood to expand the very meaning of life through audacious use of symbols, images and ideas. This may sound like a pompous claim, but it is in fact modest: Advertising, when pursued with love and talent, especially talent, can become a mass language that explains and illuminates the meaning of daily life through powerful and succinct images and ideas.

Is it possible for me to provide a formula or a set of rules on advertising? I don't think so. But I do believe that by studying my triumphs and failures, in reliving with me my year-in, year-out hurdling of the corporate barricades to give life to my work, it is possible to heighten one's sensitivities to advertising's extraordinary power, to inspire people to reach for great work rather than settle for simply "good" communication or "safe" marketing.

Great advertising comes down to The Big Idea, although I never *create* the ideas that characterize my best work. I snare them from the air as they float around me. (Michelangelo said that a sculpture is imprisoned in a block of marble, and only a great sculptor can set it free.) The common denominator of all my work is an unremitting quest for The Big Idea because The Big Idea—a surprising solution to a marketing problem, expressed in memorable verbal and/or graphic imagery—is the authentic source of communicative power. My ancestor Plato defined idea *(eidos)* as a mental image. He claimed that idea was synonymous with quality, because a thing should be as stunning in reality as it is in our mental image of it. *Idea* to him meant almost the same as *ideal.* A big idea is one that picks up force and speed because its element of surprise changes a habit or a point of view. When you come through with such an idea it has the force of poison gas. The right idea in advertising attacks the mind and body. It can floor you. And big ideas can originate from a variety of sources. They can often derive their electricity from that enormous reservoir of popular culture—the arts, sports, politics, history, today's headlines; others simply use images and design to express a clear, compelling message. In today's world of mass communications there are few ideas, big or small. Mostly, what passes for ideas are a few flashes of style, not substance.

Sounds mystical, perhaps, but ideas in advertising happen to be ignited by the sparks and sounds of our daily experiences as citizens of an expressive democracy. When I was a student at New York's High School of Music and Art, I was mesmerized by the work of the American painter Stuart Davis, who magically simplified forms and reduced them to a system of flat planes and geometric shapes. Davis was also intoxicated by the dynamism and electricity of New York City. He was a precursor of the modern art director, endowed with a peripheral vision that could visually collect subway signs, tabloid headlines, gas pumps, spark plug ads, the shapes and colors of passing trucks and so many of the other nuances of daily life. I learned that Davis, one of the first multimedia personalities, painted while playing the radio and reading newspapers. This came to me as almost a revelation, explaining much of my own life to me.

As the son of a Greek florist in The Bronx, I grew up taking in the roars from Yankee Stadium, the nonstop shriek of elevated subway trains, the sweet staccato voice of Mayor Fiorello LaGuardia reading the comics on radio during a newspaper strike. It was more natural for me to become an advertising professional than inherit my papa's florist shop in the Irish Kingsbridge neighborhood of The Bronx.

Clues were revealed in my life's journey from The Bronx to my present role as the perennial maverick in the world of advertising: I spent every available second of my early years drawing. I drew, I drew, I drew —on every paper surface from the margins of the *Daily News* to the wrappings in our florist shop. When I was not yet twelve years old, I designed a travel poster on Switzerland in my art studies class that flouted conventional communication. Alongside a photograph of the Swiss Alps I inserted an illustration of Swiss cheese in the shape of one of the Alps. Graphically, without any words, a big idea was communicated—with a piece of imagery you could taste! But alas, my teacher, an otherwise inspiring force in my life, insisted that the cheese and the mountain were not in correct proportion.

For me, The Big Idea has always been synonymous with the audacious. Later, as a student at Pratt Institute in a class on Bauhaus-inspired design, we were asked to create an original design based on the rectangle on our 18×24 pads. I readily saw a fresh new answer, and for the entire class period I stared at the pad with my arms folded. As the test drew to an end my incensed teacher parked herself behind me, putting the heat on me to come up with my rectangular design. In the last seconds I reached for my pencil and, at the lower left of the pad, signed my name. The teacher was furious and I flunked the test, but that didn't matter because I knew I had delivered The Big Idea: the 18×24 blank white sheet was the ultimate rectangular design. (My maverick solution was intensified by the chutzpah and theater of not lifting a finger for two hours—a vintage example of the style I've followed throughout my adult career: create The Big Idea, present it theatrically.)

These were the early stirrings of a belief in the creative power to make anything happen. The genuinely talented communicator must be armed with that attitude, with an unshakable belief that every problem, from the seemingly insignificant to the monumental, embodies a surprising solution—a big idea. Some people run away from problems; I rush to embrace them. You'll see this in my experiences throughout this book. To believe in this method of working is to share my deep belief that cause and effect make up the inexorable equation of creativity, that everything is possible, that you *can* go to heaven.

In 1954, fresh from the Korean War, I was cutting my teeth at CBS. The network's historic television quiz show "The $64,000 Question" drew such a massive audience that movies across America closed their doors the night of the telecast. An ad was needed to promote the appearance of a priest-contestant who had reached the jackpot stage. He could pocket the $32,000 he had won thus far (over several appearances that had made him as well known as President Eisenhower) or he could go for the $64,000. I did a simple ad of the priest's face, which everyone knew, with the question that everyone was asking: *"Will he go for the $64,000?"* That was the entire ad. I had left out the CBS Eye—deliberately—as well as the channel and the time. The priest was so famous, I wanted the ad to look like a news story. The ad exuded such confidence that by leaving out all the usual nitty-gritty we were telling the world we knew how famous this incredible show happened to be. The morning the ad ran, Dr. Frank Stanton, president of CBS, went apopleptic at my defiance in omitting the network's hallowed logo and time slot. But by lunchtime, CBS had received so many congratulatory calls on the power of the ad that its big idea panache came through to Stanton. (Sometimes the big idea is expressed by *omitting* information.)

A year later, in my first ad for an advertising agency (the late, unlamented Lennen & Newell), I was asked to prepare a message to promote New York–to–Los Angeles flights on American Airlines. At that moment, New York was traumatized by rumors that Brooklyn Dodgers owner Walter O'Malley would soon move the franchise to California. In my ad I showed a ballplayer in a Brooklyn Dodgers hat peering west under the headline, *"Thinking of going to Los Angeles?"* with a bold logo of American Airlines slapped over the bottom half of his face. This timely message angered the Dodgers' front office, but everyone caught my double entendre—they understood that I had brought the number one issue in people's minds into normally dull airline destination ads. (Bookings on American to Los Angeles jumped the next day—and, alas, the treacherous O'Malley did indeed take flight with our beloved bums.)

I mention these artifacts of my early years to disabuse any reader who might conclude that my dealings with the megafamous (Robert Kennedy, Joe Namath, Betty Grable, Muhammad Ali, Malcolm Forbes, Frank Sinatra, James Beard, Donald Trump, Salvador Dali, Edward Koch, Mickey Mantle, Joan Collins, Patrick Ewing, et al.), somehow give my work an extra dimension . . . and therefore, my creative challenges are in another league from a creative director in, say, Indianapolis. Not so. Every challenge I confront, from a simple letterhead to a network television campaign, elicits the same creative intensity, the same determination to evolve a simple, stunning piece of imagery that says it all—not only with a clarity of communication but with a richness of meaning. The thought process and the attitude that insists on portraying a rectangle as an 18×24 pad are identical to those inner forces that have enabled me to create the *"I want my MTV!"* television campaign that turned on millions of young people.

This process comes so naturally to me because I have an insatiable hunger to see, hear, taste, and experience as many of these stimuli as my mind and body can absorb. On an average Saturday, for example, I'll go to as many as seven current movies, spending about ten minutes per flick to get its essence. Most are not worth the cost of admission, but I find all movies interesting because there's always *something* that catches the eye or ear. Sometimes I drag along my wife Rosemary, so she can never complain that I don't take her to the movies. We then invade museums and art galleries, where I can drink in the beauties of art from all sources. While I'm an aficionado and serious collector of primitive sculpture (tribal art of Africa, Oceania, Northwest Coast Indians, etc.), I regard myself as an irrepressible eclectic, with an unslakable thirst for all kinds of "things" created by human hands through the millennia. *New York* magazine called me a "parlor primitive" when their reporter saw the unclassifiable collection of objects in my Greenwich Village apartment—Cycladic figures, Eskimo masks, Maori sculpture, Tiffany lamps, an Easter Island skeleton figure, a Greek vase, a Northwest Coast rattle, Fang heads, Indian bannerstones, an Asmat shield, fertility dolls, stone pipes, ivory fetishes, flaring headdresses, cult objects, reliquary heads, ceremonial staffs and other assorted primitive statuary, including a four-foot Uli (a rarity of Oceanic art from the Pacific island of New Ireland, a wooden male god with pagan Halloween eyes, large breasts and an erect penis, painted and pigmented over generations to a magical luster).

In every corner of my apartment are custom-designed bookcases to house my collection of art volumes—those huge, heavy books that are bought by a handful of perennial students and collectors like me. My books, like the "things" I collect, are an eclectic sprawl, with limited editions of the work of Georges de La Tour, Uccello, Corbusier, Della Francesca, Man Ray, Bellini, the Bauhaus, Elie Nadelman, Arthur Dove and especially Brancusi, the Rumanian peasant mystic who created those immortal sculptures *Bird in Flight, Sleeping Muse, The Kiss, Prayer, The Seal, The Fish,* all the boldest possible simplifications of form, while producing an overwhelming, unexpected emotional response. I love to study the lives and work of artists through the ages to learn whatever can be gleaned about the mysterious connections between images and human emotion.

And early every Saturday morning I play full-court basketball at the 23rd Street "Y" with jock cronies and young, serious athletes, mostly black. When they call me "the old man" and try to push me around, fists fly and I show up on Mondays at my agency with an exquisite mouse under an eye, ready for another week of exciting, crowded, intense work.

When I was a young art director at Doyle Dane Bernbach, the pioneering creative agency of the twentieth century, I never allowed *anyone* to present my work to a client. Recognizing the method to my madness, Bill Bernbach instructed his people to let the crazy young Greek do his own selling. At a presentation to a major client, I was accompanied by the agency's media director, a senior copywriter, and two account executives as I showed my work. Bill Bernbach and his partner Ned Doyle were also present. The client loved what he saw, and in a spirit of camaraderie he asked the media director, the copywriter, and the two account guys what they did at the agency. Then he turned to me and asked, jokingly, "And, George, what do *you* do?"

"I make one million dollars look like ten million," I answered. Bernbach and Doyle were absolutely floored. After that, Ned Doyle called me "The Jugular."

To be sure, not everyone in this wide world, particularly in the parochial advertising community, has the talent to make a tiny budget look humongous. That's why this book focuses on the big ideas of my career that have also achieved that seemingly miraculous effect. I can show you how the many big ideas that have marked my career (still fresh and pertinent, decades later) correlate closely with an uncompromising approach and attitude and a vigorous set of confident beliefs in the power of cause and effect.

Watch the way I have worked over the years—and please be patient with my loosey-goosey antics: these are not simply the screwball hijinks of this "bad boy of advertising." The sacrilegious and the solemn are all parts of my "method." By sharing my delights and disappointments, perhaps you will understand my ethos of creating images and slogans that not only sell products and services, but also become part of our popular culture and enter the American psyche. I always want my work to dazzle the eyes, touch the hearts and reach the minds of millions— and cause them to act.

2

A Minority
Opinion

Advertising is an art

In my deepest voice, I often say that if making ads is a science, I'm a girl. Science and technology obviously affect and shape the advertising experience, but ultimately, advertising is an art that springs from intuition, from instinct and above all, from talent.

As the post–World War II era dawned, advertising was an infant profession, and there were no formal training opportunities available in schools or colleges. The only academic training for this new mystique could be found in the graphic arts, despite the fact that language had always been the driving force of advertising; and, conversely, the best advertising slogans were primarily *visual* expressions. Look back at the early classics of advertising and you'll unearth these verbally based visual artifacts:

"Lucky Strike goes to war!"	(Lucky Strike cigarettes)
"They laughed when I sat down at the piano."	(U.S. School of Music)
"Never a bride, always a bridesmaid."	(Listerine)
"99 and 44/100% pure. It floats."	(Ivory Soap)
"His master's voice."	(RCA Victor)

We have never faced a shortage of agile writers who create clever, brilliant themes or phrases that frequently enter the language, but the blending of verbal and visual imagery—that inexplicable alchemy which causes one plus one to equal three, has been very rare during the first half of the century. During those formative decades a dynamism was occurring in the *graphic* sector, expressed in the radical imagistic movements from Dadaism to Surrealism, in the works of the Bauhaus, de Stijl, Constructivism and in those memorable design compositions of Mondrian. Visual experimentation was their common denominator, their impelling force. Dramatic innovations were occurring in the use of symbolism in the fine arts, yet during this period of ferment, advertising, a creative pursuit, had been using only one of its available tools—language —and usually in isolation from the visual strength that would spring from graphic creativity.

Meanwhile, the only "formal" training for the new mystique of advertising could be found in the graphic arts. There were always schools or courses for design and illustration and "commercial art." These were practical extensions of the fine arts into advertising-related activities such as typography, layout, poster design, fashion illustration, commercial photography. Advertising "instruction" available to artists could be loosely described as knee-jerk drills in constructing schematic advertising layouts. They were Prussian-style exercises, directed by hacks who preached the conventional wisdoms of advertising's early days: large illustration above a headline above a block of body copy with a logo in the lower-right-hand corner. Even today, most print advertising follows this vapid pattern. Small wonder that the least talented people in advertising, incapable of innovation, create advertising according to this gospel, later blessed and sanctified by the reigning magistrate of advertising, David Ogilvy.

Advertising has no rules—what it always needs more than "rules" is unconstipated thinking. The most significant advertising innovation in this century has been the Creative Revolution of the late 1950s and 1960s, when words and graphics finally merged. Until then, young artists entered the advertising world equipped with nothing more than fatuous rules on the five or six ways to do a layout.

During the second half of this century, the many artistic ferments that had been roiling the graphic communities of Europe led to the emergence of the modern American art director. One of its first pioneers, Paul Rand, boldly experimented with visual "fun" in advertising. His sense of imagery was deep and innovative. He created a bridge between the verbal and the visual that young talents like Bob Gage, Lou Dorfsman, Herb Lubalin, Gene Federico and I, all art directors, walked across into a brave new world of expressive freedom.

In Europe, in the 1930s, the poster artist Cassandre created haunting visual messages that were forerunners of modern graphic communications. His monumental head-on rendering of the great transatlantic ocean liner, the *Normandie,* set a new standard for graphic drama. Paul Rand took the logical next step into advertising, but he was almost blushingly embarrassed about being too commercial. His talents ranged widely, from the deceptively pristine IBM logo to the vivid advertising design for the 1950 movie on racial hatred, *No Way Out,* (with Richard Widmark, and Sidney Poitier in his film debut). I admit that I followed Rand with an unabashed love of selling. I was streetwise and infatuated with the enormous potential of graphic communication. Now, finally, the talented advertising writer had found his or her missing counterpart who was a creator of visual imagery, rather than simply a maker of pedestrian layouts. The emergence of the modern art director thus gave birth to modern advertising.

Decades later, advertising in the 1990s has become a hot subject for study, with special emphasis on its *rational* character, reflecting the Madison Avenue Establishment's insistence on viewing advertising as a science. Many of the scientific techniques of advertising—media planning, research, marketing strategy, budgeting, and all the nuts and bolts of planning—are certainly essential; nonetheless, the inordinate emphasis on these *logical* disciplines reinforces the self-defeating ideology of advertising itself as a science rather than an art.

Media connoisseurs, even scholars in such arcane fields as semiotics, have become important sources of interpretation for the Western world's mass media. A new breed of media pervert has emerged, ready and willing to explain, with scientific certainty, any aspect of mass communication. Increasingly, opinions are backed by numbers, numbers are supported by studies, studies are exalted in an aura of scientific precision. Advertising, that most complex of modern art forms, is disguised as a science.

But the emperor is stark naked. Advertising is an *art!*

I have always been entranced by Picasso's penetrating remark, "Art is the lie that tells the truth"—especially because I think his definition is so wonderfully relevant to advertising in market-wise America, where almost all products are comparable in quality. When advertising is *great* advertising—when it's inventive, irreverent, audacious and loaded with chutzpah—it literally becomes a benefit of the product, and Picasso's "lie" becomes the truth. Food tastes better, clothes feel better, cars drive better. If you find it hard to agree with this basic belief, you may find it extremely difficult to understand the magic of advertising. Unfortunately, the magic of advertising eludes most people—especially advertising professionals.

כשר לפסח

in the best
Passover
tradition!

GOODMAN'S
PASSOVER
MATZOS

Welcome to Heaven!

A new and heavenly haven where you'll find
great restaurants, fine stores, arts, entertainment,
gardens, plazas, parks and promenades —
all on the banks of the Hudson River
next to Battery Park City. (And there's a fabulous view
of the Statue of Liberty, too!)

World Financial Center

It's Heaven on the Hudson

Look
who's in
Heaven
so far...
Rizzoli
Bonwit Teller for Men
Mark Cross
Caswell & Massey
Barney's
Penigord Park.
Ann Taylor
Donald Sachs
Hudson River Club

Retailers: There are 90 distinctive locations
in over 500,000 square feet of retail
and public space, so there's still room in heaven!
For leasing information call Richard Levinsky,
Director of Leasing, (212) 945-2600.

By car/taxi:
FDR Drive or West Side Highway to West St.
Turn west at Liberty St. (200) Liberty St. is
first tower of World Financial Center.

By subway:
IRT line: #1 train to Cortlandt Street
BMT line: R, N lines to Cortlandt Street
IND line: E, K lines to World Trade Center

By bus:
M-9 and M-10 lines to World Financial Center

3

Don't Take
the Big Idea
for Granted

**To sell the boss, if you have to threaten suicide,
threaten suicide**

Advertising is the art of breaking rules, not the science of making them.

However, there is one rule in advertising that should *never* be broken: before you shoot from the hip (or the lip), do your homework—understand your client thoroughly. Don't limit your homework to the obvious—competitive advertising, brand share data, any research and articles you can lay your hands on. Homework is also sleuthing and snooping so that you get to know early the loves, hates, biases and predilections of the ultimate decision maker—the client, the boss, the guy who pays the bills. During the Renaissance, paintings and sculpture and palaces and cathedrals were created by artists for a patron. (If Michelangelo had a better angle on Pope Paul III, he wouldn't have had to lay down on the job so long.) Today that patron/prince is often shielded and insulated by middle managers, most of whom are committed primarily to preserving their incomes and their Connecticut commuter tickets. That's why it's so essential to understand who has the real power to say yes or no, who can bless or damn a campaign, its various merits notwithstanding.

Advertising is not an exercise in political democracy; despite all the striving for consensus as a campaign concept travels up the hierarchy of approvals, the best laid campaigns can die on the drawing board if you don't know your client. Listen to this classic case of a savvy advertising man *(moi)* who thought he had done his homework and arrived at the big idea, but lost a great campaign because of an astounding miscalculation: I had neglected to think hard enough in advance about what makes the head man tick.

The advertiser was Olympia & York, the Canadian-based developer of the World Financial Center at the southern tip of Manhattan—a dazzling complex of retail stores and restaurants, promenades, lavish public areas, and spacious buildings that house the world's leading financial service companies (Dow Jones, Oppenheimer, Shearson Lehman, American Express), with space for ninety retailers. Olympia & York's chairman was Philip Reichmann of the powerful Reichmann family of Canada, a short, wimpish looking man, an orthodox Jew who wore a yarmulke and closed his offices at sundown on Fridays, the start of the Jewish Sabbath. He had a slight tic in his right eye, an involuntary blinking that could be mistaken for a conspiratorial wink. (That wink, I think, is what did me in.)

I had worked with Reichmann on a previous venture, and regarded him as a no-nonsense executive who could make tough decisions. We assumed he was thirsting for a new kind of advertising for the World Financial Center that would immediately capture the city's imagination. (I learned later, when it was too late, that I had mistaken greed for smarts.) It was clear to us at the outset that the name *World Financial Center* conveyed visions of Wall Street and investing, not leisure, shopping, cultural beauty and a stylish respite from New York's hurly-burly. The World Financial Center was also hidden in the large shadow of the World Trade Center's Twin Towers, one of New York's most popular tourist attractions. It was apparent at the outset that any current awareness of this new complex had to be zero. To be certain we were not acting entirely on instinct, we telephoned fifty people at random and found that only two claimed to have heard of the World Financial Center, but these two were clearly confusing it with the World Trade Center. We followed this up with detailed one-on-one interviews of another fifty Manhattan adults in professional/managerial jobs with incomes as high as $80,000 —the most likely visitors to the World Financial Center. We discovered that 54% had never heard of it. Of the 46% who said they had, the vast majority had no idea what it was.

While it was probably too late to scrap their generic name, it was still possible to affix to it a descriptive phrase with instant, memorable imagery that everyone would remember . . . that would cause people to visit the World Financial Center. We also needed a theme that was pregnant with meaning and nuance that could be extended into public relations activities and would put the World Financial Center clearly on the map. We had to create imagery of a mythical place to enhance the appeal of the real place. Neil Brownlee, my brilliant copy chief, and I put our heads together and we came up with this divine theme:

"World Financial Center—It's *Heaven on the Hudson.*"

This theme also became a visual trademark, with the spread wings of an angel, depicting a heavenly World Financial Center. It was a bold solution to create swift popularity for that deadly sounding "World Financial Center" moniker, enabling us to leapfrog that generic/financial/soporific name with imaginative, memorable messages. We devised slogans that would not only reinforce the theme, but would conjure an irresistible atmosphere to fill the imagery vacuum. Here are a few:

"I spent Sunday in Heaven!"	(shoppers, tourists)
"6 ways to get to Heaven."	(directions)
"This bus is going to Heaven."	(jumbo bus poster)
"You're only two blocks from Heaven!"	(outdoor poster)
"Look who's in Heaven . . ."	(a listing of retailers)
"Get a better body in Heaven!"	(Plus One Fitness Center)
"If you love to eat, go to Heaven!"	(Le Perigord Park)

We also designed shopping bags, T-shirts, postcards, mailers and brochures. A 60 second radio spot was created, adapting one of the greatest Irving Berlin tunes, "Heaven, I'm in Heaven." Our theme was rich in applications and nuances, it would work in all media, and would create powerful visibility for this invisible complex, a visual echo effect. To be doubly sure we were on the mark, we researched the impact of our campaign among the same fifty adults who had barely known the World Financial Center, and we found that after a cursory exposure to our advertising, everyone could now describe it accurately, with heavy mentions of retailers, restaurants and cultural events. Their reaction to the theme "Heaven on the Hudson" was overwhelmingly positive and 92% said they would visit the Center.

The campaign was presented to our client's marketing people, and they reacted divinely. More meetings ensued, and after additional tinkering, polling of O&Y's internal staff, reactions from their retailers, and numerous conferences with their public relations, entertainment and real estate people, a date was set to show the refined, fly-specked campaign to Philip Reichmann. A date was set for a Friday afternoon. The Sabbath sundown was approaching. It was a good omen, I thought. The meeting was limited to the two marketing people, my partner Bill Pitts, and me. We plunged zestfully into our presentation, commencing with our research findings, paying appropriate homage to the close cooperation we received from the marketing staff, then unfurling our theme and presenting its many applications, climaxed by our rousing musical track.

While I was presenting the campaign, I noticed that the normally benign Bill Pitts was now smiling almost extravagantly, signaling me it was in the bag. But at the conclusion of my presentation, as the sun began to set, Philip Reichmann asked his marketing people *who* was responsible for giving us the direction that led to this presentation. It suddenly became stunningly clear that he *hated* the campaign. It was much too "clever," he said, and entirely unsuitable for his key tenants, especially American Express. *(Huh?)*

The top man had spoken, and my cherished campaign, if not yet dead, was comatose. I was appalled that this inspired solution to a seemingly impregnable problem could be so summarily rejected.

With chagrin, I realized that this failure was my fault, that I had neglected the most vital part of my homework. What mattered most was Philip Reichmann's reaction, but I could not accept his impossibly glib, fearful verdict. Like a condemned man, my life flashed before me as sundown hurried over the Hudson, and I retrieved from my mental dossier of triumphs and tragicomedies the memory of my first big sale when I was an upstart art director at Doyle Dane Bernbach many years before. In that formative year (1959), I had designed a dramatic poster for New York's most important maker of matzohs, A. Goodman & Sons in Long Island City. My work was a huge, gorgeous, realer-than-real color blowup of a matzoh with the headline "Kosher for Passover" lettered in Hebrew. It was scheduled to run in New York's subways just before Passover. In multi-ethnic New York, my Hebrew lettering communicated with the clarity of a shamrock in a Queens saloon. But, alas, the account supervisor of Doyle Dane Bernbach presented it to the owner of Goodman, who turned it down. I appealed to Bill Bernbach, and he grudgingly made a date with the client so that I could make a last attempt to pitch him personally. It wasn't easy. The Goodman boss was an Old Testament patriarch with a forbidding manner, and his vocabulary was limited to "I dun like it"—and "no." After what seemed like hours of fruitless persuasion, the old man folded his arms across his chest, slumped back in his chair, and shook his head at me sadly.

"There must be some way I can sell you on this," I said. I rolled up the poster and climbed out the window. I stood on the outer ledge, high above the pavement, gripping the raised sash with my left hand while I waved the poster with my free hand as I screamed from the ledge at the top of my lungs, loud enough to be heard in all of Long Island City: *"You make the matzoh, I'll make the ads!"*

"Stop, stop," cried the old man. "Ve'll run it, ve'll run it. You made your point already. Come in, come in, please!" I climbed back into the room and thanked the patriarch for the nice way he had reviewed my work. As I was leaving, he called out after me, "If you ever kvit edvertising, young man, you got yourself ah job as ah matzoh salesman."

Now, almost thirty years later, I was deep in déjà vu. When I had gone to Long Island City, I had done my homework. The Goodman patriarch, I had learned in advance, was a mulish old man, but somehow capable of being charmed. With Philip Reichmann, I was weaponless. I had neglected to anticipate his reactions, having placed all my confidence in the accuracy of his underlings' judgments—while I had worked from day one on the assumption that my client was a hot-to-trot shaker and mover. But I was wrong, and I was shockingly checkmated. I searched for a window that would allow me to hang out over midtown Manhattan so that I could shout at Philip Reichmann, *"You make the World Financial Center, I'll make the ads!"* Unfortunately, in this age of architectural modernism, the windows were flush with the walls and could be opened only by a nuclear detonation. It was all in vain. The top man had spoken, and despite my frenzied rejoinders, he ended the meeting abruptly as the sun dipped behind the Watchung Mountains in New Jersey, ending a maddening episode in my career. Philip Reichmann adjusted his velvet yarmulke and left the room. The next week he fired his number two marketing person and our agency spent the following year trying to recoup our out-of-pocket costs. Going down in the elevator, I asked Bill Pitts why he had looked so confident.

"Reichmann kept *winking* at me," he said. "I thought he was *relishing* the campaign."

"That was no goddam wink," I said, apoplectically. "That was his goddam *tic.*"

The lesson was clear: I should have tried to get inside Reichmann's head before we lifted a pencil. From now on I'll never try to sell heaven to a man with a yarmulke.

Over the next two years, with a hefty budget, the World Financial Center finally ran an ad campaign—(not mine, believe me) possibly the most cryptic advertising of the twentieth century. I realize I may sound like a lover spurned. *Manhattan,inc.* subsequently devoted three pages to an analysis of this advertising as a distinctive example of "mysterious" work on behalf of a potentially great client. At the time of this writing, the world is still massively ignorant of the World Financial Center.

Agencies live or die by the kind of clients they attract. My fierce determination to come up with big ideas that make miracles attracts those tough entrepreneurs who want big results, who understand the power of persuasion. Throughout my career I've done my best work for clients like these, all rugged individualists with huge egos and a passion to succeed in a big way.

For too many agencies, the wooing of a client is all flattery, entertaining and the kissing of ass. But once the prospect becomes a client, he becomes the *enemy*—too demanding, too critical, too cost-conscious, too dumb to appreciate the agency's mediocre work. These relationships are corrosive and destructive, but that's what so much of the agency business is like—which has absolutely *nothing* to do with creating great advertising.

That's why in this chapter I've begun the story of my career by describing one of my startling miscalculations—mistakenly assuming that I would be working for an entrepreneurial personality with balls and passion. I was completely wrong, and our great work fell on the deaf ears of a bureaucrat. The Big Idea should be reserved for clients of imagination and chutzpah—who can recognize talent and are determined to milk that talent to its limit.

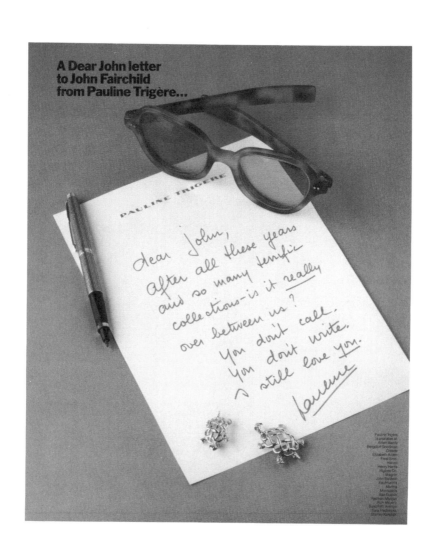

A Dear John letter
to John Fairchild
from Pauline Trigère...

Dear John,
after all these years
and so many terrific
collections—is it *really*
over between us?
You don't call.
You don't write.
I still love You.
Pauline

4

How to
Simplify
Marketing
Mumbo Jumbo

Define the problem in one short sentence

When speaking of a client's "marketing problem"—an obstacle that must be overcome or a competitive challenge that must be dealt with— many advertising people lapse into doubletalk or spew statistics. *Marketing* is a voodoo word that suggests complexity and even mystery, but if you're thinking clearly, you should be able to distill a marketing problem —which precedes the *advertising* solution—into one simple sentence. If you can't, you don't understand your subject. If you can, that "problem" can become a thrilling opportunity for inventive work. Here are two choice examples:

In 1959, Volkswagen became a client of Doyle Dane Bernbach. This runty-looking German car bore an evil legacy: Volkswagen was the car Adolf Hitler had launched as the "people's car" of the Third Reich. World

War II had ended just fourteen years before, and memories of those horrendous times were still raw. Before Volkswagen chose DDB, they had spent many deutsche marks with a major New York ad agency and had managed to sell about three cars. Bill Bernbach's young, maverick agency had been handed an onerous challenge. As soon as we were awarded the account, a contingent of creative and account people were sent to Germany by Bernbach to look, listen and learn so that we could be properly oriented on the virtues of Hitler's car (which had been designed by Dr. Ferdinand Porsche). I looked and listened, but I know I didn't learn anything new because I had felt the answer in my gut before we had left American soil, and no amount of well-intentioned orientation could possibly change it. When I returned from our German tour of Volkswagen, I went to see Bill and told him, with my youthful arrogance, that I had figured it out.

"The *advertising?*" Bill asked with astonishment. "No, Bill," I said, "the *marketing* problem." Bernbach looked at me with a half frown, never really certain I was ever serious.

"Yeah, Bill," I said, "I figured out the marketing problem. Here it is: *We have to sell a Nazi car in a Jewish town.*"

The Volkswagen, by almost any standard in those days, was an ugly car, and its homeliness had become an impossible obstacle because everyone knew that it was a German car, created by Der Führer. In New York City, the major initial market for Volkswagen, with its large Jewish population, the painful awareness of this German car's origins made it an impossible sell. To compound the problem, the American car industry was marketing full-sized cars almost exclusively, so entirely apart from the political currents that swirled around Volkswagen, Americans were simply not buying too many small cars. The campaign that ensued—the still famous "Think Small" and "Beetle" and "Lemon"—took all the negatives of Volkswagen and turned them into positive appeals through the use of charm, simplicity, warmth, and winning irreverence. (These breakthrough ads were written by Julian Koenig, a matchless copywriter whom I met at Doyle Dane Bernbach in 1959. During that unforgettable year, Koenig and I walked away with a slew of medals, including one for Volkswagen, in the prestigious New York Art Directors Club competition. The next year Koenig and I went off to start Papert Koenig Lois, the world's second creative agency after Doyle Dane Bernbach.) Through this brilliant strategy, the deeper issue of Volkswagen's origin as the people's car of the Third Reich was submerged, and receded into history.

Every day of my life I bump into a new marketing challenge, but thirty years later, I ran into a doozy. The legendary couturiere Pauline Trigere, the Paris-born fashion designer, an elegant lady of a certain age, who had appeared for me in a multi-celebrity television campaign I had created to promote Greek tourism, joined me at The Four Seasons for a luncheon pow-wow. She had called me with some urgency to say that she had to talk to me. Peering at me through her tinted tortoiseshell glasses, she did what few marketing professionals are ever able to accomplish: she defined her marketing problem in one short sentence—in fact, in just five short words: *"George, people zeenk I am dead!"*

The inimitable Pauline Trigere, a forthright, unpretentious, aristocratic lady, with her strong face and impervious Gallic accent, was dead right—and to define her predicament so candidly was a revealing clue to her honesty and courage. During the fifties and sixties, Pauline Trigere was properly regarded as one of the great couturieres in the world. By 1988 she was no longer a chickadee, and her longevity problem was compounded by an intramural industry vendetta: The most influential trade paper in the fashion world is *Women's Wear Daily,* the flagship journal of Fairchild Publications, headed by the dynast John Fairchild, whose opinions carry enormous weight and who has been known to banish any mention in *Women's Wear Daily* of anyone who has offended or slighted the Fairchild power. The New York weekly *7 Days* (November 22, 1989) provided some background on the Fairchild/Trigere estrangement: "Fairchild's feud with designer Pauline Trigere dates back into the mists of time—1970. Remember the ill-fated midi? Fairchild was enthusiastically boosting that fashion disaster, which he called the 'longuette,' and Trigere was brave enough to deride his pretentious term in a TV interview. She has been persona non grata ever since in all Fairchild publications."

Even the origins of her banishment have misted over. According to Pauline Trigere, in an interview with *Newsday* (September 21, 1988), Fairchild's displeasure was more recent: "About three years ago, Crain's *New York Business* interviewed my son, Jean–Pierre, and they asked him what he thought about Mr. Fairchild—do you think he is fair? And he said, 'No, how can he be fair when people like so-and-so are out.' Jean–Pierre dared criticize Mr. Fairchild." Her son was referring to Fairchild's banishment of Geoffrey Beene. At one time or other, Fairchild has also excluded any mention of Hubert de Givenchy, Giorgio Armani and Bill Blass. According to James Brady, a former publisher of

Women's Wear Daily, most of them "have kept their mouths shut and taken it on the chin." Not Pauline Trigere.

I realized that night how accurately she had described her marketing problem. When I got home from the agency I asked my wife Rosemary, who has purchased a few Trigere dresses during our long marriage, what she knew about my newest client, knowing that Rosie had seen Pauline on television in my recent Greek tourism campaign. "I think she died a few months ago," said my wife.

I was shocked, but not really surprised. I then asked Rosie to call several of her friends to add depth to my consumer survey. After dinner she called eight friends, all fashion-savvy women. Six were certain that Pauline Trigere had passed away; two assumed that if she had not expired, she had surely retired. Earlier that day, when Pauline had described her predicament to me at lunch, I knew at once that the only way to turn this tough challenge into an opportunity would be to write an open "Dear John" letter in the form of an ad that everyone in the fashion world would see. It would be a reverse handling of the "Dear John" message during World War II, when a GI would receive a letter from his erstwhile sweetheart, telling him their love was over, usually because of another man.

When I next met Pauline, at my agency, I told her that her marketing assessment, lamentably, was totally accurate, and that she had a very, very serious problem—which called for a creative solution of great audacity. The time had come, I suggested, to deal with the Fairchild banishment head-on, but without being aggressive or offensive. I showed her an ad, which was simply a handwritten letter from Pauline Trigere to John Fairchild. The letter was surrounded by Trigere artifacts: her tortoiseshell shades, her fountain pen, and two diamond turtles (Pauline is a world-class collector of turtle jewelry and sculpture). The letter, under the double entendre headline, "A Dear John letter to John Fairchild from Pauline Trigere . . ." in Pauline's red-ink handwriting, went like this:

> *Dear John,*
> *After all these years and so many terrific collections—is it really over between us? You don't call. You don't write. I still love you.*
> *—Pauline*

Pauline was stunned—and delighted—in equal parts. I was casting her in the role of Seventh Avenue's Joan of Arc. She was reluctant to be burned, but she was ensnared by the ad's audacity and she loved its charm. Her budget was zilch, but she was prepared to dig up enough moolah to place a four-color ad in *The New York Times Magazine*, which would be running a widely read fashion section for the fall season. Understandably, Pauline had to do some serious ruminating about running an ad that would harpoon John Fairchild, the fashion world's white whale. After an anguished weekend of reflection and Seventh Avenue realpolitik considerations, Pauline told us, with a mournful face, that she could not possibly go ahead with this approach because her son and Geoffrey Beene and all her friends in the business warned her that this ad would be her ruination. "But you must understand, George," she said, "I'm *crazee* about it!"

I could sense that Pauline was strongly attracted to the chutzpah of my approach. I was therefore doubly determined to win her over. I emphasized the delicious improbability of such a statement coming from the empress of fashion (the trade later referred to her as the doyen of couturieres when writing about this campaign), while the tantalizing double entendre of the "Dear John" salutation, I insisted (modestly, to be sure), was the sheerest brilliance, and would bring her not only renewed prominence in the fashion/retail world, but would also make her the object of adulation among the many people in her business who understood how tough it was to take on the powerful John Fairchild. Pauline relented slightly, promising to think about it further. A few days later she called to say that she still loved the ad, but this time her banker was worried. I told her to tell her banker to go on making money and I'll make the ads. Sensing my rising impatience, Pauline retreated one more time, and promised to think about it still further.

The next day she called Bill Pitts from her Park Avenue apartment. "Listen," she said, almost surreptitiously, "I have decided to go ahead with George's ad. My son doesn't know, my friends don't know, my banker doesn't know. But screw it, Beel, I want to run it!" "Dear John" ran in *The New York Times Magazine*'s "Fashions of the Times" section at the end of August. A few days before, spotting the ad in a preview copy, the *Times*' alert marketing columnist Randall Rothenberg ran a lead piece on the front page of the *Times* business section (August 17, 1988): "From Pauline Trigere, a Dressing Down." He reproduced the ad, summarized the background and ended with a choice quote from Pauline: "This is not a feud. I wanted to prove to the world that I'm still alive and kicking."

A new day had dawned for Pauline Trigere. She was the new heroine of the fashion world as congratulatory letters and phone calls were received even from as far as Jerusalem, where Mayor Teddy Kollek placed a call to Pauline, whom he had known for many years, to express his admiration of her courage. Pauline Trigere became hot copy, the source of ongoing stories for the *New York Post*'s "Page Six," for articles in newspapers in Washington and Los Angeles and San Francisco. *Newsday* ran a two-page interview of the suddenly pertinent and vital Pauline Trigere. When Bill Pitts called her during all this tumult to show her a possible next ad, she replied impatiently, "I am too busy, Beel. A photographer is coming any minute from *Manhattan,inc.* to take my picture for a big story." A big story it was:

The Perils of Pauline
Tired of being snubbed by John Fairchild, designer Pauline Trigere decided to strike back at the WWD publisher.

The publicity value of this modest campaign has been estimated by public relations professionals as wildly out of proportion to its minuscule ad budget. Some said it had to be worth *millions,* with a steady flow of articles in national media. John Fairchild has not yet restored Pauline Trigere to grace (although he embraces her with impressive warmth when they cross paths at The Four Seasons); and fully a year later, Connie Chung ran a feature on CBS on the notorious Trigere/Fairchild incident, in which Fairchild said, almost contritely, that the "Dear John" salvo "sure was good publicity for her!" Whether or not he eventually lifts the banishment of Pauline's name from *Women's Wear Daily,* this admirable lady has proved decisively, and with considerable courage and style (like her clothes), that she sure ain't dead. She had become the undisputed heroine of the fashion world, batting her Gallic eyelashes while disarming the Establishment and putting new life in her business.

When we suggested follow-up variations of "Dear John," she threw up her hands and asked in dismay, "Boys, who can handle all ze customers zese new ads would cause for me? I still can't handle all ze orders from my dear customers who came back to me after ze *first* ad!"

5

The Pricking
of "Positioning"

Or . . . Always unzip your fly before
you take a leak

Once upon a time, my advertising agency was awarded a new product from UniRoyal: a leathery vinyl fabric called Naugahyde. It was a superb leather substitute that quickly spurred many imitators. Retailers were soon awash with fake leather, causing considerable confusion among shoppers, who could not distinguish marvelous Naugahyde from its many inferior imitations. A strategy was needed for Naugahyde to be correctly perceived at the very mention of its name as the most leather-like vinyl on the market.

Whenever possible, the answer to a marketing problem should be *surprising*. If the answer is obvious, it's probably a clinker. The right answer will surprise both client and consumer. My solution to the Naugahyde challenge was a classic example of a creative surprise. I created a mythical beast called the Nauga, a new species that shed its hide once a year for the good of mankind (and UniRoyal). The Nauga was also very, very ugly. (The Nauga was not an animated creature, but a real, three-dimensional character.)

In my mind's eye I had a clear image of Nauga and its many applications. The Nauga would be taller than a basketball player, and would become an unforgettable spokesman for Naugahyde on television. All seven feet of the Nauga would show up at UniRoyal's many sales meetings, where he would woo furniture retailers. The Nauga would also be a surprising hangtag and a twelve-inch doll for kids.

Our client at UniRoyal, Jack Trout, a bright, enthusiastic executive, liked the Nauga concept and fought the good fight in his company to bring the sweet, ugly Nauga to life. Drawings of the Nauga in all its incarnations were presented to the brass of UniRoyal and received ringing approval. Their lawyers, however, shook in their boots, certain the Federal Trade Commission would decide the Nauga could be mistaken in our advertising for a live species and its vinyl hide perceived as genuine leather. They therefore counseled their management to abort our beloved Nauga, convinced that UniRoyal might be cited for deceptive advertising.

"Kill the Nauga?" I exclaimed with parental horror. "Over my dead Greek body!" Action was called for to prove that the Nauga would not be regarded by consumers as a real-life species. My agency immediately conducted one-on-one research among a hefty sample of consumers. We showed them our Nauga ads and asked, "Is this a real animal?" Our respondents' replies boiled down to: "What are you, nuts? That's just a big, fat, ugly creature with a cute tush!" Armed with this intimidating research, Jack Trout helped us persuade UniRoyal's brass that my Disneylike creation was perceived for what it was: a cartoon character. UniRoyal's lawyers were miffed at me, but logic prevailed and the ugly Nauga (a pre–E.T.), with its sweet, mournful eyes, was born.

A few days after our first ads ran, retailers began to clamor for the hangtags because the kids were collecting them and were steering their parents to Naugahyde-covered furniture—while the parents, despite their clear understanding that the Nauga was an imaginary character, wanted to be certain this vinyl-covered product came from the hide of a Nauga. The Nauga was classic, smart, imaginative "positioning," years before that word had entered the lexicon of advertising.

This campaign for Naugahyde demonstrates the power of persuasive imagery, visual and verbal. Great advertising should have a memorable *visual* image, a kind of graphic mnemonic (the Nauga)—and unforgettable *words* that sit on the tip of your tongue ("The Nauga is ugly, but his vinyl hide is beautiful"). If you create both visual and verbal imagery, one plus one will equal three. Powerful imagery, moreover, can stay alive for decades: Twenty-five years after this extraordinary campaign, I came upon a twelve-inch Nauga doll in a posh new antique toy store on Manhattan's Upper East Side. It was on sale—for $1,500.

Jack Trout was proud of our work. Later, he left UniRoyal and founded his own advertising agency, Trout & Ries. (Ol' Jack and Al Ries adopted the Nauga and made him their own—the Nauga became the distinctive creative achievement that helped launch their new shop.) Over the ensuing years, Jack Trout and Al Ries positioned themselves as the high priests of "positioning." In their 1981 book, *Positioning: The Battle for Your Mind,* Jack and Al handed down this imposing definition of their new religion: "According to positioning theory, the human mind contains slots or positions which a company attempts to fill. This is easy to do if the position is empty, but difficult to do if the 'position' is owned by a competitor. In the latter case a company must reposition its competition if it wants to get into the mind." In that seminal treatise, Trout and Ries concluded: "Today, creativity is dead. The name of the game on Madison Avenue is positioning"—and all the time we were pushing the sweet, ugly Nauga together, I never heard one mention of "positioning" from the lips of Jack Trout.

At the zenith of "positioning"'s notoriety, *Manhattan,inc.* asked me to comment on this latest Madison Avenue revelation. I responded with my customary intellectual gravity: "To speak of positioning is so obvious, it's like telling me to unzip my fly before taking a leak." As far back as the late 1950s at Doyle Dane Bernbach, where instinct and talent fueled their breakthrough creative work, "positioning" and "strategy" were regarded, almost unconsciously, as the first *implicit* steps of the creative process. These concepts were *givens* that were accepted and understood. "Positioning" and "strategy" were the natural beams and flooring of original work; if anyone dared to speak of the wonders of "positioning" at Bill Bernbach's agency, he would have been marked as a posturing buffoon.

The best "positioning" should evolve intuitively and spontaneously out of a clear understanding of an advertiser's problems and opportunities. Pauline Trigere was "positioned" as the Joan of Arc of Seventh Avenue. The World Financial Center was "positioned" as a heavenly retreat from Manhattan's hurly-burly. Goodman Matzoh was "positioned" as a mandatory Passover staple. Volkswagen was "positioned" as a new idea: a small car. "Positioning" obscures the primacy of creative thinking in the advertising process and seduces lazy minds. The problem with "positioning" is its facile reduction of the creative mystique to a seductive buzzword, while obscuring the need for the big idea—leading too many advertising people to believe they have found truth and beauty by merely unzipping their flies before taking a leak.

Particularly in political advertising, "positioning" and "image" have become high-cachet words. A schmuck is "positioned" to appear noble, a boor is "positioned" to sound humble, a crackpot is "positioned" to seem moderate, a crook is "positioned" to seem honest, a wimp is "positioned" to look macho. These obvious stratagems often work, and among our elected officials we can always find schmucks, boors, crackpots, crooks and wimps. While Americans are incredibly smart and perceptive about *product* advertising, they are not always brilliant in their responses to political candidates, whose advertising can fool most of the people some of the time. Packaging political candidates like a bar of soap —"positioning" them so that they appear to have a certain persona— works only *some* of the time. The best political advertising conveys candor, a truthful essence of the candidate. This can only be done by avoiding the traps of "positioning," even by focusing on a candidate's weakness and turning it into a strength, but it must be done with the audacity of truth.

In 1964 I handled the New York State senatorial campaign for Robert F. Kennedy. His brother, President John Kennedy, had been assassinated the previous year. Bobby had become, in Jimmy Hoffa's chilling phrase two days after the assassination, "just another lawyer." An exile from Lyndon Johnson's cabinet and uncertain about his future course in American politics, this lifelong resident of Massachusetts announced he would move to New York and run for the Democratic nomination for senator against the fatherly Republican incumbent, Kenneth Keating, a benign gent with flowing white hair. The press and Bobby's political enemies immediately clobbered him as a "carpetbagger," a not entirely unjust knock, despite Bobby's claim that he was a constant visitor to Manhattan.

Nonetheless, Bobby Kennedy was believed by many (including me) to be an ideal candidate who should retain a prominent profile in national politics and would someday run for president. He was also a powerful presence in Washington despite his current joblessness. It was therefore essential that his advertising sweep away the "carpetbagger" label or his candidacy could be stillborn.

In working with the ruthless carpetbagger, he struck me as an honest, principled leader who was desperately needed by New York, even if he came from a different state. Bobby Kennedy was ruthless enough to twist arms and grab lapels for a state that was always getting minimal help from Washington. Months before any political advertising blitz normally begins, we plastered New York State with this straightforward message: "Let's put Robert Kennedy to work for New York"—a swift counterattack against his big liability. Our strategy of up-front honesty paid off as the "carpetbagger" handle evaporated. We had taken a potentially lethal attack and correctly portrayed candidate Kennedy as a gusty potential benefactor for New York instead of a grasping parvenu from out-of-state.

As the campaign entered its final days, we sensed that Bobby might lose to Keating because of a large undecided bloc, including many voters troubled still by the "ruthless" label, so we created a 20 second spot that caused voters to think hard—as they heard and saw words moving against a dark screen:

> When you're in the election booth, think about this . . .
> Which of the candidates for the United States Senate . . .
> has the better chance of becoming . . .
> a great United States senator? . . .
> A _great_ United States senator.

It was a mind-expanding way to tell people: Even if you think the guy is ruthless, so what? He would make a great senator while Keating would go on being an amiable hack. Kennedy defeated Keating. (In 1968, his valiant run for the Democratic presidential nomination made him the likely nominee. It all came to an end with his assassination that dreadful night in Los Angeles.)

A more complex problem beset us in 1985 when we became the agency for the Greek National Tourist Organization (GNTO). This was mission impossible: we were up against international terrorism _and_ the White House. That summer, skyjacking and hostage-taking in the Middle

East had become rampant, and tourists to Greece were canceling their reservations en masse. The U.S. Department of State issued an advisory, warning Americans against traveling through Athens International Airport. Then came the clincher: President Reagan warned in a news conference against traveling to Europe. Later, the *Achille Lauro* episode raised anxieties to a feverish level. On a more subtle but possibly more urgent front, Greece had no important legislators in Washington to speak up for an avowedly "neutral" country in those pre-glasnost days, when "neutral" was akin to being a vassal state of the Evil Empire. Turkey was the beneficiary of Washington's NATO—directed policies, at the obvious expense of Greece.

A miracle was needed—a miracle that *can* happen, through the power of great advertising. First, this personal preface before I reveal how we made that miracle: As a proud Greek–American, the son of Greek immigrant parents and a former true-blue member of the Bronx chapter of the Sons of Pericles, a teenage boys club for children of Greek families, I had been fuming with frustration during all my years as an advertising professional—often described in the trade press as the "Golden Greek" and even the "Gorgeous Greek" (that's redundant!)— maddened by the inexplicable fact that I had never been asked to promote tourism to my parents' beloved Greece. As a certified workaholic and a passionate Hellenophile, I had taken only two vacations in twenty years, both to Greece. During my career I've worked for products and services that form an ethnic rainbow. I've created advertising campaigns for matzohs (risking life and limb to sell my work) . . . for housewares from Denmark (Dansk) . . . for tires and typewriters from Italy (Pirelli and Olivetti) . . . for cars from Japan (Subaru) . . . for a Nazi car in a Jewish town (Volkswagen) . . . for a beer from Holland (Orangeboom) . . . for wines from France (Mouton Cadet, then for the trade association Food and Wines From France) . . . for television programming from Britain (Granada) . . . for the official airline of Morocco (Royal Air Maroc) . . . for the most famous Irish bistro in New York (Charley O's) . . . for the most popular French bistro in New York (Brasserie) . . . for the finest South American restaurant in town (La Fonda del Sol) . . . for the katzenjammer German fast-food chain (Zum Zum). But never did this loyal Son of Pericles receive a call from the Greek government to apply my talents for the land of my fathers.

Finally, in the fall of 1985, I knew Zeus had struck me with his lightning bolt when I received an invitation from the Greek National

Tourist Organization in New York's Olympic Tower to present my agency's credentials for their advertising account. The new agency's assignment: contain the almost terminal damage to Greek tourism. Hotels were begging for guests, cruise ships were being beached, and nobody was dancing in the aisles of Olympic Airways or on the isles of the Aegean.

At our first meeting with our potential new client, I played my guilt card shamelessly, almost berating the GNTO people for having ignored, over all these years, America's celebrated "crazy Greek of advertising." They endured my pistol-whipping like valiant Hellenes, unflinching and unapologetic—and invited us to submit a creative proposal in two weeks. This is the campaign we created:

"I'm going home . . . to Greece!"

You might infer from this theme that I had intended to recruit famous Hellenic–American personalities such as Telly Savalas, Jimmy the Greek or Olympia Dukakis. Not so. I made a 180 degree turn from the obvious. I proposed instead that we show many famous Americans, all of *non*–Greek ancestry, who were "going home to Greece," the birthplace of democracy, "where it all began." I envisaged a cavalcade of famous Americans from sports, movies, television, fashion, theater—all expressing their love for Greece after revealing that their forebears came to America from Norway or Italy or England or France or Spain or any country whose most humane traditions and values could be traced to ancient Greece, *"where it all began."*

The GNTO people understood our campaign's powerful possibilities and promptly convinced the Athens bureaucracy to approve the campaign. Without missing a beat, we got on the phone to line up four or five celebrities for our television spots in exchange for trips to Greece. At first, talent agents and celebrities thought we had lost our minds. After all, the U.S. State Department had issued an advisory, warning Americans against traveling through Athens International Airport—and President Reagan warned in a news conference against traveling to Europe! So the fear of travel to the Mediterranean, and especially to Greece, was intense, yet we were asking these famous people to appear for *no money!* But we persisted. We cajoled, propagandized, begged, and used every persuasive gambit until we were able to win over two or three celebrities. We appealed to their sense of justice. We argued that Greece must not be allowed to be punished because of their position at that time as a "neutral" between the U.S. and the U.S.S.R. We also pointed out that whoever appeared in our television spots would be able to speak of his or her own ancestry, a proud opportunity for anyone who rejoices in the pluralistic roots of America, nation of immigrants.

Word spread through the talent grapevines of Hollywood and New York, and soon our unlikely challenge caused a celebrity stampede. No less than thirty-eight famous Americans came forward to appear in our campaign. Many had never appeared in any television advertising, even when offered megabucks *(millions* of dollars for some). One of America's finest actors, the octogenarian Ralph Bellamy, yearned for a taste of the Greek experience before he died, and welcomed this opportunity as the answer to a lifelong dream. The distinguished E. G. Marshall, a devotee of Greek culture—and fiercely opposed to the Reagan administration's Cold War obsessions (his daughter was a volunteer church worker in Nicaragua)—became an ardent participant. The popular actor Cliff Robertson, another Grecophile, who was being paid several million dollars by AT&T as its television spokesman, enthusiastically joined the entourage. Many of these celebrities were edgy about traveling to Greece, but they all went—not for money, but out of a genuine urge to visit the birthplace of Western culture.

Word about the campaign spread quickly, and once on the air, it triggered extensive media coverage, especially on television news programs, where our commercials were given free exposure as striking examples of how one country hurt by terrorism was coping effectively with a difficult challenge. The campaign was of particular interest to the news media because it hit squarely at the fear issue by showing that many of America's prominent citizens were not afraid of traveling to Greece. (One talent agent advised his client not to appear in the campaign for fear of being sued if a terrorist episode caused American deaths, but his client wanted to go to Greece and accepted our offer.)

In their delivery of that now-famous line, *"I'm going home . . . to Greece!",* our celebrities imparted a sincerity that gave to the campaign yet another element of power and conviction. We produced fourteen commercials, featuring thirty-eight celebrities. They ran in GNTO's major American markets, including Washington (to be sure that America's politicos, strongly pro–Turkey, would be more evenhanded in their treatment of Greece).

The big idea of using Americans of *non*–Greek lineage, rather than obvious Greek–Americans, exerted a mysterious tug on almost all thirty-eight celebrities, which I could not quite pinpoint until I watched them describing their ancestry. Unlike any other advertising I can recall, this campaign gave to its participants, all famous Americans—even those whose ancestry (like Lloyd Bridges and Peter Graves) went back centuries—a sense of being "rooted" for the first time. This remarkable experience—whether the celebrity's ancestry went back to Italy or Scotland or Spain or Hungary or Sweden—became an almost mystical illumination, and imparted emotional strength to the campaign.

(So much of our ability to line up all these celebrities resulted from the extraordinary talent of my television producer for the last twelve years, Christine Crowley, who has never learned to take no for an answer, and knows every talent agent in the world. I regard Chris with the same kind of deep familial affection that I feel for the other tough, loving women in my life—my sisters, Paraskeve and Hariclea, and my indomitable wife Rosie. This Irish firebrand comes into my room every day and pushes me around shamelessly [she thinks!]. If you let her, Chris Crowley will run you over with a tank—but she always does the impossible, and invariably makes it possible to implement our big ideas.)

Within weeks, bookings leaped, Olympic Airways planes were filled, travel agents and tour operators were back in business. The depressing state of Greek tourism had been stunningly reversed. All this occurred while tourist anxieties were still intense—and they persisted as an important news topic in all media for many months.

The lesson to be learned from these three diverse marketing challenges can never be distilled to that one glib word, *positioning.* I make this modest claim: The brightest marketing minds in the world could never have figured out these "positionings" for Naugahyde, Bobby Kennedy and Greece. Those solutions derived from an intuitive understanding of what was running through people's minds. In each case—with the ugly Nauga, with the deflating of Bobby Kennedy's carpetbagger/ruthless image, with Mayflower pilgrims going home to Greece—we went against the grain; we used an element of surprise. The problem with the pseudoscientists of "positioning" is their deification of logic and linear thinking. The best "positioning" ideas invariably derive from breakthrough advertising, from surprising, disarming *creative* solutions. A logical, rational methodology handcuffs any possibilities for a thrilling creative solution that can make miracles.

The logical, rational "positioning" of Naugahyde:
This is the best leather substitute on the market.
The surprising solution:
Create the little Nauga and establish a new, mystical presence.

The logical, rational "positioning" for Bobby Kennedy:
He's a carpetbagger, but let's pretend he isn't.
The surprising solution:
Let's admit he's a carpetbagger and take advantage of his clout.

The logical, rational "positioning" for tourism to Greece:
Tell the world it's safe to travel to Greece.
The surprising solution:
Show famous Americans of non–Greek lineage traveling to Greece, unconcerned about terrorism—because they are responding to that deep attraction of Greece as the cradle of Western civilization.

When the high priests of "positioning" describe "slots" in the human mind as the targets of their magic solutions, they are talking pseudo-scientific nonsense. They have formulated a neat, rational methodology that would pre-empt the creative primacy of advertising. But advertising, I insist, is never that logical. The best solutions to difficult marketing challenges defy the straitjacket of "positioning" and spring unfettered from the creative imagination—because advertising is not a science, but an art.

"You're some tomato.
We could make beautiful Bloody Marys together.
I'm different from those other fellows."

"I like you, Wolfschmidt.
You've got taste."

Wolfschmidt Vodka has the touch of taste that marks genuine old world vodka. Wolfschmidt in a Bloody Mary is a tomato in triumph. Wolfschmidt brings out the best in every drink. General Wine and Spirits Company, N.Y. 22. Made from Grain, 80 or 100 Proof. Prod. of U.S.A.

"You sweet doll, I appreciate you. I've got taste.
I'll bring out the real orange in you. I'll make you famous.
Kiss me."

"Who was that tomato
I saw you with last week?"

Wolfschmidt Vodka has the touch of taste that marks genuine old world vodka. Wolfschmidt in a Screwdriver is an orange at its best. Wolfschmidt brings out the best in every drink. General Wine and Spirits Company, New York 22, N.Y. Made from Grain, 80 or 100 Proof. Product of U.S.A.

6

Why a
Trend
Is Always
a Trap

Beware of precedents—
they block the creative juices

The absence of rules in advertising is a terrifying situation that causes many ad people to thrash about in search of something "safe." Because advertising is an art, the solution to each new problem or challenge should begin with a blank screen and an open mind, not with nervous borrowings of other people's mediocrities. That's precisely what "trends" are—a search for something "safe"—and why a reliance on them can lead to poor work.

At the start of each new year, as the press scans the horizon for newsworthy departures from the past, I'm usually asked by reporters from America's newsweeklies: "What do you think the trends in advertising will be in the coming year?"

My answer is always identical to what I said the previous year: "Beats the shit out of me. I'll know it when I do it."

Timidity and imitation are not peculiar to advertising. The legal profession lives by precedents until an imaginative or courageous legal mind challenges the past and creates a newer precedent. Medicine is probably the ultimate trend-driven profession. The current emphasis on nutrition and fitness happens to be an extremely *new* attitude. (When I worked at Doyle Dane Bernbach in 1959, cigarettes were advertised on television; in 1990, the Surgeon General testified that 400,000 deaths each year can be traced to smoking.) In previous centuries, bleeding was an accepted treatment for various ailments, with elaborate theories on where to drain the patient's blood in relation to the location of the pain. We live and die with trends.

Picasso was the greatest artist of this century because he expressed his own magical perception of reality, always ignoring "precedents" and "trends," but never forgetting that inspiration could spring from the art of antiquity, from the native forms of African and Oceanic art, from the great works of his Iberian antecedents. More than anyone alive, Picasso understood that art was an intensely personal expression, totally apart from the whims and conventions of contemporary society. Each of his "periods" then became a "trend."

"Trends" should be anathema to anyone who treats advertising seriously, in an artistic way, using elements of mystery and magic to sell a product. How do you ignore trends? It depends on the kind of problem you're up against.

1. To push for a new solution, start by saying no to conventional rules, traditions and trends.

Television advertising for package goods inevitably focuses on the package and visualizes the benefits. In the 1960s, showing a bare foot in a television commercial was taboo. It was considered tasteless. Well, how was I supposed to advertise Ting, a new product for athlete's foot? It was okay with the networks to show an animated foot, but hard-core photographic nudity was out. Undaunted (but outraged), I sent the networks a storyboard concept based on filming a real foot. ("You got some pair of *cojones,*" said my design colleague and alter ego, Denny Mazzella.) The paralegals at the networks were angered by my gall, but I wasn't about to play footsie with them; I went ahead and shot the commercial. A doctor's hand pointed to different spots at the bottom of a bare foot—nails, arch, metatarsus, heel—showing where and how Ting killed athlete's foot. His lecture was accented by restrained (but infectious) offscreen giggling by the patient. It was an amazing feat.

When I showed the finished spot to the network clearance people, they tried, unsuccessfully, to stifle their own giggles. Without a word of discussion, they okayed the nude foot, ushering in a new era of visual permissiveness. When the bare foot ran, it may have been one small step for mankind, but it was a giant step for advertising. This spot also started a new trend: America's television screens became trampled by naked feet, a new "must show" for any athlete's foot product now that Ting had created a new precedent.

2. When facing a fixed formula, expect that the human angle has become fossilized. Start by bringing back humanity.

The incontrovertible musts in packaged goods advertising: show the product, the package, the logo, and list all ingredients. Also, try to hit the viewer on the head, preferably with a hammer. This trend was ushered in by Rosser Reeves, the father of USP (the Unique Selling Proposition—a product difference that sets it apart from other brands in its category). Reeves, a classy individualist and brilliant thinker, fathered the obnoxious school of packaged goods advertising, typified by his celebrated Anacin spots of the 1950s that showed a cartoon cutaway of a human head being subjected to Torquemada tortures. (Incredible—these were the inventions of advertising's gifted Renaissance man!) Many advertising campaigns for over-the-counter pharmaceuticals followed Rosser Reeves' hammering trend.

I happen to be a sensitive soul who hates to look at sinus cavities and nasal passages. In 1961 I was able to demonstrate a more civilized way to advertise packaged goods. I created an ad for a fine cold relief medication for children called Coldene which excluded the product, the package, the logo, the ingredients and the hammer. I showed just a darkened bedroom, where a sleeping couple had been awakened by their coughing child. Actually, I showed nothing—just a black background with some white type. The all-type message against the nighttime darkness was a brief piece of dialogue:

"John, is that Billy coughing?"
"Get up and give him some Coldene."

This ad was a new and fresh way to sell because its method was unashamedly *human,* and its humanity was visualized in a new and startling way. (It was also a prefeminist statement. Today the wife, who probably works, would bark out an order for her old man to get up and take care of the kid!)

3. When competitors all show stiffs at a cocktail party, stiff that cliché.

With the end of World War II and America's transition from a war footing to a consumer society, liquor advertising began to evolve a certain fanciful imagery: a world that was crowded into a mythical penthouse with skinny, stylish couples, always white, having a cocktail party—but where women were forbidden to hold a glass. That was the "trend" in the early 1960s when we were assigned Seagram's Wolfschmidt vodka. Had I stuck with this social cliche it would have been impossible to solve a tricky marketing problem facing Wolfschmidt. The vodka market was dominated by Smirnoff, with its smart advertising claim, "Leaves you breathless." Here was a double signal: To noontime lushes it said drink Smirnoff and nobody will smell booze on your breath. To vodka drinkers it said yes, all vodkas taste the same, but Smirnoff is the smoothest.

We had to put across the simple thought that you *could* tell one vodka from another. Our solution was a radical departure from the chic snobs in penthouses. We showed a vertical Wolfschmidt bottle talking to a luscious red tomato. *"You're some tomato,"* said the (ahem) erect Wolfschmidt bottle. *"We could make beautiful Bloody Marys together. I'm different from the other fellows."* The tomato answered, *"I like you, Wolfschmidt. You've got taste."*

The campaign conveyed three messages: Wolfschmidt vodka had taste, you had taste if you bought Wolfschmidt, and it was the daring vodka for mixed drinks. The following week we ran a follow-up ad showing a horizontal Wolfschmidt bottle pointing to the navel of a ripe orange. *"I've got taste,"* said the Wolfschmidt bottle. *"I'll bring out your inner orange. I'll make you famous. Roll over here and kiss me."* The orange answered, *"Who was that tomato I saw you with last week?"*

Follow-up ads, week after week, showed a lemon, a lime, an onion, an olive, a stirring stick and all of the sexually relevant paraphernalia seen on a bar, each talking a blue streak with the Wolfschmidt bottle, always in sexy double entendre. Wolfschmidt was quickly perceived as the "fun" vodka, thanks to its catchy, playful advertising associations—which also served as the script for double entendre passes by guys (and dolls) on the make at parties.

4. Use your media options creatively to add power.

In 1988 the French trade association, Food and Wines From France (FWFF) chose our agency to reverse the downward trend of French wines in the U.S. and Canada. After years of prosperity in North America, sales of French wines were being hurt by the weak American dollar since the crash of 1987 and by the aggressive promotion of California wines.

The cornerstone of FWFF's advertising had been a once-a-year *Wine Guide*—a multi-page booklet on French wines that was inserted in magazines such as *Gourmet* and in liquor trade magazines—but when we spoke to FWFF's customers, the wine importers, they said the inserts, paid for cooperatively by them and FWFF, were a waste of money. We had to figure out how to give our client a bigger bang for the buck—how to make it affordable for French wines to be advertised on television. (FWFF's previous agency said they would need eight million dollars to be on television. I've always said I could make a million dollars look like ten million—so we had enough dough!) Here's how we solved this seemingly insurmountable challenge:

First, we compared French wines to the world's greatest paintings, a unique treasure of French culture. Our theme became *"French Wine is French Art."* Then we produced a pool of 30 second television spots, each selling a different group of French wine brands. No importer could possibly afford to go on television. Now it was possible. In each spot, each time a brand was mentioned, the wine bottle emerged from a great French painting in the background—a Degas or Seurat or Manet or Monet or Toulouse or Cézanne. A sample spot:

The commercial begins with the voice of an announcer, asking this question: *"Can you name these French works of art?"* We then see a ravishing French impressionist painting as the announcer tells us what we're looking at: *"The painting: Renoir."* A bottle of French wine then emerges from the painting as the announcer names and describes it—with a French accent that is easy for Americans to understand: *"The wine: Mouton-Cadet Bordeaux White, Light, with an intriguing bouquet."* We then see a classic painting by another French master as the announcer says: *"The painting: Monet. The wine: Mouton-Cadet Bordeaux*

Red. Full-bodied, classic Bordeaux." A third French painting appears as the announcer continues: *"The painting: Manet. The wine: Mouton-Cadet from Baron Philippe de Rothschild."* By now we've seen three great French paintings and three different bottles of Mouton-Cadet wine, each clearly pronounced so that we can see, hear and *learn* all at once. A final scene shows a young American couple dining out, toasting each other with French wine as they say: *"French wine . . . is French art!"*

Note the pattern: three works of art, three Mouton–Cadet brands. We created sixteen 30 second spots that featured forty-eight brands from sixteen importers. Each brand name was shown clearly on the screen so that it could be read as the voice-over announcer lovingly said it—a quick but vital lesson in French pronunciation to encourage the ordering of French wines by self-conscious Americans.

We also showed that it was entirely possible to be on television by using cable. With a budget that was normally consigned exclusively to print because it was assumed that television was much too expensive, we were now able to get extensive coverage on CNN, Arts & Entertainment, TBS, ESPN and other cable channels. Rather than confine ourselves to the limited audience of FWFF's traditional inserts, we were now in a mass medium, with custom messages for each of sixteen importers. We found that cable advertising would deliver *eighteen times* the number of impressions compared to the impact of the *Wine Guide* approach—383 million compared to 21 million impressions.

After one year, this campaign's impact on sale of French wines was perfectly clear: While sales of all imported wines in the U.S. dropped 5%, the sixteen importers of French wines in our spots saw their sales rise by 12 to 15%—a remarkable 17 to 20% spread from the trend. *"French Wine is French Art"* demonstrates how a big idea can help an advertiser make a million dollars look like ten million.

Trends can tyrannize; trends are traps.
The fact that others are moving in a certain direction is always proof positive, at least to me, that a *new* direction is the only direction.
Defy trends and don't be constrained by precedents.
Stay loose.

"I want my

MUSIC TELEVISION™

"Don't give up the ship!"

7

You Gotta
Have
a Slogan

The *word* comes first, then the visual

When giving lectures to aspiring young art directors I'm often asked to reveal my "formula" for creating advertising. My answer: start with the word. This may sound like an anomaly, coming from an art director. Let me explain:

Art directors, presumed to be illiterate, are expected to think visually—and most do. They sift through magazines to find visuals, however disjointed and inappropriate, to help them get started. Most art directors, unfortunately, do not sit and try to write the *idea;* they usually wait for a writer to furnish the words, which may not be visually pregnant. By contrast, a handful of great art directors are authors of some of advertising's finest headlines—or they work intimately with gifted writers as they conjure with words. Conversely, even when a writer works solo, his words must lend themselves to visual excitement—because a big campaign idea can only be expressed in words that absolutely bristle with visual possibilities.

The concept of visual imagery springing from words may sound odd, but in advertising (as in real life) this happens to be the strongest way to communicate a clear idea that will stick in people's minds and memories. To be sure, a picture can be worth a thousand words. But if that picture also happens to be the spontaneous visual extension of a strong theme or slogan, its power is enormously enhanced. A visual by itself might be communicative and moving—but could still mean different things to different people. I want to permanently implant an image in your head and place words on your lips. I want everyone to receive the same message.

In 1968 I created a 30 second television spot for Maypo cereal that gave fresh new life to its retired theme line *"I want my Maypo!"* The obvious imagery this line suggested was a kid wailing at his mom for Maypo, but obvious imagery can also be boring and therefore invisible. Compulsively, I made a 180 degree turn away from the obvious. Instead of kids crying the line, I used hulking superstars of professional sports to sell Maypo to small fry, five to twelve years old. I showed Mickey Mantle, Oscar Robertson, Wilt Chamberlain, Johnny Unitas, Ray Nitschke, Don Meredith and Willie Mays—the most thrilling names of their day from baseball, basketball and football—all in one television spot, crying for their Maypo and shedding lifelike tears. Here was the ultimate sissification of the American macho sports icon, a deliberate twisteroo on the unconscionable hustles by too many jocks who manipulate kids through hero worship. Instead, the superstars in our spot sold obliquely, displaying self-mocking wit.

"I want my Maypo!"—with a sub-theme that was tied directly to our advertising: *"The oatmeal cereal heroes cry for!"*—sold a lot of cereal and was heard in ballparks all over this land. Don Meredith and Mickey Mantle told me when they arrived at any ballpark for a game, the fans chanted at them, with mock tears in their eyes, *"I want my Maypo!"* (On the other hand, the humorless Willie Mays had to be coaxed and wheedled into shedding tears; in the imperishable words of that immortal baseball great, who preferred to speak of himself in the third person, "Willie don't cry.")

The words and visuals—superstars crying *"I want my Maypo!"*—gave the campaign extraordinary power. A single-minded merging of words and pictures had been accomplished, resulting in riveting imagery. That word *imagery* is too often associated purely with visuals, but it is much more than that: *imagery is the conversion of an idea into a theatrical cameo, an indelible symbol, a scene that becomes popular folklore, an iconographic image; and this imagery can be expressed in words or visuals or, ideally, both.*

Fourteen years later, in 1982, when those five- to twelve-year-olds who had cried *"I want my Maypo!"* had become the 18 to 35 generation, I used that petulant, demanding theme again to tap the reservoir of imagery of their childhood years. Our client was a new Warner Amex 24-hour video music cable network called MTV (Music Television), a fledgling concept facing crib death. Despite an introductory period of advertising by a large marketing advertising agency, the radical concept of a music video channel was scorned by cable operators, who hated rock 'n' roll, especially round-the-clock; many operators also believed kids who went for rock 'n' roll were heavily into drugs. Record publishers were convinced MTV would kill their business if allowed to prosper (as if they never knew what radio had done for them), and refused to allow their titles to be transformed into music videos. And predictably, advertisers and ad agencies looked down their noses at this new cable concept as a frivolous fad that attracted only kids as young as ten and twelve, and ignored this upstart medium.

I figured the line *"I want my MTV!"* would stir up the richest kind of déjà vu among its target audience. The whiz kids at MTV, led by the post-pubescent Bob Pittman, thought I was a wily old fox for bridging the years so cunningly with this updated line, and they gave it their warm amen. Their faith in me was rewarded, as my intuition proved to be on the nose. With our theme—*"I want my MTV!"*—delivered by rock superstars Mick Jagger, Peter Townshend and Pat Benatar, we ignited a firestorm of popular demand for MTV within minutes after the commercial ran. The clincher in each commercial was this windup sequence as a voice-over announcer says:

> If you don't get MTV where you live,
> call your cable operator and say . . .
> (We then cut to Mick Jagger—or Peter Townshend or Pat Benatar—
> who bellows into a telephone:)
> "I want my MTV!"

We did not list a phone number; all those callers who phoned their cable operators and blared out our slogan (à la Mick Jagger) had to find the phone numbers themselves. Beset by a clamoring public, cable operators reversed themselves within days and sought out MTV for their cable systems, music publishers began to stand in line to promote their titles on MTV, and the ad world rose from its lethargy to take notice of this new cable medium with its intensely responsive audience. This was an *advertising* feat, pure and simple. Years later, after MTV's battle for acceptance, many an advertising maven concluded that MTV had been an idea whose time had come. Oh yeah? When I started to work for MTV, this new music video concept was a dead duck. Without cable operators to accept this new network there would have been no MTV. Our advertising compelled cable operators to demand their MTV and success ensued as night follows day. Without this campaign, MTV might have expired in its infancy. Instead, "I want my MTV!" led to the most spectacular pop culture phenomenon since the advent of cable television —and, arguably, since the invention of the tube itself.

An ideal theme can also be rich with multiple meanings while sending a single-minded message. A contradiction in terms? No. In 1973 I created a campaign for Cutty Sark scotch whiskey that hit the bullseye with buckshot.

Cutty Sark's management was thrashing about for a creative breakthrough to regain brand leadership in a tightening scotch marketplace. They were considering a clean break with the past by scuttling Cutty's famous logo, whose widely known visual trademark was the tall sailing ship (which, er, also happened to have been a slave ship). For over thirty years, more than a hundred million dollars had been spent to promote Cutty Sark in an ad that showed a painting of the ship.

Speaking like the accomplished marketing pro that I am, I told Cutty's brass, "Don't give up the ship. Any trademark with a hundred million bucks behind it is worth at least a hundred million bucks. A hundred million here and a hundred million there adds up to a lot of money." I focused on the simple, old-fashioned drawing of the ship on the label as the visual centerpiece of any new advertising campaign, while seizing as its verbal theme, *"Don't give up the ship,"* the enduring battle cry of the American naval commander John Paul Jones during our Revolutionary War.

"Don't give up the ship!" became our clarion call for Cutty Sark.

Each ad and poster had a blowup of the ship on the Cutty Sark label, with its own salty headline that was raffishly fashioned for each magazine or market and exploited the multiple meanings of this theme:

For *The New Yorker:*
You want the boxing match and she wants the ballet?
"Don't give up the ship!"

For Father's Day:
The best advice I ever got from my Daddy was . . .
"Don't give up the ship!"

For a poster in New York subways:
When you've had it up to here with graffiti . . .
"Don't give up the ship!"

"Don't give up the ship!" became one of the best known and most talked about campaigns in the booze business, and Cutty's sailing ship sailed back into the black.

A strong theme compresses everything into one knockout punch. Themes are constructed from words, the basic tool of communication. Too many advertising professionals believe the visual image, the picture, is our common language. Not so. I'm a designer, who obviously has a vested interest in graphic expression but, to me, our common language is always *language.* That's why my life is a search for a combination of three, four, five or six *words* that express the big idea.

Advertising is commercial propaganda that is based on a big truth, not the big lie. Joseph Goebbels knew what he was doing by introducing the concept of propaganda to our century, but the propaganda of Nazism was a demonic technique based on the big lie to seduce the German volk to follow their Führer mindlessly. Advertising, an American invention, is imaginative propaganda to stimulate commerce in a free market.

The right words focus the market's attention on your brand by communicating a powerful, attractive big idea. That idea about your brand helps build front-of-mind, unaided awareness. The right words that communicate this unexpected idea give your brand a vitality and a freshness that continue long after the advertising sails into the sunset.

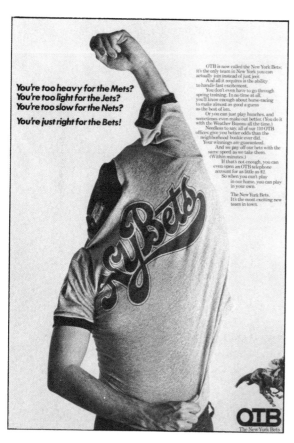

8

How to Sell
Mass
with Class

How come so many dumb messages are
aimed at so many smart people?

People are smart.

I'm convinced this is a minority opinion in the boardrooms of most advertising agencies. I've suffered through a few multi-martini lunches with other agency chairmen, and I've been shocked and angered by the patronizing attitude of these communications biggies. Their recurring complaint is that people are stupid. An insidious logic then flows from this elitist arrogance: research is cited to nail down this canard as truth, and once this bogus truth is revealed, it follows as surely as night follows day that bright, witty advertising is verboten because "they" simply "won't get it."

Therefore, it's not only permissible (if you follow this reasoning), it's *essential* that their agencies create mediocre advertising.[1] Stupidity is not the flaw of the advertising, it is argued; what causes advertising to be dumb (it is further argued) is the natural inferiority of the slob in the street or his missus in the kitchen. Many if not most package goods companies accept as gospel this presumed simple-mindedness of American consumers and they trot out intimidating research to prove it. Hence the proliferation of anxiety-inducing messages, particularly during daytime television, aimed at housewives, the most patronized souls of the marketplace. Wax on floors, stains on fabrics, residue on dishes, lint on clothes, rings on collars, slipping dentures, leaky diapers (for babies and the elderly) and other terrors of domestic life assail the American housewife. Insulting stuff.

Many television spots, especially for package goods, are scientifically "measured" and evaluated, second by second, with readouts that look like electrocardiograms, accompanied by precise insights into the meaning of each dip and rise of the telltale needle during the course of these 30 second illuminations, showing the exact second when the consumer reaches a peak of involvement, like an orgasm, followed by a waning of interest, all of which reveal awareness, retention and purchase intent. It's all edifying and awesome, but despite the scientific presumptions of all this research, is this any way to run an airline?

The fact remains that almost all package goods products are rigorously tested, and after their weak spots are corrected and tested again, they are pronounced kosher to compete in the marketplace. Reality then intrudes and the best laid plans go awry. Look at it this way: if everything that runs on television has been so thoroughly researched, how come most advertising sucks? And how come most new products bite the dust? What's going on?

Too much advertising is predicated on the snobbish assumption that people are dumb, so why give them smart advertising? Feed them predictable, banal work that may score well in research but will probably get clobbered in the supermarket. Intelligent, disarming, fresh, bright work can only be done if you really think people are smart enough and sharp enough to "get it." I think people are absolutely brilliant about advertising. They have a microchip in their heads that places a television

[1] This reasoning was wonderfully expressed during the 1970 Senate battle over Richard Nixon's nominee to the Supreme Court, Harrold Carswell. Nebraska's Senator Roman Hruska defended the nomination because he approved of Carswell's *mediocrity*, arguing that the mediocre people of America needed a spokesman.

commercial in its marketing context with lightning speed, enabling them to judge astutely what they see.

Moreover, they always respond to an *idea*—a strong central concept or image—especially if the idea is presented in a warm, human way. *"When you got it, flaunt it!"* is an American colloquialism that is familiar to everyone and has become a standard entry in anthologies of American sayings. It was created in 1967 by my agency as the theme for our memorable advertising for Braniff—a zany, outrageous campaign that featured some of the world's oddest couples, exchanging the screwiest and most sophisticated chatter heard on television. I paired pop art guru Andy Warhol with that mean heavyweight Sonny Liston . . . pitching great Whitey Ford of the Yankees with the surreal Salvador Dali . . . the ageless black baseball legend Satchel Paige with the flagrantly young Dean Martin, Jr. . . . ear-splitting singer Ethel Merman with publisher Bennett Cerf . . . the British comedienne Hermione Gingold with Hollywood tough guy George Raft . . . fey movie critic Rex Reed with the irrepressible Mickey Rooney . . . and the poet Marianne Moore with crime writer Mickey Spillane. For the kind of dialogue not normally encountered in television advertising, listen to this odd couple—Marianne Moore and Mickey Spillane, who reveals to her: *"Well, I'll tell you frankly. What I really wanted to be all my life was a poet. Only, I couldn't think of any of the rhymes. You know what I mean?"* The ever-polite Marianne Moore replies, *"I know what you mean."* Then listen to how the voice-over announcer blends the presence of these two "odd couples" into a pitch for Braniff: *"Tough Mickey Spillane and the great Marianne Moore always fly Braniff. They like our food, our girls, our style. And they like to be on time. Thanks for flying Braniff, folks."*

Marianne Moore then delivers our theme: *"When you got it, flaunt it!"* The spot winds up with this postscript line by Mickey Spillane—*"You know, you got a way with words."*—that fits in nicely with their dialogue while drawing attention to our theme.

We presented the campaign to the chairman of Braniff, Dallas tycoon Harding Lawrence, a powerhouse entrepreneur with all the mercurial unpredictability one should expect of tycoons. Lawrence was surrounded by a large staff of highly paid and highly insecure top executives. We showed the group how our theme could introduce every innovation Braniff could flaunt—painted planes, leather seats, Pucci uniforms, jazzy new terminal in Dallas, new computer system, new routes. After two hours of rapid-fire selling, covering every aspect of the Braniff system, we were rewarded by Lawrence's staff with silence, then with mushy doubletalk, nobody taking a position, all waiting for the boss of Braniff to demolish the campaign and plaster me against the wall. Harding Lawrence finally spoke: "I'll tell you what I think. I think starting today, Braniff is gonna flaunt it!"

Harding Lawrence was one of those clients who genuinely understood advertising. Many don't. He responded instinctively to wild work, often with a "nifty," while slipping his hand into his shirt and pulling the hairs on his chest. Imagine: the chairman of this Dallas-based airline approved this maverick campaign without diluting any of its wackiness, the source of its power. Take the spot with Andy Warhol and heavyweight champion Sonny Liston. It opens on a tight closeup of Warhol giving this outré spiel: "Of course, remember there is an inherent beauty in soup cans that Michelangelo could not have imagined existed." Camera pulls back, showing him seated next to a big, brooding black man as the voice-over says: "Talkative Andy Warhol and gabby Sonny Liston always fly Braniff. They like our girls. They like our food. They like our style. And they like to be on time. Thanks for flying Braniff, fellows." Warhol winds up with our theme: "When you got it, flaunt it!" Liston never opens his mouth while giving Warhol a "What the hell are you and what planet did you come from?" look.

This campaign broke down barriers and flouted precedents—and was widely perceived as audacious, original, *charming* advertising—causing a swift ascent of Braniff's business. But one frown from Harding instead of twenty "nifties" would have torpedoed the entire effort. Fortunately, he saw its power, as many instinctual entrepreneurs can spot a gold nugget among the recycled garbage that goes under the heading of "advertising." *"When you got it, flaunt it!"* entered the language, and remains part of our American argot almost twenty-five years later.

If you think this campaign was more appropriate for sophisticated consumers than the hoi polloi, America's increasingly mass culture confounds that demographic distinction. Since the advent of the jet age, air travel in particular has become a mass experience. "When you got it, flaunt it!" was a *mass* line that was directed at intelligent people who happened to be the mass of Americans, our market.

Often there are great opportunities to be found by talking *up* about a client, when talking *down* has marked its advertising. Take the case of New York City's Off–Track Betting (OTB).

People like to bet—so much so that anyone with clear lungs runs the risk of instant emphysema in any smoke-filled OTB parlor in New York. In 1973 my wife Rosemary, an adventurous sort, called me out of a conference with a client to tell me on the phone that her sister had just called her with a fantastic piece of news: a horse running in the fourth race at Aqueduct was named "Joe and Laura"—the names of their parents. It was like a religious miracle, Rosie insisted, and urged me (e.g., *ordered* me) to place a bet at the nearest OTB parlor. I had to do it, my wife explained, because she wouldn't step within ten feet of those smoke-filled stores. As any dutiful husband would, I placed the bet, but the horse finished last (so much for religious miracles). What did connect was the obvious need to make betting through OTB an acceptable experience for every social class in New York—from hard hats to middle class housewives in Queens to swells in Manhattan swinging briefcases. We therefore created a new *team* for New Yorkers, the "New York Bets," which rhymed beautifully with three of New York's major teams: the New York Mets (baseball), the New York Jets (football) and the New York Nets (basketball). Because it was a natural, look how smoothly it was expressed in our advertising:

You're too heavy for the Mets?
You're too light for the Jets?
You're too short for the Nets?
You're just right for the Bets!
OTB's new nickname is the New York Bets.
It's the one team anyone can join.

With one swing at the bat we made betting respectable by turning it into a *sport.* OTB was then New York City's third-largest retailer. It was big business by any measure, but most of this impressive volume came from gambling *freaks*—a small fraction of our potential market. The "New York Bets" opened up gambling to everyone. New Yorkers who wouldn't be caught dead talking to a bookie joined the New York Bets because betting on the nags was now socially okay. New York Bets T-shirts became the most popular of that crowded genre (and are collectors' items today). We created a stampede of telephone accounts.

We were also able to attract superstar celebrities to appear in our ads free, just for plugging their shows when they came to New York—first Carol Channing, then Rodney Dangerfield, Bob Hope, Jackie Gleason and for the coup de grace, the "chairman of the board," Frank Sinatra. A year later we were able to place our advertising on television, shattering a long-standing taboo—promoting gambling on the tube had always been verboten. In two years OTB's handle (revenues) tripled. A lot of people had apparently joined the New York Bets. This was a mass idea that was also sharp and smart, and the hoi polloi ate it up. I was also blessed by having the ideal client, OTB's chief, Paul Screvane, formerly New York City's Sanitation Commissioner, a no-garbage, no-bullshit guy who understood a big advertising idea.

In the early sixties, Xerox was catapulted from the schlocky back room to become the company with the classiest image in American industry. Our advertising made it all happen. When Xerox began to advertise, it was a new, unknown company with a very small budget and a certainty about where its advertising should run. It had a splendid new copier, the Xerox 914, that a child could operate in seconds without smudging a pinky. At our presentation in Rochester, we urged Joe Wilson, the president of Xerox, to show his amazing product on television so that overnight, his copier would become a household name. But Wilson was tough to sell. Like almost every client in those years, when TV was relatively new, he seemed to regard us as plunderers, out to squander his ad dollars in one quick binge on this "expensive" new medium. He had to be shocked out of his hang-up. I told Wilson his product would be perceived as schlocky without television to show its magic—and his chair almost hit the window. "Most businessmen think of duplicating as a schlocky, sloppy mess, with a slob in their back room splattering ink over his white socks," I continued amiably.

It was the only way to unsell Wilson on his belief in selling copiers solely to a few thousand purchasing agents with ads in trade magazines. We insisted to Wilson that only television, the first real hoi polloi medium, could turn his miracle machine into a showroom product. We wanted millions of secretaries to see how the Xerox 914 worked so they would bug their bosses to get one fast. We wanted Xerox to become a household name . . . to become *famous!* We proposed that Xerox sponsor six television news specials on "CBS Reports." It was quite a trick to spread Wilson's thin budget of about $300,000 over six network shows, but we would reach millions of people on a trade ad budget—a far cry from talking to a few thousand purchasing agents. Wilson thought I was nuts and fired me. But after a decent night's sleep he called me in the morning and said, "Okay Lois—shoot the little girl."

We made Xerox a household name by going on "CBS Reports." After that, when the company's salesmen made cold calls they were no longer mistaken for Zerex antifreeze or for a Japanese laxative—people knew who they were, and suddenly, business offices were including "Xerox rooms" in their floor plans. But alas, after our first commercial on the 914, we plunged Xerox into hot water. We showed a little girl, asked by her father to run off a copy of a letter on a 914. She skipped over to the Xerox, holding a rag doll under her arm. She made a copy of the letter, then placed the doll on the 914 and pushed the buttons again. Out came a crisp copy of her doll. To see a perfect copy of a letter or document come out of a machine was an astonishing experience in 1960. When the little girl brought the original letter and the Xerox copy to her father, he asked, quite pompously, "Which one is the original?"— a valid question because the 914 was a superb copier.

When that spot ran on "CBS Reports," the duplicating company A. B. Dick (aptly named) charged that it was a hoax and complained to CBS and the Federal Trade Commission, insisting that no duplicator could work that easily. We were therefore ordered to yank the commercial off the air. To show that we weren't playing with mirrors, we scheduled a new shooting for CBS and the FTC. Instead of calling back the little girl, we told our casting department to get us a monkey. When the cameras began to roll, a chimpanzee waddled to the 914, plunked the letter on its glass surface, jabbed the buttons, and scratched its armpits while the 914 clicked out a copy of the letter. The chimp picked it up, grabbed the letter, and waddled back to the father for approval. Once again the father examined the original and the Xerox copy and asked, in the same pompous voice, "Which one is the original?" The chimp scratched his head and grunted.

The outrageous idea of a chimp operating business equipment (he did it with greater ease than the little girl) made Xerox a famous name instantly. Even a monkey could run a Xerox machine! While the country went ape for Joe Wilson's machine, our simian spot was not loved by everyone. After the chimp was first shown on TV, an angry letter was received at Xerox from an embarrassed secretary, urging the company to discontinue that spot because the morning after it ran, she brought some work to her company's Xerox machine and found a banana waiting for her on the 914.

It was the use of television and our bold approach to this young mass medium that freed Xerox from the back room and made it more famous than famous. Six months after we started the advertising, America was becoming known as the "Xerox culture." We insisted that Xerox sponsor prestigious television shows, with a consistent emphasis on public service and cultural programs. We were proposing mass with class, but the networks had met their quota of cultural shows, so Xerox became producer as well as sponsor of "Death of a Salesman," "The Glass Menagerie," "The Louvre," "Mark Twain Tonight" and "The Kremlin" during the dark days of the Cold War—the first time any Western television crew was allowed there.

Conventional wisdom: advertising should be properly "targeted" so that every dollar spent reaches the ultimate user. Minority dissent: if advertising were a science, that would make sense, but advertising is the art form of the people and television is its ultimate medium. When advertising makes a product "famous," it makes the whole world aware of what's out there. "Famous" advertising reaches the target consumer *and* the target consumer's wife (or husband), kids, mother, brother and neighbors. How do you then measure the impact of advertising on the ultimate user? Beats me, and nobody really knows.

I can say this: In our commercial world, it's good to be famous. It's not good to be invisible. Making a product famous is the result of an almost emotional bonding between the product and the person creating its advertising. Advertising that floors the world with a big idea can only come into being from these deep wells of imagination and belief.

We're here
to tell you
the truth.

The truth is, there's nothing on television
more important, more entertaining, more thrilling
than the true human drama of the news.
And because it's the most important part of your day,
we're here to tell you the <u>truth</u>.

EYEWITNESS NEWS 7

9

How to
Reach Slightly Ahead
of the Product

Gertrude Stein to Picasso: *"I don't look like that."*
Picasso to Stein: *"You will."*

Advertising should lead the product. Advertising should never be a mirror. Advertising can be a compass that points its arrow toward new standards of consumer satisfaction. To some this will sound mystical. Advertising haters will gag at the very thought. To me, this belief is a vital aspect of the advertising life; it adds force to my raison d'être and depth to my work. I have a priceless tale that sheds light on this seemingly presumptuous concept:

Picasso had been laboring for months over a painting of his grim-faced patron, Gertrude Stein. His portrait of this bizarre lady finally emerged as a work of sublime art in a mask-like African style, punctuated by the fierce accents of Picasso's ancient Iberian origins. This work is now universally revered as a milestone in the history of art. But when Gertrude Stein finally laid eyes on her long-awaited, commissioned portrait, still wet, her heart sank. "My dear Pablo," she lamented, "I don't look like that!"

Picasso shot back, *"You will."*

That's how I feel about a great advertising campaign. We should portray what we feel in our hearts the product can grow to *become*. The advertising imagery should be ahead of the product—literally—not in a way that assails credulity, but in a sensitive way that inspires belief in the product's benefits and imparts a greater sense of purpose to those who produce it and sell it. Artists, in their magical clairvoyance, show their subjects as their inner characters will eventually define them; similarly, advertising can sometimes portray its subjects as they can *become*. There are instances, particularly if the product is a service that is undergoing a transition, when advertising can legitimately portray what can become, without overpromising. Here are three examples of how advertising reaches just slightly ahead of the product, and leads the product to a new reality:

In 1963 Lewis (Bud) Maytag, Jr., the thirty-six-year-old president of National Airlines and a former jet pilot, wanted a striking, visible campaign to help save his young, troubled airline. He wanted advertising to fill seats on National—people were staying away in droves. We began by searching for a theme that would say National runs its airline in a lively way: it dressed its stewardesses in outfits by Oleg Cassini, it came out first with fan jets, it introduced special meals on certain flights. We wanted to draw attention to all this while coaxing National into newer innovations. Inspired by the old American expression "Is this any way to run a railroad?", this became our theme:

Is this any way to run an airline?
You bet it is!

Almost overnight, this company that was about to go out of business suddenly looked sharp, like a winner, and the New York–to–Miami market ate it up!

National had a Hialeah flight that left New York and arrived in Miami in time to catch the races. We suggested a Gambling flight. We proposed that National route a flight fifteen miles beyond the offshore limits, gut the plane's interior and install gaming tables. Our television spot would show a lovely stewardess saying, "Is this any way to run an airline? You bet it is." She would then plunk a ten-dollar bill on the table. Despite assurances from our lawyers and National's that it was workable, the first flying crap game never got off the ground. Nonetheless, this outlandish idea was an important clue to what could happen and our theme became the fuel that propelled the airline industry, not just National, to new possibilities.

We took airlines out of timetable advertising (print messages that focus on flight schedules) into television as National became the first airline to move heavily into the new medium, with 60% of its budget in television spots, a bold move in the early sixties. (Sporadically, one could see television spots for airlines in those early years, but they were visually skimpy ten second timetable announcements of certain flights or schedules, never a sustained image campaign. National was the first airline to run image advertising on television.) We pushed for matzohs during Passover on National's crowded New York–to–Miami route. We were the first airline to feature a stewardess as spokesperson on television, a lovely aspiring actress, Andrea Dromm (who went on to become a lovely but uninspiring actress), whose down-home Doris Day prettiness is still vivid to those who saw the commercials so many years ago.

Those indefinable currents of morale, esprit and attitude were strengthened within the National Airlines family as employees and managers vied to justify their company's advertising theme, *"Is this any way to run an airline? You bet it is!"*

In 1988 New York's Channel 7, the ABC television network's flagship station, was floundering for want of a clear identity. During the seventies the station's Eyewitness News flourished with a format that placed manic emphasis on laughing anchors and upbeat reporters. All was fun and games with the Eyewitness News team. The novelty of this euphoric departure from conventional newscasting did not wear off as quickly as one might have guessed. For many years Eyewitness News had been a formidable number one in the ratings, with irreverent Roger Grimsby, straight-arrow Bill Beutel, the bubbly, boisterous Roseanne Scamardella with her unmitigated New York accent (inspiration for the late Gilda Radner's "Rosanne Rosanna-Danna" on "Saturday Night Live"), the loose cannon weatherman Tex Antoine and other inmates of that happy academy. Ultimately, however, all the happy talk began to wear thin as New Yorkers showed they were no longer amused by the smiles and banter of Eyewitness News, switching their loyalties to Channel 2 (CBS) or Channel 4 (NBC) or one of the three independent channels aggressively pursuing New York's news-hungry population.

By the mid-eighties, when WABC–TV's primacy was clearly lost, the news staff, from anchors to writers, fell victim to self-doubt and corrosive second-guessing. The station needed therapy as much as it needed a great advertising campaign. We delivered both. We created a disturbing and almost provocatively controversial campaign: *"We're here to tell you the truth."* This theme blatantly restated the station's raison d'être and explained in the clearest possible way why Grimsby, Beutel and the entire staff of Eyewitness News came to work every day. This daring theme touched raw nerves at WABC–TV and set off an extraordinary session of self-examination at a free-for-all group grope. The station's entire staff bared their souls in a family-style exorcism of all those self-doubts and conflicts that sometimes plague earnest people whose ideals and values have been diluted or compromised or lost. Some believed this campaign would return their station to new leadership based on news quality, while others felt they simply could not handle a theme that laid down such a high-minded standard. The pressure would be too much, they argued. "We're here to tell you *the truth!*"?

Imagine the scene: thirty or so of WABC–TV's key people sitting on a set at the station's studios on Manhattan's west side, with famous names speaking out, challenging, confessing, pleading, finding themselves—all because of an *advertising theme,* for chrissakes. I was witnessing an honest-to-God psychodrama that had come to pass because our advertising had crystallized in a few words what their calling was all about. "Here we are not afraid to follow truth wherever it may lead," said Thomas Jefferson. We also quoted Harry Truman ("I never give 'em hell. I just tell the truth. They think it's hell.") and Mark Twain ("When in doubt, tell the truth.") and other great historical figures.

The campaign finally ran, but not for long. It caused too many of the Eyewitness News clan to wonder if they could do their work according to this ideal standard. "We're here to tell you the truth," as obvious as it may sound, got to the marrow of television journalism. That powerful word *truth* was often invoked by the elder sages of the business, such as Walter Cronkite and Eric Sevareid, when discussing their purpose as electronic journalists. While the Eyewitness News people were not inclining to lies instead of truths, the burden of that mesmerizing word unhinged too many otherwise rational souls at the station.

The campaign enjoyed a short but glorious life before the discomfort that gripped the station's staff compelled their management to ask for a less provocative campaign. I swear, that's the whole truth, and nothing but!

When real estate mogul Peter Kalikow purchased the *New York Post* from Rupert Murdoch in 1988, it was widely assumed that he was interested solely in the newspaper's real estate assets, without any sensitivity to its journalistic potential. This ailing newspaper was beset by dwindling circulation, advertiser resistance, and a Murdoch-inherited schlock image. ("Mr. Murdoch," went the apocryphal remark attributed to a famous Manhattan retailer in response to Murdoch's pitch for ads in the *Post,* "Your readers . . . are our shoplifters!") Such was the scuttlebutt in the Big Apple when Kalikow took over, following an impressive line of previous owners before Murdoch that included Dorothy Schiff, Franklin D. Roosevelt (one of a consortium of owners in the 1920s), Oswald G. Villard, William Cullen Bryant and Alexander Hamilton.

To lay to rest this damaging rumor and to convince New Yorkers that the *Post* was headed for renewed prominence in the city, I established at the outset a strong sense of commitment to the newspaper's heritage. We redesigned Kalikow's newspaper, beginning with a fast-paced masthead, and on the new masthead I slapped an oval engraving of its founder, Alexander Hamilton, overlooking the newspaper he had founded in 1803. Simultaneously we created a jumbo bus shelter poster that was seen throughout the city, boldly delivering this message:

> *A reassuring word to Alexander Hamilton,*
> *the founder of the Post . . .*
> *Don't worry, your paper is in good hands!*

This poster may well have prodded Kalikow to commit himself to the new *Post.* Indeed, I believe our "Hamilton pledge" helped keep the *Post* alive—it was a breath of fresh air, it shored up morale, it was a meaningful message to the world that Kalikow was serious . . . and probably stiffened his resolve.

Then came our coup de grace: our television advertising campaign, with its bold theme:

We're keeping the sizzle but adding the steak!

This advertising forced the *Post* to look closely at its editorial makeup to be sure its new management had really added "steak" (new columnists, new features, new reporters) to its "sizzle" (the sassy tabloid style that had made the *Post* distinctive over the years). Kalikow brought in the liberal columnist Pete Hamill to add some balance to the *Post*'s conservative coloration. He also hired Jane Amsterdam to be the *Post*'s editor, bringing with her a brilliant reputation at *Manhattan,inc.*, of knowing how to put meat into a publication. She was the only woman editor of any major newspaper in the area—a meaningful indication of Kalikow's willingness to break rules in pursuit of quality journalism.

As the *Post* quickly assumed its new, vital personality, we created two 60 second television spots starring no less than thirty-four (!!) *Post* reporters eating steak at a famous New York restaurant. In short order, our advertising theme became the standard against which many of the *Post*'s editorial decisions were measured. "We have to add more steak!" became a rallying cry in the corridors of 210 South Street, and when ads were flown or telefaxed to Peter Kalikow on his yacht off the waters of the Bahamas, he would bark back on his ship-to-shore phone, "There's not enough steak in this issue to pour ketchup on. I paid for a three-pound porterhouse and you guys give me a hamburger." The *Post* kept adding steak until New Yorkers understood that Kalikow was an altogether serious angel. Circulation went from 460,000 to 600,000, while the crass image of the Murdoch years (Wingo-hyped circulation, lurid headlines, typified by the classic "Headless man in topless bar") had been upgraded. Can advertising lead the way? You bet it can!

Advertising receives a lot of knocks for hucksterism, for dishonesty, for selling out—and much of this criticism happens to be valid. Nonetheless, there is much honest work and mostly honest people in our business, striving to bring intelligence, humanity and wit to advertising.

Show me a great campaign and I'll show you people who care about their work and their fellow men.

Section Two

Nourish the Big Idea

1

The World
Always Says,
"Be Careful"

But my inner voice often says, "Be reckless"

My earliest childhood recollections were punctuated by these three words (in Greek) from the lips of my immigrant mother, Vasilike Thanasoulis Lois: "George, be careful." They have been a refrain throughout my life—a sincere admonition from the lips of people who have always meant well but have never fathomed my attitude toward life and work. In the art of advertising, being careful guarantees sameness and mediocrity, which means your work will be invisible.

Better to be reckless than careful.

Better to be bold than safe.

Better to have your work seen and remembered. Your work *must* be seen and remembered or you've struck out. There is no middle ground.

When I turned my back on the expectations of my father,

Haralampos, that I would become a florist and take over the family store in the west Bronx, he said to me as I headed out for a career in art, "George, be careful." He knew I could make a living at the store, but a career in art was another matter.

When I dropped out of Pratt Institute after just one year, heeding the advice of my mentor Herschel Levit, a peerless teacher of graphic communications who told me to go to work and sent me off to my first job (which he got for me) because he was convinced there was nothing more to be learned in his classes at Pratt, my sisters, Paraskeve and Hariclea, said to me, "George, be careful."

When I was drafted into the U.S. Army to go to Korea and kill Oriental kids my fellow GIs called gooks, slopes, and dinks, I went off to war determined to fight the U.S. Army instead, and my young bride, Rosemary Lewandowski Lois, said to me, "George, be careful."

When I left Doyle Dane Bernbach after just one year and gave up a great career opportunity at the world's first creative agency to start the world's second creative agency—Papert Koenig Lois, with Fred Papert and Julian Koenig—my normally ballsy boss, Bill Bernbach, said to me, "George, be careful."

Throughout my career in the advertising arena, my partners, my lawyers, my colleagues, my clients, and my friends have all cautioned me at one time or another, "George, be careful." It's understandable, because talent gets you in trouble, especially in advertising. I'm always pushing for a creative idea that has more grit than one has a right to expect, that rubs against sensibilities, that drives me to the edge of the cliff. That's how you bring life to your work. The fact that something hasn't been done does not mean that it can't be done. Safe, conventional work is a ticket to oblivion. Talented work is, *ipso facto,* unconventional.

In 1972 I wrote a book about a Greek florist's kid in the roughhouse world of advertising. I called it *George, Be Careful.* Whenever I'm asked to autograph a copy, my inscription sometimes reads:
"_____, be reckless."

(If you're in advertising, write in your name. If you're not in advertising, write in your name.)

2

How to
Sell
the
Big Idea

If you don't sell it, it won't run

A source of tension and rage among creative people is their awareness that everything they do must ultimately be approved by the person who pays the bill, the client. Advertising, a vital aspect of our free market economy, must defer to the judgments of clients. Like you and me, clients are human beings, their titles, power and wealth notwithstanding. My presentations are made in that spirit, never forgetting that clients are people—who happen to be shopping for miracles.

Advertising is also theater, and must be well directed. I present my work to a client (or prospective client) only when it is fully developed and will cause my listener to rock back in semi-shock. Like it or not, the art of advertising is profoundly dependent on the art of selling and the "sale" begins by stirring up a sense of expectation in the bosom of the client that a giant idea will soon be released from the genie's bottle.

When the client arrives at my agency, he or she is always accompanied by several key colleagues. Anticipation begins as they enter our conference room, its walls thoughtfully bedecked with noteworthy campaigns, current and past, for our various clients. A large black circular conference table sits in the center of the room. There are no windows. There are no distractions. Ample soft drinks and ice sit on a side table. If the meeting is in the morning, hot coffee is ready and my wife's home-baked cake greets our visitors. Everything is served on good china. (The client and his aides are coming into my home, and I treat them like guests at my table.) Blowups of the work we will present face the wall behind my chair, neatly stacked. The client knows something tantalizing will soon be revealed. I never use slides or those sleep-inducing overhead projectors. My emphasis is always on eyeball-to-eyeball contact, on person-to-person communication so that conviction, belief and passion are conveyed. Cunningly, I delay the revelation of our big idea with boisterous small talk, fortified by many jokes—several quite dirty and, I contend, all very funny. Other than a good opportunity to try out the latest jokes, it's all intended to loosen up the client. As a compulsive cup-filler, I dart out repeatedly to our kitchen, to replenish the fresh-brewed coffee (nicely flavored with a cinnamon stick) or to bring new ice or to fill special requests such as herb tea, honey, skim milk or Ovaltine. As I lunge from the room on one such expedition, I can hear one of my staff telling the client that our chairman, chief executive officer and creative director (yours truly) is also the agency's premiere domestic. My strategy to create a loosey-goosey ambience is proceeding apace.

I am in the process of reeling in the client as the small talk and the stories and the refreshments run their course, but I delay the presentation of our campaign for yet another interval as I recall one more apt anecdote or one more ribald joke. Delayed gratification can drive someone nuts, but properly handled it makes The Big Idea much more magical when it is finally unveiled. In the meantime we keep talking, darting from one eclectic reference to another. (My agency's inventory of references is bottomless: in addition to the wonderful variety of campaigns we are doing at any given time for our various clients, my savvy staff can deal with such wide-ranging subjects as perestroika, the Knicks, the greenhouse effect, the Laffer curve, graphology, political rumors, Donald Trump, South American literature, Andrey Sakharov's meeting with Lavrenti Beria, feminism, the savings and loan scandal, AIDS, the misadventures of George Steinbrenner, Cycladic art, World War II, Saddam Hussein's Ba'ath upbringing, Kasparov versus Karpov, current museum shows, the opera, Ivan Boesky's beard, Nancy Reagan's astrology, Cole Porter's lyrics, Akira Kurosawa's films—and more. This is not simply a display of eclecticism for its own sake; to be in the company of people who are tuned in to the real world is powerful reassurance that our *work* will not be theoretical or "blue sky," but strongly connected to reality—*marketing* reality.) The client is now at the edge of his seat, ready to dive for the stack of presentation boards facing the wall behind me. When I can see the drool on the client's tie, I begin our presentation.

The first part is usually handled by one of our marketing mavens, who sums up cogently and in plain language the marketing situation out there, the problems facing the client, the opportunities to pursue—and sets up the creative answer. No slides, no overhead projectors, just straight talk based on thorough homework, supported by a minimum of key-point blowups. Our focus is always on the client's business. His situation is conveyed with candor and clarity by our marketing director, the person who is expected to understand the client's company. The focus during our presentation is never on those audiovisual crutches that telegraph uncertainty, insecurity, or waste.

The marketing analysis fires up an intense need for a big, pregnant idea to solve the client's problem—the essential prelude to my solution. I then present the big idea. I start with the theme, a few powerful words, set in type on what I call "concept boards." I linger over the theme, explaining why it is the magical solution. I make sure it is rolling on the client's lips before I proceed further. Then I gradually reveal the mountain of work stacked against the wall, a careful unfolding of the big idea's extensions and possible applications in all media. If it's called for, a demo music tape is played, either original music or an adaptation of a famous song, using our theme. We also show the results of research we have done to make certain that our idea sends a clear, convincing message. I don't "sell" in a conventional sense. I marshal all my arguments and show the strong logic of what I'm proposing. (Even the most incisive advertising-oriented people need some help.) I inundate my client with every possible application of the big idea. No gaps remain in his perception and understanding of the concept. If I have a "selling technique," I would describe it as a three-step pattern:

1. *Tell them what they're going to see.*
2. *Show it to them.*
3. *Tell them what they saw.*

I also make a promise of success. I assure my client that our campaign will work. I promise and assure without conditions or qualifiers—because success is what I *know* will happen. Most advertising agencies never come close to making such a promise. They don't want to be held to any words or thoughts that might be interpreted as a guarantee. Most agencies are very, very careful. I willingly promise success because I'm excited about our big idea and I know in my heart and mind that my work will work.

The creative presentation is followed by a media plan and a budget summary, including an educated guesstimate of production costs. We then give each person a presentation book that contains copies of every creative item we have shown, from theme to television storyboards to T-shirts, plus a plainly worded marketing analysis and research summary, as well as our media plan and budget. I make sure my staff gives special emphasis to this presentation book. It is our statement and spokesperson. It often winds up in the client's home and is read by his wife or even by friends and neighbors. (If it's done well, it reads like a suspense novel that you can't put down.)

During the presentation, many in the client's coterie add a lick or a stroke to the idea, posing the serious problem of polishing a concept until its edge is gone, but logic, facts and passion usually save the day and one more big idea is now ready to be implemented. Often I keep explaining and pushing the idea even after it has been bought by the client. I admit that I have a problem being overzealous, and I sometimes go on and on in a kind of rapture about our campaign, savoring its brilliance and repeating our magical theme. This has led several of my clients to rap my knuckles—sweetly, to be sure. Charles Revson once cautioned me, "Lois, don't knock on an open door." I was also told by Gannett's boss Al Neuharth (who created *USA TODAY*), "Lois, you can't take yes for an answer."

At the end of our meeting I acknowledge the importance of the questions and reservations that may have been raised—ever alert, however, to this kind of reaction: "I love it, but I'm afraid of *one* thing—" and that one thing is the heart of the idea I've presented. That's when I recall the famous line of Beethoven's patron on hearing the Fifth Symphony: "It's vunderful, Ludvig—except for the first four notes."

Often, the meeting is followed up by additional consumer research to assure my client that our campaign communicates effectively. And I'm always asked to present the campaign to other levels of management, to obtain maximum consensus. In rare instances, regardless of how thorough your preparation and despite the finest of presentations, a client says no, adamantly and irreversibly. That hurts. But after the initial shock of rejection we regroup and work our tails off to come back with an even bigger idea. Nobody's gonna push *me* around!

3

Winning Over
Reluctant Clients

Don't give up until you're thrown out bodily
(then send a telegram)

I don't always have to stand on a window ledge to sell my work, but I would do it all over again if that were the only way to sell a campaign to a reluctant client.

When working closely with a client in a cozy spirit of teamwork and partnership, when it's clear that the answer to my client's problem is the advertising I create—I'm the doctor. Presumptuous as this may sound, I do know what's best for these well-intentioned moguls who are either too close to their problems to understand that a solution is possible or cannot see the solution when it's served up to them on a platter. Here are three examples of how I convinced reluctant clients to do the right thing:

*How I convinced Quaker Oats
to create a successful new product by taking advantage
of its hallowed brand name.*

These days you don't have to study market share data to know that Aunt Jemima pancake mix and Aunt Jemima syrup—products of Quaker Oats —are among the top brands in their respective categories. And while Aunt Jemima is one of America's greatest brand names, there was a time when Aunt Jemima *syrup* did not exist, although many people were certain that such a product had been on the market for years.

In the 1960s, while working on various Quaker brands, I couldn't believe that Aunt Jemima had never marketed a syrup. I asked the young product manager, Bill Smithburg, how come. He gave us several reasons, but they weren't compelling. Quaker's management seemed to be stuck in the inertia of their highly successful business, with nobody willing to shake them up so they could see their own untapped strengths. Nobody in that large bureaucracy would make a move unless they had hard evidence to justify action, so we decided to make the first move. We went ahead on our own with detailed consumer research on pancakes, which included one question on syrup. We asked consumers to mention the syrup brand they used most recently—and we included Aunt Jemima syrup among a list of ten brands, even though there was no such animal. Our findings: a huge percentage of the women we interviewed said the syrup they used most recently was Aunt Jemima!

We rushed back to Quaker, cornered Smithburg, and convinced him to set a date with Quaker's marketing bigwigs. An agenda was prepared, including the usual status reports on our various projects—but with no mention whatsoever of our plans for creating an Aunt Jemima syrup. At the meeting, departing from the agenda, we pulled out our research and launched into a pitch for creating Aunt Jemima syrup. This new product couldn't miss, we argued, because there were so many women out there who think they've *already bought it*—and here's the research to prove it. Smithburg's bosses were stunned at first because syrup was not on the agenda and was therefore not an issue to be addressed. But our findings were staggering and our proposal for creating a new product that people already believed was on the shelf had a logic that was entirely puncture proof. So Quaker plunged into the syrup business. The slogan for our advertising campaign became the simple question, "Aunt Jemima . . .

what took you so long?" (Today the chairman of the board of Quaker Oats is Bill Smithburg, propelled by his brilliant coup.)

*How I broke a corporate logjam and caused
a major investment in a new product line by not taking no
for an answer.*

In the late 1970s, when the diet/health/fitness trend was a speck on the marketing horizon, we acquired a new client, Stouffer's frozen foods. At our "nuptial" dinner with Stouffer's brass I asked politely (to show that I understood their business) if they planned to go into frozen diet gourmet foods. They replied politely (to show that *they* understood their business) that diet foods was a back burner item that required expensive ingredients and eked out low profit margins. Yes, they had done some R&D, but it was improbable that anything significant would materialize. I pointed out that we were in the midst of an emerging health trend and that more and more American women were working. Wouldn't Stouffer's at least want to protect its flanks, I asked, in case someone else in frozen foods decided to market a frozen diet/gourmet line? Could Stouffer's develop a quality product, I persisted, if only as a defensive move? Yes, they allowed. Stouffer's could certainly come through with a good product, but they had canned the project.

Over the weekend I experimented with names of a diet/gourmet line of frozen foods with my wife Rosie. One of the names we came up with was "Lean Cuisine." We both gasped at the sight and sound of this mind-boggling name. On Monday I set Lean Cuisine in lean type and sent it by Federal Express to my dinner guest from Stouffer's with a short note asking him to take a peek at how a diet/gourmet line should be named. When he opened the package he saw at his very first glance a whole new business take shape in front of his eyes. The concept needed no selling, no persuasion. "Lean" said thin, "Cuisine" said delicious and together these two words rolled off the tongue. He immediately called a meeting of his staff, showed them "Lean Cuisine" and announced that the diet/gourmet project was being moved to the front burner. Stouffer's consumer research on the name *Lean Cuisine* broke the bank, and all signals were go. Lean Cuisine was launched, became an immediate success and went on to become the great brand of the frozen food category. Fourteen years after my reluctant client Stouffer's decided to act after seeing the name Lean Cuisine set in type, sales of this new product line still exceed $300 million!

A top honcho at Stouffer's later told one of my colleagues, "Lois's name *Lean Cuisine* saved my career." Also, *The Wall Street Journal* (November 28, 1989) named Lean Cuisine as one of the top marketing milestones of the decade. Those two words, *Lean Cuisine,* set in type, said *everything* that had to be said to describe and sell this new product line—to my client and to millions of diet-conscious consumers.

How I sold a campaign to a global bureaucracy
by keeping it simple, by conserving my energy—
and by being supremely patient.

A common denominator among America's most successful entrepreneurs is indefatigability—which means they work their asses off. Indefatigability is also essential in selling a large corporate client who seeks a consensus among its many echelons and generalissimos. Franchise organizations are notorious for decision by consensus, but an international hotel chain can be even more difficult because you need the blessing of a hotel manager in Khartoum for a campaign that will run in America and Europe.

Inter–Continental Hotels asked me to come up with a creative concept for its chain during a time of terrorism anxiety among tourists and a faltering dollar. The $42 billion American hotel industry was also plagued by colossal overbuilding and growing competition for business travelers, Inter–Continental's customer base. Sheraton, Hyatt and Marriott were spending lavishly to capture this market, while awareness of Inter–Continental (not helped at all by its generic-sounding name) was near zero. We were given a mandate from Inter–Continental's top management: "Capture the soul of our operation and get the message out to the world."

When we looked at the chain's research, we were struck by a revealing statistic: 75% of its customers came back to Inter–Continental after their first visit. We then traveled around the world (literally) visiting nineteen hotels, and we came upon another revealing fact: all nineteen general managers told us, proudly, that their guests kept coming back because of Inter–Continental's superb quality. This led to our theme:

Inter–Continental, Again and Again.

In its bare, simple language, this theme communicated extraordinary consumer loyalty while its rhythmic sound reinforced the motif of returning to a wonderful experience. Everything pointed to this approach: the client's research, the unanimous emphasis on quality by the nineteen general managers around the world, the need for a memorable theme that would make Inter-Continental a front-of-mind brand for business travelers—and would work anywhere on the planet.

However, nothing ever flows as smoothly as my logic. There were layers and levels of management people to win over before anyone would give the campaign a final okay. After winning the approval of Inter-Continental's marketing chief, the sensible Peter Smith, I was summoned to Paris on twenty-four-hour notice with Ted Veru (an ex-client, fellow Greek, and now president of our agency) to present the campaign to a conclave of Inter-Continental's European and Middle Eastern hotel managers. They bought the campaign, but I had stirred a hornet's nest by recommending that we "star" a different manager of an Inter-Continental hotel in each television spot. I wanted to underscore the individualistic character of each hotel, but some of these characters (I learned later during the shooting) were overindulged prima donnas who needed stroking and coddling.

After selling all of Europe and the Middle East, I then had to present the campaign to individual managers of Inter-Continental's American hotels—in New York, Washington, San Francisco, Miami and Hilton Head, South Carolina. Inter-Continental's corporate owners, Grand Met, in England, also needed to see what the wild Greek was doing to turn around their business.

When the campaign was fully okayed globally, I made plans to fly around the world again to shoot Inter-Continental hotels and their managers on every continent, but right up until boarding our Pan Am flight I had to fight off guerrilla attacks from the chain's linguists who insisted that "Again and Again" could not be translated properly into German or Swahili. My agency's documentation on the global translatability of "Again and Again" was dense enough to rate a seminar by the Modern Language Association. After successfully fending off the chain's bureaucrats and snipers, I was finally given the okay to produce the campaign in English and adapt it for use around the world. Tse-tse flies, Montezuma's revenge, and malaria were easy to handle after all this corporate infighting. "Inter-Continental, Again and Again" became "Inter-Continental, *Encore et Encore*" in French, *"Wieder und Wieder"* in German, and was translated into umpteen other languages. The campaign was produced and under way. (I was especially proud because all the print photography was shot by the talented Luke Lois—my kid, you bet!)

The evidence that ensued showed "Again and Again" to be a solid success for Inter–Continental: an upsurge in 800 number bookings, a powerful leap in awareness, a solid jump in revenues. Creating this campaign was a quick, joyful experience; *selling* the campaign to this ultra cautious, hydra-headed client required the most intense mental and physical discipline as I logged hundreds of hours of flight time and endured perpetual jet lag. But it was worth it. As I've said again and again, I'd do anything to sell a great campaign.

4

How to
Protect
Your Work

**I'll use every trick in the book to save my big ideas
(and I have!)**

Conventional wisdom: It takes courage to sell outrageous work.

Wisdom: It takes courage to sell lousy work.

Here's how to spot lousy work: If you can't see it or if you can't remember what you've seen or if it doesn't knock you down . . . it's lousy work. A great campaign stops you in your tracks—but because great campaigns are so visible, they are in danger of being extinguished after a short life. As I go about my work as advertising's enfant terrible, I often feel I'm playing Russian roulette with five bullets. I'm in danger of being shot down *as* I create a campaign, and even after the campaign is okayed by my client I'm still skirting the edge of catastrophe. Great advertising springs from intuition and audacity—which can be very short-lived. (A campaign can be gangbusters and the client's sales may be going through the roof, but one letter from an outraged consumer, for example, can cause havoc.) Yet the right moves or the right words can save great advertising.

How to use mass seduction—the only way to sell a "group" client and keep everyone sold.

A group of 87 Pontiac dealers in the New York area voted to pool their ad dollars for a unified ad campaign. My agency was invited to make a pitch for their business to a committee made up of a dozen car dealers. Each Pontiac dealer had his own ad agency, run by his cousin. My instincts told me to stay away; I could be eaten alive by these barracudas. But I know something nobody else does: the easiest guys to sell are salesmen.

I had to create a campaign that would bring people into their showrooms, and obviously, it would have to be a campaign they would *all* like. I decided to recruit all 87 dealers into a choir that would belt out parodies of popular folklore melodies. While Pontiac's national advertising out of Detroit talked about the car, I would have the 87 Pontiac dealers singing about themselves as nice guys who made good deals. Angelically, to overcome the popular image of car dealers as con artists, I called my new client the Pontiac Choir Boys. In each spot the camera panned over the faces of 87 Choir Boys as they sang a parody of a heartland American song. Here's what they sang to "My Bonnie":

> *Last night you walked into my showroom*
> *We tried very hard to agree*
> *If you really want that new Pontiac*
> *Then bring back your money to me*
> *Bring back, bring back*
> *Oh bring back your money to me to me*
> *Bring back, bring back*
> *Oh bring back your money to me*

This was not only a harmonious creative solution, it was also a shrewd answer to a complicated challenge. Neighbors stopped into Pontiac's showrooms to say they saw their Pontiac Choir Boy on television, and once inside the showroom, they were fair game for a sales spiel. More important, by creating a riveting image on the home screen, my advertising had an extraordinary impact on dealer traffic and sales.

As the campaign hummed along I thought of an inspired follow-up: instead of the Choir Boys, I would assemble a chorus of their wives. I was drunk with success—if I could get 87 dealers to sing, I should have no trouble corraling their ladies. To win over the wives I sent roses to all of them, but my good intentions led to acute embarrassment. I learned to my horror that several divorces were pending, while quite a few Choir Boys weren't on speaking terms with their Choir Girls, or vice versa. Quickly, I rounded up the 87 Pontiac Choir Boys, gave them a new tune and told them to sing. It was a lot easier that way. I had come up with a spectacular solution to a difficult challenge, but because I couldn't take yes for an answer I had almost kiboshed the whole production. So the Pontiac dealers sang, and I felt a lot better. (Besides, whenever they talked, they gave me a headache.)

When a client is a bully, force him to respect your talent... and build billings out of bile.

The Ronson Corporation made electric razors and made life difficult for its ad agencies because of the tyrannical ways of its founder and top dog, pit bull Louis Vincent Aronson II. My partner Julian Koenig knew from the start of our relationship with Ronson that the domineering and arrogant Aronson would not be overjoyed by the presence in his chambers of the street fighter Lois. Koenig therefore became the demilitarized zone between us.

During an occasional tranquil interlude in our relationship, we would manage to sneak in some wonderful ads for this troublesome client. One simple, strong print ad in a small vertical space took the voodoo out of electric shaver advertising with this arresting message: *"No brush. No lather. No blades. No blood. No push. No pull. No bull. All you get is the shave that's rated best."*

But these productive respites from the maddening kibitzing by Aronson were the exceptions to the rule. Normally, our encounters were more than I could stomach. During one meeting, after many ads were presented, Aronson hammered away at one of our layouts for a two-page ad, which he'd been looking at for months. "Hey, Julian," he said, "how would it look as just one page?" Julian held up the two-page layout and said, "Here's how it would look"—and he tore it in half.

It ran as a two-page ad.

If you let a client get too involved, it's your fault.
If you can't keep your client at a friendly distance,
wear him out by making him a "partner."

During the newspaper wars of the early 1960s, the *New York Herald Tribune* became my client and I joined its uphill struggle to win readers from *The New York Times.* The *Tribune*'s publisher, Jock Whitney, brought in a big-league editor, John Denson, who transformed its tombstone image into a lively, with-it journal. In fact, the new *Trib* looked so different and so unusual that it became suspect to many New Yorkers who weren't buying it because they were confused by all the changes. Julian Koenig and I therefore created the still-famous theme, *"Who says a good newspaper has to be dull?"*—which caused an immediate, dramatic spurt in circulation, while the *Times* got really nervous!

The sense of immediacy and vitality that this memorable slogan conferred on the new *Trib* was carried over into our nightly television spots that focused on the front page of the next morning's issue. Each nightly spot came on exactly at eleven, just before the CBS news, scanning the still-wet front page, with teasing references to the news behind the headlines. Now for the clincher: A few seconds before our spot came on, the CBS announcer said, "Stay tuned for Douglas Edwards and the news—but first this message:" As the videotape cameras scanned the front page of the *Trib,* we said, " 'James Meredith starts classes at Mississippi.' That's the headline. But there's more to the news than the headline, because now there's a new way to edit a serious morning newspaper—the *Tribune* way. It gets rid of long gray columns of unevaluated news." We hit the high spots of the front page, but never told the news. Instead, we said, "There's more to the news than this headline—and there's more to it than you're going to hear on this program." Doug Edwards then came on with the evening news.

At 8:15 each night in the *Trib*'s city room, less than three hours before air time, we grabbed the first proofs of the next morning's front page. In a cab from the *Trib* to the CBS studio, writer Ron Holland and I wrote the copy and worked out the camera shots. We were allowed just 30 minutes taping and editing time at CBS to do our spot—no small order—but we pulled it off, working with three cameras. Each night each spot was an original idea, reflecting the unpredictable explosiveness of New York City life. I then scooted home to catch the finished commercial on my own TV set, and I watched with amazement as the announcer said, "There's more to the news than this headline—and there's more to it than you're going to hear on this program." I couldn't believe that CBS was letting us get away with this scam night after night. Months later, when the chairman of CBS, William Paley, finally caught one of our spots just before his favorite news program, he was also amazed—and infuriated. He ordered us never to use that line again.

Tough as it was to turn out a polished commercial night after night, it was tougher having an audience of *Trib* brass and bureaucrats at the CBS studio watching us work, reviewing and okaying everything we did while we sweated bullets, our eyes on the clock. But under the pressure of nightly deadlines, our kibitzing section became thinner and thinner very quickly. We wore them out, just by doing our work. The best way to overcome this kind of problem is to get into your foxhole and start lobbing grenades.

Reality can be lost in a group grope discussion.
A pinprick of humor works wonders to restore it.

Jiffy Lube is a household name today, but when we started to work for this pioneering quick oil change company in 1982 it was unknown, with a handful of locations in a sprinkling of states. (Today Jiffy Lube has over a thousand locations in most of the fifty states.) Despite its small size in those formative years, this struggling new company had gone through a half dozen logo designs, all eyesores on the American road. As a prelude to our advertising campaign, I convinced Jiffy Lube's swashbuckling founder, ex-football coach Jim Hindman, to let us create yet another new logo that would be *the* logo for *all* Jiffy Lubes into perpetuity, so help me God!

I designed a circular "J" in the form of a directional sign, a striking curved red arrow that almost forced you to make a turn off the road into the Jiffy Lube driveway. I called it an "action logo" because it grabbed your eye, especially while behind the wheel, almost like a traffic sign, with its striking red arrow curling around and its arrowhead pointing to the entrance to Jiffy Lube. Set in type across the horizontal thrust of the red arrow was the white *Jiffy Lube*. I explained this was an "action" logo —with the curved red arrow as its basic shape, a design that induces movement into Jiffy Lube—as compared to conventional, "passive" logos, usually geometric designs that just sit there, invisibly. I also gave a quick lecture on the economics of logo design, how companies specializing in "corporate communications" create designs that look like computer graphics and communicate no idea or image, but usually carry an enormous tab—anywhere from $200,000 to a million and up, depending on the depth of a client's pockets.

It was one of my proudest logo designs, and I had already won over the support of Jim Hindman, his marketing director, and others of his inner circle. To obtain consensus from Jiffy Lube's corporate staff in Baltimore, Hindman asked me to present the logo to his management committee. Several of us went to Baltimore to make the presentation. At Jiffy Lube's headquarters we were ushered into a large conference room, where a variety of corporate executives we had never met awaited our presentation, including their head of operations, their sales director, their financial officer, their personnel chief, and their legal counsel.

I took them through the mottled history of Jiffy Lube's atrocious collection of undecipherable logos—wondering with crossed fingers if we were insulting any of the people in the room, some of whom may have been proud parents of those graphic mutations. I then delivered a passionate dissertation on the importance of a powerful logo, how such a logo in all their locations would cause one plus one to equal three, how it could become as well known as the CBS Eye (designed with Bill Golden by my long-time associate Kurt Weihs) and could contribute substantially to the image of Jiffy Lube as a modern, uniform chain with standardized quality control and all the rest. "Some day you'll have a thousand stores," we told them, "so it's imperative that you have a terrific, clean, consistent look and are not weighted down with the present grab bag of dreadful logos."

They listened attentively, and as I began to reel them in, I unsheathed our new Jiffy Lube logo, strikingly printed in brilliant red against a white blowup card. I explained how and why it would be a great Jiffy Lube asset—and I began to feel glowingly *complete*. I had covered every base, and I knew I would not kick myself later for having omitted an important selling point. Confidently, I asked Jiffy Lube's management committee, "Do you like it?" They applauded, and my guys exhaled with relief. Their legal counsel, Arnold Janofsky, a short pudgy man, raised his hand and I gratefully gave him the floor, figuring that a ringing statement of support from their legal beagle would wrap up the sale. Instead, he threw us a curve:

"George," Janofsky said haltingly, "don't you think that your design

. . . with that curved arrow . . . has a kind of *phallic symbolism?"* I was aghast. *Me,* a purveyor of subliminal pornographic messages?

"Well, Arnold," I said seriously, "I don't know what *your* peepee is shaped like, but *my* peepee sure don't look like that!"

They bought the logo. It's now a household graphic. It could have fallen to earth if I had tried to answer Arnold's question seriously.

Having to protect your work with people sniping at you from every angle ain't my idea of having fun. But it usually turns out all right because even if the big idea is ultimately rejected, you usually come away from the experience with at least one funny story!

THE 4 GREAT AMERICAN DESIGNERS FOR MEN ARE:

R_____ L_____
P_____ E_____
C_____ K_____
T____ H_____

THIS IS THE
LOGO OF THE
LEAST KNOWN OF
THE FOUR

In most households, the first three names
are household words. Get ready
to add another. His first name (hint) is Tommy.
The second name is not so easy.
But in a few short months everybody
in America will know there's a new look
in town and a new name at the top. Tommy's clothes
are easy-going without being too casual,
classic without being predictable.
He calls them classics with a twist.
The other three designers call them competition.

282 Columbus Avenue
at 73rd Street
New York, New York 10023
(212) 877-1270

© 1985 MURJANI

5

Beware
the
Legal
Beagles

How a big idea can create
a new legal precedent

Advertising is a highly regulated activity, governed by a legal clearance process that is serious and thorough, particularly on television. No commercial can run on any television station in the United States without having been approved by the station or by the continuity clearance department of the network with which it is affiliated.

The need to make one's work conform to legal requirements can impose clear limits on the creative professional. There is little room in the real world of advertising for creative concepts that flout the basic rules: claims must be substantiated, copy cannot be libelous or slanderous, privacy cannot be invaded, competitive messages are not allowed to "ashcan" other brands, trademarks must be respected, testimonials require an affidavit confirming use of the product. In addition, television commercials must not violate station or network "policy," that large, subjective area of *taste*—a highly ambiguous province.

Advertising law, like constitutional law, is a constantly changing body of rules, reflecting the profound impact of Madison Avenue's small minority of influential creative people, who create great advertising that shakes up the Establishment and alters precedent. But that's the exception; most advertising agencies work very hard *(too* hard) to make certain their work *conforms* to legal guidelines. They want, above all, to avoid controversy.

My attitude toward legal clearance has always been subversive. Most people in advertising sigh with relief when the networks okay their work and get nervous if objections are raised. It's the reverse with me. If my storyboards are okayed without a ripple, I'm in trouble. It's a signal that I might be going senile. It doesn't bother me at all if my work throws lawyers into a panic; in fact, I love it. When a lawyer screams, it's a vital double-check on my artistic integrity: it tells me a new legal precedent may be aborning.

To squeak through the legal curtain and create a new precedent, a sliver of light may be all you need.

The Alexander's department store chain, for decades a fixture of New York's frenetic retailing scene, needed image resuscitation. By 1982 its reputation as a mecca of values, particularly in women's apparel, was fading. Alexander's was coming to be regarded by consumers and retailers as a declining brand, as a schlock chain.

The owners of Alexander's, the feuding Farkas brothers (Robin and Steve), heirs of the original Farkas who founded the chain a half century earlier, appointed my agency to rebuild their image. They plied us with several pounds of research, which proved what any savvy New Yorker knew instinctively: the chain's image was lousy, but a lingering admiration persisted among female shoppers for Alexander's special values. To get to the heart of the matter, we did our own research among women shoppers—one-on-one interviews in depth that encourage people to speak with great candor, thus bringing socially sensitive attitudes to the surface—and found that many women were closet fans of Alexander's: they bought their clothes there, then replaced the Alexander's label with a hot-stuff name, such as Bloomingdale's or Saks Fifth Avenue. These findings corroborated the "closet fan" syndrome we had detected among female staffers of our agency.

Having done our homework, we did our campaign and submitted our concept to the Farkas brothers. The big idea was to show a chic working woman in a 30 second television spot prancing through New York's top stores to check them out, but buying at Alexander's while singing these words to an original tune:

> **I browse at Bloomingdale's**
> **I breakfast at Tiffany's**
> **But I buy at Alexander's!**
> **I buy at Alexander's!**
> **I'm sauntering through Saks**
> **Meandering through Macy's**
> **But I buy at Alexander's!**
> **I buy at Alexander's!**
> **I never forget to go to the Met**
> **But I buy at Alexander's!**

The feuding Farkases did not react to our campaign with similar levels of enthusiasm. Robin loved it, but Steve only *liked* it. After Robin adjusted his opinion downward—he now *liked* the campaign but no longer *loved* it—Steve revised his opinion upward, declaring he now *loved* the campaign. In clout and pounds, Steve carried more weight than Robin, and we got the go-ahead.

In the course of legal clearance, we submitted the script to the networks before going ahead with production. All three networks were plainly flabbergasted, admitting they did not know how to deal with this baffling exception to all their rules on competitive advertising. We were not guilty of "ashcanning" (derogating Alexander's competitors), they said, but our commercial, somehow, was not entirely kosher. All three networks arrived at the same non-decision: each said they *might* okay the campaign if the other two networks said yes. Accordingly, I instructed our account supervisor to tell a white lie. Obeying his leader, the account supervisor called ABC and announced triumphantly that NBC had approved the campaign. ABC hemmed and hawed and okayed it. The account supervisor then told NBC that ABC had approved the campaign. NBC okayed it, enthusiastically. CBS was now a shoo-in, and we were ready to shoot our commercial—but with a new set of obstacles:

We wanted to shoot on the actual doorstep of the enemy—Bloomingdale's, Saks, Gimbel's, Macy's, and other well-known New York retailers—with our singing model belting out "I saunter through Saks" or "I browse at Bloomingdale's" or "I meander through Macy's." At the outset we enlisted New York City's police in our cause; they gave us permission to shoot those exterior locations as our abundantly manned and fully equipped crew stopped and blocked cars and pedestrians in front of these major high-traffic stores. Our smoothest shooting was in front of Saks Fifth Avenue, a few feet from world famous St. Patrick's Cathedral. Impressed by our huge and fast-moving television taping crew, Saks' enthusiastic doorman helped us with gusto, determined to see his store properly filmed in this apparently big-buck *Saks* production.

In front of Gimbel's, another high-traffic location, our large crew caught the attention of the store's advertising manager, a bright fellow with whom I'd once worked at CBS Television—and he smelled a rat. He knew this production was not in *his* budget and ordered us to scram, despite our police permit. We told him to be reasonable—after all, this was a free country and I was a veteran. We almost had the guy buffaloed —but he stormed into the store to check with Gimbel's lawyers. A few minutes later he returned, demanding that we leave—his lawyers said we had no right to shoot one inch of Gimbel's. I promised him we wouldn't do it *again*—(we had completed the shot while he checked with his lawyers). We struck the set and ran like hell.

We got the job done by thinking and moving fast. We did nothing illegal, but in doing scenes that defied precedent, we ruffled feathers at every step. A few department stores lodged unpublicized complaints with the Farkases, but none wanted to be pegged publicly as a spoilsport, knowing the publicity would benefit Alexander's.

After the first television flight, "I browse at Bloomingdale's but I buy at Alexander's" became the best known retail television campaign in memory. (At a businessman's lunch, Mayor Ed Koch spotted one of the Farkases and sang the complete jingle, having seen the spot on television.) This powerful campaign caused the chain's top-of-mind awareness and their image to improve dramatically, and the gang at Alexander's sang our praises.

When the rules have the slightest sliver of daylight, I'll drive through it like a truck. Especially as it applies to advertising and many creative efforts, the law is always in flux, often in response to creative troublemakers. Today, advertisers readily reel off the names of competitive brands in their advertising and even show their logos—not just in competitive comparisons, but to speak openly and frankly about the marketing jungle out there.

You can make an unknown client famous by associating his name with the big winners. It's legal now.

Murjani International, the successful marketer of Gloria Vanderbilt jeans, employed a restless young designer named Tommy Hilfiger, talented but anonymous despite an impressive line of stylish leisure apparel that bore his label. The company's chairman, Mohan Murjani, decided to provide needed advertising support for an unknown Tommy Hilfiger store that had opened on Manhattan's West Side. In 1985 we were given a tiny budget to promote the Tommy Hilfiger brand and the Tommy Hilfiger store. With my wonderfully talented copywriter, Elaine Kremnitz, who knows all the ins and outs of the fashion world, I created the ultimate teaser ad that would also run as a telephone booth poster and as a giant billboard on Times Square: *THE 4 GREAT AMERICAN DESIGNERS FOR MEN ARE: R____ L_____, P____ E____, C_____ K____, T____ H_____.* Without showing any of Hilfiger's designs, this message thrust our unknown designer into the company of Ralph Lauren, Perry Ellis and Calvin Klein. Before we ran it I asked Mohan Murjani and Tommy Hilfiger, "Are you sure you're selling a great product? There's gonna be a run on your clothes, so they better be terrific—because the best way to kill a bad product is through great advertising."

"Marvelous product," said Mohan. "Don't worry about it."

"Do we really have the nerve to run this, Mohan?" said Tommy apprehensively. Then he gave me a nervous sidewise glance and said, "G . . . G . . . George, you better be careful." We ran it. My shameless gambit of success by association set off a firestorm of publicity while traffic to the store was choking the street and phone calls in response to the ad/poster never stopped. (One of New York's tabloids asked, "Who the hell is T____ H_____?") A few months later Mohan Murjani decided to invest a few more bucks to further promote his young designer. For this second phase in Tommy Hilfiger's swift ascent from anonymity, I proposed a 10 second television commercial and a six-page magazine ad that described three groups of America's great designers: the pioneers, the next wave—and now, the new wave, personified by guess who?...

First there was Geoffrey Beene,
Bill Blass and Stanley Blacker.
Then Calvin Klein, Perry Ellis and Ralph Lauren.
Today, it's Tommy . . . Tommy Hilfiger.
Time marches on!

"No way," said our agency's lawyers. "You'll probably get sued by every designer you mention—and by every designer you left out!"

"Are you nuts?" asked Murjani's shell-shocked lawyers. "We'll get hung by our nails."

The counselors had reason to be nervous. I had begun to work on this concept by showing *photos* of Beene, Blass, Blacker, Klein, Ellis and Lauren, which might have suggested that I was trafficking in real live personalities, a clear invasion of privacy as well as trademark infringement, both serious crimes, I kid you not.

"When I'm about to commit a crime," I shouted at my lawyers, "don't talk to me of punishment. Just show me how to fake out these no-good, rotten Nazi bastards."

A practical compromise came about: if I dropped the photos but mentioned only brand names while adding the right disclaimer, we might be in the clear. The photos were killed and this disclaimer was added: *All the names mentioned in this advertisement are registered brand names.*

While the lawyers continued to speculate on the possibilities of being sued, Mohan Murjani gave me the okay to run the campaign, and by this time, after the explosion of publicity and the runaway sales, Tommy had become a hawk for our "controversial" approach.

In clearing our 10 second storyboard through the networks, one of their more perceptive legal beagles observed that we appeared to be trading on the reputations of successful designers to enhance the name of the unknown Hilfiger. "Nonsense," we shot back. "Our television spot happens to be an accurate historical insight into the evolving waves of au courant designers in the volatile apparel world—and it is a fact that Tommy Hilfiger is the contemporary personification of the new wave." They bought our argument and the spot ran. (I assume they understood what we said.)

The impact of this teeny-weeny budget campaign that ran on a few New York television stations and in selected magazines was extraordinary: *The New York Times* ran a major piece, "The Making of a Designer," on the front page of its business section and reported that

Stanley Blacker sent Tommy flowers "to congratulate him on his boldness and brave advertising." The *Times* also noted: "Mr. Hilfiger's advertisements are better known than Mr. Hilfiger's clothes." The *New York Post* observed ominously, "The top menswear designers are not too happy with the new kid on the block, Tommy Hilfiger. Tommy, a comparative nobody, is trying to become a somebody by comparing himself to the established stars of the fashion world." *Newsweek,* in a long article, "A Flashy Upstart—Tommy Hilfiger's ads outdo his clothes," estimated that our ad budget was $20 million. When the fact-checker called to confirm that figure, I told her to delete one zero, then cut it in half (our total budget was less than $1 million), but they had already carved $20 million in concrete. *People* magazine, too: "With brash advertising and a $20 million boost, Tommy Hilfiger takes on Seventh Avenue titans" was the headline of a two-page article, prepared by three writers. (I've always said great advertising can make a $1 million budget look like $10 million, but I never said it would make it look like *$20 million!)*

As his presence in national and local media became ubiquitous, the Tommy Hilfiger line of apparel flourished and Tommy Hilfiger became, for the moment, a serious name on Seventh Avenue. If it's handled correctly, "success by association" can be an audaciously effective strategy, but subtlety and wit are essential. It also pays to have the right disclaimer in your hip pocket. And thanks to this campaign, a legal precedent has been carved out for "success by association."

When a client wants to declare war on a competitor, be sure he intends to follow through or you might get burned.

Once upon a time there was a hot electronics chain in the New York City area called Crazy Eddie. Their unforgettable advertising theme, "Our prices are *insane!"* delivered by a hyped up, fast-talking pitchman who played Crazy Eddie and became the company's vivid trademark, built this chain into a major retail operation. Crazy Eddie owned the electronics market in the New York tri-state area, but this hefty franchise soon became a target for competitive retailers such as Circuit City, which embarked on a strategy to cut into Eddie's formidable market share.

Our agency competed for Circuit City, called Lafayette in New York, and we won the business with our campaign (1986) that said to the haggling-weary (our research showed that most people hated to bargain): *"Why haggle? The new Lafayette Circuit City is nationwide, with brand-name buying power ten times greater than Crazy Eddie. There's no haggling for our lowest price. We're so positive ours is the lowest, we'll refund the difference plus 10% if you find one lower."* One of the television spots starred the King of Hagglers, boxing promoter Don King. In his inimitable pitchman style, with the camera tight on his face (without showing his trademark fried hair), King says: *"Some people say I'm the entertainment impresario. Some say I'm a haggling wheeler-dealer. They're both right! Like the time I went to Lafayette Circuit City, ready to haggle. I found great brand-name TVs and stereos at low guaranteed prices. And they said if I found a lower price, they'd refund the difference* plus 10%. All that and no haggling. I was so "shocked"—at this point the camera pulls back to reveal his fried hair, standing straight up, as King tells us—*"it made my hair stand on end!"*

We developed the "no haggling" theme from all angles, and I knew we had a gangbusters campaign that would put Circuit City on the New York map against stiff odds, although it would be an uphill struggle—Crazy Eddie with his memorable slogan, *"Our prices are insane!"* seemed impregnable. But now Lafayette Circuit City had a campaign that could make big inroads.

A few weeks into the campaign, our client revealed to us exultantly that it had Crazy Eddie by the short hairs. Its dogged marketing operatives in New York had come up with proof positive that its competitor's products were deceptively coded. Let me explain: a VCR at Crazy Eddie might have a price tag of $200. A separate code on the tag tells the salesperson how far down he could negotiate before reaching his final price—let's say, to $150. The customer is led to believe he could haggle down Crazy Eddie by $50, but the true "lowest price," coded and set, was a lot lower than the so-called "final price." The fix was in. The "haggling area" was rigged—while at Circuit City, the same VCR sold for less than the $150 base price without haggling. There was a lot that went around in the dark at Crazy Eddie besides Santa Claus.

This smoking gun had the Circuit City guys climbing the walls, and we were urged to kill, kill, kill—to go straight for Crazy Eddie's jugular. I couldn't disappoint our client, and I came back with a killer anti–Eddie campaign. I cast Crazy Eddie as the supplicant at a confessional. "This is even stronger than going for the jugular," I assured the Circuit City hawks. "This campaign goes for Crazy Eddie's *soul!"*:

In a confessional booth, the camera shows a guilt-ridden Eddie revealing his sin: *"I try to convince people my prices are insane. But even if people haggle like crazy, they won't know if they got my real lowest price because I use a coded price tag system."* This was followed by Circuit City's claims about their honestly discounted prices.

When we sent the script to the networks, they went for their nitroglycerine. We not only said Crazy Eddie was a fraud, we were also satirizing the confessional, however good-naturedly. The networks saw this as a litigious message, bursting with possible slander or sacrilege or both, but we quickly set them at ease when we laid out the black-and-white evidence of coded tagging, including a citywide study of competitive pricing, which proved our point.

Zestfully we went ahead and produced the spot. As I sat back and waited for the unconditional surrender of Crazy Eddie, something unexpected happened. After only a few days of advertising our client told us to pull the anti–Eddie spots off the air. Legal papers had been served against Lafayette Circuit City by Crazy Eddie, claiming trademark dilution because our commercial parodied its television spokesman/symbol. *Hullo?* We had even produced a spot for Christmas with a young Crazy Eddie as a loudmouth brat, sitting on Santa's knee while haggling with him over the price of a television set he wants Santa to drop down his chimney—but this little masterpiece would never run because Crazy Eddie had threatened a lawsuit. A resolution of *l'affaire jugular* was arrived at quickly and without publicity between Crazy Eddie, plaintiff, and Circuit City, defendant. All our commercials were to be destroyed and Crazy Eddie's lawsuit would be withdrawn. Case closed.

Somehow, Circuit City had gotten spooked, and our client the tiger had been transformed into a pussycat. Not too long after that surrender Circuit City sold off all its Lafayette stores and beat a retreat out of the New York market. It was a sobering moment that changed my life. I've become, as lawyers like to say, litigious. I'll now sue at the raising of an eyebrow or the dropping of one false word.

Hurdling the legal barricades goes with the territory if you're committed to creative, innovative work. The body of rules and precedents that governs advertising simply reflects what has occurred up to now. Too many young creative people regard the networks' rules and codes as The Law, and their work becomes stiff and constipated in deference to this imagined Final Authority. *The only final authority on your work should be you.* If your work challenges the legal status quo, you may have enhanced and expanded the law. It is the responsibility of creative people to find every legitimate way to overcome legal hurdles by translating these challenges into creative solutions without diluting or disemboweling the work itself.

no ex**cuses**
AWARD OF THE MONTH:

Dedicated to the principle
that to err is human,
but to take the heat and
make no excuses for it,
is divine!

To Leona Helmsley

Hey...since when is it a crime to redecorate?!

no ex**cuses**
AWARD OF THE MONTH:

Dedicated to the principle
that to err is human,
but to take the heat and
make no excuses for it,
is divine!

To Exxon

For moving The Black Sea
to the Alaska coastline.

6

A Full-Color Ad
on a Front Page
...*Free?*

How a great ad campaign is, *ipso facto,*
a public relations bonanza

A great advertising campaign should aim for an explosive unity between the product and popular culture. This can ignite (not every time, but when it happens, it's unforgettable) a kind of magical alchemy that causes the advertising to enter the culture. National politics is a reservoir of mass fascination that replenishes itself gloriously every four years. Show business and the sports world are other rich sources for mythmakers, but politics, the stuff of history and power, is the best reservoir of them all. And when politics is agitated with affairs of the heart, a universal front-of-mind myth is created. For the bold, discerning advertiser who seeks that explosive unity, seek no further.

In the 1988 race for the Democratic presidential nomination, Gary Hart was the clear front-runner until it was revealed that he had been monkeying around with a bimbo named Donna Rice on a boat named *Monkey Business* off Bimini. After Senator Hart had fallen from grace and Ms. Rice had risen to celebrity, she was signed up by an imaginative entrepreneur, Neil Cole, the president and founder of New Retail Concepts, to be the spokesperson in an advertising campaign for his No Excuses jeans. That campaign created instant awareness for No Excuses.

The raison d'être for Donna Rice—an attractive model-type who sinned and showed no remorse—made it clear to me that No Excuses would have a tough time finding a new bimbo to succeed her as spokeslady after Rice had lived out her fifteen minutes of Warholish celebrity. The new spokeslady would have to be a sculptured beauty who would fit snugly into No Excuses jeans while proclaiming to the world that she made no excuses for her naughty behavior. Those requirements painted No Excuses into a corner. The successor to Donna Rice turned out to be Joan Rivers, a caretaker choice who was skinny enough to look passable in jeans, but hadn't done anything particularly sinful that warranted her defying the world with a bold, "No excuses, folks!"

As the campaign was running out of steam, I ran into Neil Cole. "What do you think of my advertising?" he wanted to know. I told him it did nothing to win me over or charm me, but at least it had lots of publicity value. "At least you're doing advertising that wakes people up," I said. "So I wouldn't say your advertising sucks, but it sure needs the right focus."

Subsequently I received a call from Cole. "I know you're no fan of my campaign," he said, "but I need your help. I'm in a crisis situation. I'm trying to come up with a new No Excuses bimbo, but there are no bimbos in sight. America is in desperate shape, George." I'm a sucker for that kind of challenge. Here was a ballsy advertiser who wanted to stick his neck out, who wanted a campaign that was directly wired in to pop/gossip culture, who wasn't afraid to make waves. My first task was to create an advertising idea that would keep No Excuses in everyone's front of mind, especially the retailing trade, always alert to smart promotions but usually suspect of an advertiser whose campaigns fizzle after one short burst. Neil Cole told me we had a paltry $100,000 to pull off the impossible while waiting for the successor to Ms. Rice to capture America's attention. It was hardly enough dough to rock the nation, but I got big results.

Our solution was to create a "No Excuses Award of the Month" that would be "given" to a public personality right out of today's headlines who "made us remember that to err is human, but to take the heat and make no excuses for it, is divine." Each monthly award would run as a full-page ad in *Women's Wear Daily* only, starting in January 1989. *(WWD* was such a dominant voice in the apparel world, no other publication was needed.)

As I moved into that gray area where "invasion of privacy" could rear its nasty head, I was cautioned from every corner, "George, be careful"—but I said the hell with it and convinced Neil Cole that if the world caved in around us, we would occupy the same jail cell and reminisce (since we would have lots of time) about bimbos. I began our campaign by choosing our Vice President-elect, J. Danforth Quayle, to be the first recipient of our "No Excuses Award of the Month." Not yet inaugurated, the inexperienced Quayle had been laboring to appear serious and statesmanlike. This was our timely tribute:

> *Eager for his place in history,*
> *he is industriously doing his homework,*
> *crossing his i's, dotting his t's,*
> *getting ready to lead.*

The day before the ad was scheduled to run, a reporter from *USA TODAY* pointed out that federal law bans using the likeness of a president or vice president for commercial purposes. But there's always room for a new precedent, and we decided to give Quayle his Award of the Month because, in the perceptive words of our client, Neil Cole, our ad was "good spirited." We had also sent to the veep-to-be a bronze statuette of jeans and planned to send a dozen pair of No Excuses jeans (which he might give as gifts to some of his golf groupies). The Quayle ad was reported on the front page of *USA TODAY,* on the wire services, and was featured on *Entertainment Tonight* and other television and radio shows across America. Quayle played the good sport. His deputy press secretary was quoted as saying, "That sort of thing happens all the time," although the statuette was returned and No Excuses was advised that government rules require that the jeans go to the National Archives. There was no further flak, while No Excuses was off and running with its nonbudget campaign that would generate astonishing publicity.

We followed up with one newsmaker after the other: LaToya Jackson, fresh off a *Playboy* spread *("For showing us that any resemblance to her famous brother is from the neck up.")* . . . Frank Lorenzo during the Eastern Airlines strike *("Who, when he writes the story of his life, will probably not get past Chapter 11.")* . . . Exxon for its Alaska oil spill *("For moving the Black Sea to the Alaska Coastline.")* . . . Actor Rob Lowe for his videotape caper in Atlanta *("How Lowe can you go?")* . . . Convicted tax evader Leona Helmsley *("Hey . . . since when is it a crime to redecorate?")* Our August selection was Malcolm Forbes at the crest of his notorious publicity for that singular seventieth birthday party in Morocco, an internationally publicized bacchanal that outdid anything the world has seen since Nero and Caligula. Under his photo I ran the caption: *"To Malcolm Forbes: For feeding 880 hungry people in Africa!"* I must admit I was concerned about possibly sacrificing my friendship with Malcolm Forbes, but I would rather lose a friend and run a good ad than keep a friend and lose a great ad. The morning our ad ran, my pluperfect secretary, Emily Paxinos, screamed at me, "George, Malcolm Forbes just called to say he *loved* the ad, and wants 880 reprints!"

None of the ads showed or discussed any No Excuses jeans. We were, however, making a connection between No Excuses and its primary market—major retailers—who simply wanted to know that Neil Cole was at it again, making the bold moves to keep a high awareness level for No Excuses jeans. These were sassy, wiseass messages that attracted national attention and appealed to retailers by flattering their intelligence through timely, *hip* references to the headlines, with copy (however brief) that challenged their grasp of language and their sense of humor.

Meanwhile, there were no lawsuits and no personal vendettas or contracts on Neil Cole or me. There was nothing but good, wholesome publicity that kept the name No Excuses right up there while we waited for the successor to Donna Rice to emerge in America's headlines. Where oh where was she? She would have to be someone who would make no excuses for something scandalous—tough specs to fill, but we were patient. Nobody had yet emerged in the tabloids to wear Donna Rice's crown, until Donald Trump gave us the perfect candidate.

With the breakup of The Donald's marriage to Ivana, Botticelli's clamshell opened up and out stepped our Venus: the "other woman," Marla Maples. She was young, a model, attractive, and she had sinned, but without bowing her head. She was a natural, the answer to a Seventh Avenue maven and an advertising man's dream.

When we contacted her agent we got the clear impression that she could use the money and wanted to help her daddy, a struggling wheeler-dealer in Georgia. At the peak of the extraordinary publicity about Marla Maples, Neil Cole and I met with her in her hotel room on Central Park South. She struck me as a shrewd young lady, until she said, "I'd just love to do a commercial on the environment." Warily I glanced at Neil and said very tentatively as my eyes hooded over, "Hey, *terrific*—you young people are really tuned in to what the world needs. Let me mess around with that idea and see if I can come up with . . . uh . . . an interesting way to handle it." Neil Cole grunted a "Huh?" in disbelief. As we left the hotel he asked me, "Can you actually do something with the environment so we all don't look like fools?"

"To every problem there's a solution," I said. "Every cause has an effect. Every beginning has an end."

"You're a fucking mystic," said Neil.

"I'm Greek," I said. "Same thing."

I was serious, of course. I knew there was an answer to this seemingly impossible problem. The key to its solution was to make certain that the message wasn't *serious.* When I showed our solution to Neil Cole and to Dari Marder, his bright marketing head, they understood what I was getting at. Then we showed it to Marla Maples: a television storyboard and print layout with Marla in No Excuses jeans tossing the *National Enquirer* and the *Star,* with their brutal headlines about her affair with Trump, into a trash basket. Marla says, in a serious tone: *"The most important thing we can do today is clean up our planet. And I'm starting with these . . ."* She then tosses the *Enquirer* and the *Star* into a trash basket and concludes witha smile: *"Things are looking better already."* The country girl from Georgia understood that this tongue-in-cheek approach not only had wit, it also cast her in a fighting-back role by taking the environment message and turning it into a sassy statement of revenge. Cole and Maples made a deal.

We announced the big news at a press conference at The Four Seasons restaurant. Most press conferences are not fully attended, although if they take place at The Four Seasons you can always count on a large turnout. The joint was mobbed as Neil Cole announced the signing of Marla Maples, dressed demurely in a white, snugly fitted No Excuses T-shirt and No Excuses jeans. When she announced that she would be doing a television commercial on the environment—"Because it's important to our future"—a deep moan rose from the reporters as photographers shot the first "live" photos of the notorious but sheltered Marla Maples, making her first public appearance since the affair began.

The news of the signing of Marla Maples made the front pages and all the television news programs—all focusing on the fact that Donald Trump's girlfriend would be plugging the *environment!* The entire situation was sliding from satire to absurdity—unless the advertising could somehow redeem all this misdirected hoopla.

I knew the networks would surely turn down the spot because of its flagrant ashcanning, even though it was done with a broad smile that said, "Hey, folks, don't take us literally. We're doing funny, self-mocking shtick about a dull subject." But if the networks busted our chops, I knew we would be able to run the spot on cable, which had opened up a whole new world to advertisers, with a flexible attitude toward legal clearance, and on several independent stations, particularly Channel 5, the flagship station of Fox, fighting to become the fourth television network. As expected, the networks gave us a hard time. CBS said it "denigrates another product." NBC proclaimed, "Our facilities are not to be used to resolve private disputes." ABC ducked and did nothing. Neil Cole then sent out a news release that told the world of his turndown by the networks. As reported by advertising columnist Joanne Lipman in *The Wall Street Journal* (July 30, 1990):

> New York's Newsday, *a metropolitan daily, ran a full-color picture of the ad on its front page. Almost every TV station in the land, including some that rejected the ad, aired it on the nightly news. As George Lois, whose ad agency created the commercial, says candidly, "If we don't run one commercial, it still looks like we spent $50 million. How do you buy this publicity we're talking about?"*

If *Newsday's* conversion of its entire front page into a reproduction of the ad—*in color*—were the only dividend to result from this flap, that alone would have been worth a fortune in free publicity. To my knowledge, this is the first time a major metropolitan newspaper has run a color ad as its front cover! In addition, our "notorious" television spot that had been banned on the networks was shown as a news feature on their news shows, on *Entertainment Tonight,* on talk shows, on local television stations, in newspapers everywhere, and reported on radio news shows.

This was the textbook case to outdo all textbook cases on why and how a great advertising campaign is also a great public relations campaign. Neil Cole spent $600,000, which included his payment to Marla Maples, the press conference at The Four Seasons, the cost of the television shoot and production of the four-color print ad—a genuinely tiny budget that produced a mushroom cloud of free publicity. *Adweek*'s Barbara Lippert made this observation in her "Adweek Critique" column (July 30, 1990):

> . . . *this commercial actually makes Marla look good. She's not allowed to blather. Instead, she does what's bearable: she makes fun of herself . . . The genius of the spot is in George Lois' art direction. The setting is lush, like Eden, with Maples a modest Eve. With a waterfall behind her head, she's Botticelli's Venus in freshly pressed jeans . . . As a commercial it's terrific . . .*

In aiming for an explosive unity between the product and popular culture, a kind of magical alchemy can be ignited that sometimes causes the advertising to enter the culture. Marla Maples is now a cultural artifact. A new entity was created when we wed No Excuses jeans to *l'affaire Trump.* (If you can't follow me on this, you might want to look into a career in accounting.)

Ipso facto, a great advertising campaign is a *great public relations campaign.* If you don't think your advertising has the spin to become a topic of conversation for everyone in America, you forfeit the chance to be famous.

7

A Creative
Approach
to Research

If everything you see on TV has been tested,
how come so many campaigns suck?

For years creative agencies have had to live with the unfair rap that they are opposed to research. As someone whose entire career has been dedicated to the proposition that a creatively led advertising agency is the only organizational setup to consistently create great advertising, let me summarize how I believe research can and should be used.

I regard research as an essential discipline of the advertising life, but I also believe that when research is used to excess it can smother inspiration. A sensible balance is needed so that the science of research can strengthen and even inspire the creative process, rather than control it. I believe that advertising, an art, cannot be predicted or predicated on the basis of any *scientific* methodology. But research is an essential resource for any serious advertising professional if it is used to dig out *market data* and to help the creative professional understand if his or her television or radio commercial or print ad *communicates.*

Market *data*—competitive brands, market shares, long- and short-term trends, consumer attitudes, price factors, trade scuttlebutt, competitive advertising—intelligently obtained and organized, can provide a useful summary of the marketplace. All of this belongs under the heading of *homework.*

Given the necessity of homework, my passion for the advertising life makes me strive for a creative answer that communicates a theme or message in a memorable way—and causes people to act. Whenever possible, I aim for a magical connection with myth and/or popular culture that endows the product with an irresistible aura. That's why *communications research* is so important—it can tell creative people if their work is working . . . if people receive their themes and remember them . . . if the product's brand name is communicated in a memorable, positive way . . . and if the consumer associates the advertising with favorable images. Communications research can deliver the answers, but you cannot test if the advertising is "good"—if it has that mystical power to *grab* people in a deep, emotional way. You can get *some* indication of quality by measuring *awareness* of your advertising. If more people are aware of your message than those of other brands in the same product category, this provides at least some indication as to the comparative power of your advertising.

Its ability to *persuade* is another key indicator intraditional advertising research. To advertising people, that familiar phrase "top two boxes" —the percent of consumers who say they will *definitely* buy the brand in your advertising (the top box in a research report) and *probably* buy the product (the second box in the report)—is often the do-or-die statistic. If these scores are high, combined with high recall (awareness) of the advertising, the commercial is probably doing something right. Most advertising, however, scores low in awareness—which means that a good score in "top two boxes" may not be worth crowing about. Before you can knock people down, you have to be visible. Most advertising is *in*visible.

Research can be a terrific tool, if it's handled with common sense. Research by the numbers leads to invisible advertising. (Sex can also be terrific, and it's certainly good for you, but it can be pretty dull if it's done by the numbers.) Spontaneity is essential. In research, that means including the agency's creative people in the research process.

No television commercial that is prepared for Procter & Gamble or General Foods or for most of the giant package goods companies is ever allowed to run unless it has been research-tested. They are probing for involvement, motivation, persuasion—for those aspects of advertising that are directly connected to imagery and artistic invention. In the ad agency world, creative people are paid to conjure images and symbols to make products desirable in the marketplace. That artistic "magic" is what consumers experience in their homes as they watch commercials on television—without ever being able to articulate *why they are reacting that way.* That undefinable experience is what scientific marketers try to uncover in their research, but they'll never get close to that secret of secrets. In peer discussions, people disguise their inner feelings, which are often unconscious to begin with. Those feelings emerge only when people watch advertising *in the privacy of their homes.*

Most television commercials that are pretested are ignored by consumers when beamed into their homes. Much of this baaad advertising is an insidious byproduct *of testing itself.* The prevalence of pretesting in the evolution of advertising campaigns (and in product development) forces too many creative people to seek the bland middle ground. Many shrewd advertising professionals decide early in the game that nothing can be gained by bucking the system, so they join 'em rather than fight 'em; rather than resist the rule of technocrats, they break the research "code" and create advertising *that will pass research tests.* In most agencies, account people and research experts determine what kind of research should be done and what questions should be asked, while the agency's creative people, who are best able to visualize the reactions and responses of consumers to their work, are excluded. And when the research findings are in, they are *told* to change this scene or that wording or to start from scratch and create a new campaign. Research done that way absolutely smothers any glimmer of a big idea. Yet, research can be used sensibly to strengthen communications and awareness . . . while preserving the campaign's creative essence.

When a client is desperate and running out of time, shirtsleeves research can save time and money while providing management with documentation for a new advertising approach.

Purolator Courier was an ailing $600 million company (1986), struggling to survive in the overnight express delivery business, dominated by Federal Express. A miracle was needed to get Purolator's phones to ring and boost revenues *immediately,* or they would be out of business in a matter of weeks. I knew we needed some kind of symbolic spokesperson who would make Purolator's advertising look and feel unmistakably different from the "lobotomy school" of advertising (showing dum-dum businesspeople in commercials who look lobotomized) that dominated the overnight express delivery category. But who? We needed a personality who needed no introduction (there wasn't a day to waste in building endorser awareness) and could personify Purolator's swift service as well as its underdog efforts to compete against Federal Express.

We created the needed miracle in our choice of the cartoon character Road Runner as the symbol of Purolator. This desert bird—called a road runner—only twenty inches tall, scoots across the ground at lightning speed; the cartoon Road Runner leaves behind a trail of smoke and says only two words: *"Beep Beep!"* Our copy said: *"The Road Runner works for Purolator. We run rings around the Coyote Courier!"* (Guess who!) We also devised a toll-free number to outdo all toll free numbers: 1-800-BEEP-BEEP. (It had eight digits, but who cares? The last digit was meaningless and had no effect on the dialed number.)

Our astute marketing chief Jon Tracosas and our creative people put their heads together and came up with a research model to answer these key questions:

1. Do people know Road Runner?
2. Do adults know him as well as kids?
3. Do they know who Coyote Courier is based on?
4. Do they like these cartoon characters?
5. If they were users of overnight delivery services, would this advertising cause them to call Purolator?

We then sent our agency researchers out into the field with a simple questionnaire and an illustration of Road Runner in a Purolator Courier hat, honking "Beep Beep!" Here's what they learned:

1. All thirty people they interviewed knew Road Runner instantly. If they were in their twenties or thirties, they had grown up with Road Runner on television. If they were in their forties they knew Road Runner from the movies, where people would burst into applause when this plucky, wiseass desert bird showed up on the screen.
2. Twenty-six of the thirty knew that the Coyote Courier was based on Wile E. Coyote, and twenty-seven of the thirty spelled his name correctly.
3. They all loved Road Runner and Coyote, with feelings ranging from passionate love to adoration. At the very sight of the illustration of Road Runner many launched into unrestrained "Beep Beep" sounds, temporarily derailing the interviews.
4. All said they would consider Purolator the next time they needed an overnight delivery service.

Realistically, not one additional interview was needed, but to prove to Purolator's brass that Road Runner would be a big, instant advertising and marketing success, we interviewed an additional hundred people. The results were the same—Road Runner was clearly one of the most popular American personalities of them all, and would perfectly symbolize a new, revitalized Purolator.

A meeting was arranged to present our campaign and our research findings to Purolator's board of directors, which included such august public luminaries as Nicholas Brady, formerly the head of Dillon Read, then senator from New Jersey (and now in 1991 Secretary of the Treasury in the Bush administration), and General Brent Scowcroft, America's leading authority on missile deployment (and now national security adviser to President Bush). The other directors were also of awesome pedigree, all clad in somber tailor-made suits, men of obvious wealth, with white hair and jowls—and one lady, a distinguished Margaret Thatcher type. They were living caricatures of the Protestant power elite —and were also the few human beings in America who were *not* familiar with Road Runner. My imitation of this swift desert bird and my delivery of "Beep Beep" woke up a few dozers. The group chortled politely, an expression of steamy passion for these gents, although Scowcroft smiled judiciously, the way a general should, and Brady smiled tentatively, as though waiting for the latest Dow before committing himself. My research director then presented the findings of our interviews, with enthusiastic imitations of all those interviewees (you won't get a "respondent" out of me) chirping "Beep Beep." We then played a vintage

Road Runner cartoon. It was an astonishing spectacle—America's corporate elite watching a kid's cartoon in the middle of a business day to decide the fate of a great American corporation.

In truth, we knew we were plugged in to a genuine icon of mass/pop culture after the first thirty interviews. This was borne out further after I gave the story of the campaign to the *Times'* Phil Dougherty. The next morning he ran a prominent story on our advertising. Our toll free 800-BEEP-BEEP number was buried in his copy. The same day the article ran, the phones rang off the hook—unfortunately, it wasn't yet our number. Negotiations were still under way to obtain the number from the current owner of those digits, the American office of a German chemical company—and calls flooded their lines. To appease them, a dozen Purolator executives rushed off to man their phones.

As soon as we officially owned the number, we ran our TV campaign and Purolator's phones jingled off their cradles from the moment we started our television campaign. An incredible 15,000 phone orders were received in a single day. When our Road Runner spot ran in any market, the next day's phone orders shot up an average of 58%. Purolator's turnaround was happening—and fast. In a few months its improved health led to a friendly takeover by Emory, and Purolator's major stockholders found themselves awash in overnight riches. Common sense research enabled us to convince Purolator's management that our campaign would work, and the astonishing sales results showed the accuracy of our overnight research.

Because the account came and left our agency in a flash, many people in the business thought we had a failure on our hands. Instead, an astonishing transfusion of success had occurred that led to a lot of guys pocketing a lot of money on the takeover.

How to change the advertising direction of a national institution.

Time magazine changes advertising agencies infrequently—in fact, once every half century. By the late 1980s, however, times had changed dramatically and newsweeklies, even *Time,* were feeling the pinch. The time had come to look for new approaches. Readers generally are overwhelmed by a ceaseless tidal wave of information, and nobody alive can keep up with essential reading—while the inroads of television and particularly cable are staggering. (The average television household in 1989 had 27.7 available channels!) Similarly, advertisers are beset by a dizzying number of media choices that have dimmed perception of *Time* as a "must choose" publication among the ad world's decision makers.

Time's publisher, Chip Weil, an unorthodox type, called me to ask if my agency would like to compete for their business. It was an offer I couldn't refuse—*Time* was at the pinnacle of magazine publishing, and I was thrilled that they might do more aggressive advertising.

We knew instinctively, without having done any research, what *Time*'s problem was: who the hell has time to read these days—not only because there was so much reading material, not only because we go home each night to so much news on so many television channels, but also because of our incredibly pressured lives. Indeed, I felt slightly guilty that with each new month it became increasingly difficult for me to read *Time,* a superb weekly summary and analysis of news, sports and culture, as thoroughly as I would have liked. The problem with *Time* was *time.* If I intended to read it every week, I would have to make time for *Time.* I knew in my bones that this was the creative theme they needed:

Make time for Time

—a four word slogan with the product name used twice! To make certain we were headed in the right direction, we conducted one-on-one interviews of readers of magazines and newspapers whose demographics closely approximate the readers of *Time.* We found that while readers revered *Time,* the intensity of their loyalty was weakening under the pressures of the information explosion and by an insistent feeling that there was "not enough time" to read *Time.*

"Make time for Time" was the call to action that would infuse their magazine, we argued, with a new relevance, a new urgency and a needed "hip" flavor. (These days a national treasure or a national institution is seen as more of an icon than an exciting read.) *"Make time for Time,"* we pointed out, was also an active line that asked for the sale—that acknowledged how busy we all were, and strongly suggested that readers carve out some quality time for *Time.* It was fun to say—and to sing. It was also wonderfully euphonious, and a cunning mnemonic that everyone would remember.

Our agency was awarded the account and became *Time*'s second advertising agency in fifty years. *"Make time for Time"* was kicked off in major markets during the fall of 1989. In addition to creating the big advertising idea—*"Make time for Time"*—we also came through with a big *media* idea that enabled us to show America the cover of *Time* on television before it hit the newsstands. It was a logistical tour de force: the actual cover of each weekly issue—that appears on Monday—is not available before Saturday afternoons. We therefore wrote our commercials on Friday afternoons, and produced finished television spots Saturday evening so that we could run on Sunday, in shows like "Meet the Press," "Face the Nation" and "60 Minutes." We wanted to be on air *before* the magazine hit the newsstands. We wanted people everywhere to see *Time*'s spanking new cover on Sunday, *before* it appeared on their newsstands on Monday mornings on their way to work.

We got over forty television stations to accept a satellite feed of our commercial as late as eleven o'clock on Saturday night. A similar miracle occurred in preparing our newspaper ads, scheduled for Monday mornings and trafficked by satellite to newspapers across the country. Creatively our big idea, *"Make time for Time,"* gave this great magazine a new driving urgency and relevance. And by equally inventive, aggressive *media* planning, we did the impossible by telling America on Sunday what they normally wouldn't see until Monday. We had delivered a big idea creatively, while our big media idea was mind-boggling in its resourceful use of new technology to meet impossible deadlines that would enable us to sell more issues of *Time*.

After our media miracle, the industry wanted to know how we managed to pull off the impossible. It wasn't hard, fellas—we simply used existing technology, but with imagination and aggressiveness. (And despite my abhorrence of awards, our don't-take-no-for-an-answer media director Chris Tinkham was so proud of his department's coup for *Time,* he twisted my arm to let us enter a media awards competition. "Only if you don't have to rent a tux to receive your prize," I insisted. A few weeks later, in a business suit, Tinkham received for our agency the 1990 *Adweek* award for the most creative use of local television.)

Research played its proper role throughout the evolution of this campaign. By interviewing advertisers and agency people in three major cities and by using the technique of "adjective selection" (a useful research tool in gauging attitudes before and after the advertising) we were able to confirm our assumptions from the moment we began thinking about how to advertise *Time*.

I gotta tell you, most research that's done for our clients—whether by our agency or by outside research organizations—jibes exactly with our strategy and approach. It's few and far between when we learn something startling or unexpected that radically changes the direction of our work. Research is, after all, talking to people and finding out what they think and how they react to your advertising—and particularly in doing research for *Time,* I'm probably the ideal demographic model. I'm an advertising professional, and I like to read everything I lay my hands on—but I'm pressured by not having enough time, and I always feel slightly guilty when I can't get to essential reading . . . like *Time.* When we came up with *"Make time for Time"* I was addressing this message to *myself*—and the only difference between my reactions and those of my counterparts in other cities across the U.S.A. is that I express myself in a more elegant accent. But don't get me wrong: when research *confirms* a concept that I know is right, that's very, very important—because clients expect third-party confirmation of creative people's instincts and assumptions. For *Time,* we did our research by the book and everyone went home happy.

Now in its second year, *"Make time for Time"* has given this great publication that extra muscle so crucial in one of the most intensely competitive periods since World War II for magazines in general and newsweeklies in particular.

Research is an invaluable resource for creative people by revealing, in advance, if a campaign communicates accurately and if it has the potential to stick in consumers' minds and cause them to act. But alas, for many small talents in our business, research is a "test" that has to be "passed" to get one's work produced. Television commercials for package goods are the most exquisitely tested of all advertising—and most (indeed, almost *all)* package goods commercials we see on television have made it to the home screen by having "passed" their research tests. Life is so smooth in package goods heaven—ah, if the real world were just as controllable! (If 99% of most package goods advertising has been tested, how come 98% of it sucks?)

If we create advertising to pass a research test, the "science" of advertising will have won the whole ball game. *"I want my MTV!"* would have flunked commercial pre-testing. *"When you got it, flaunt it!"* would have flunked commercial pre-testing with a vengeance. *"Think small"* would have flunked with breathtaking speed. Fortunately, Bob Pittman of MTV and Harding Lawrence of Braniff and the head hun of Volkswagen followed their instincts. And may God protect General Scowcroft and Secretary Brady from learning about animatics.

8

Tackling
the Ego Problem

You'd be paranoic too
if people were out to get you!

Revisionism is a hazard of the advertising life. Credit for a big idea and disputes about who said or wrote what when can drive you up the wall if you let that kind of backbiting get to you. Advertising attracts intense personalities who thrive on the heat of confrontation, the thrill of victory and the agony of defeat. Advertising also attracts many untalented personalities who pretend to creative ingenuity, who take credit for work they could never have authored. Several times a year I receive portfolios from creative people that include some of my work. I shrug and go about my business.

More than in most professions, the ego factor is a rampant force in advertising, and I don't say this in a negative sense. All our great innovators (in and out of advertising) have been men and women of towering egos. The ego is the furnace of great work, but you can't let its steam scald you. Everything I do is a collaboration with other people, all extremely conscious of who did what or who originated what great theme or who suggested what visual. I can understand these concerns, but I won't get sucked into that zoo.

I also have to live with the "factoid factor"—the conversion of anything that appears in print, however wrong or untrue, as *fact.* Once something appears in print, no correction in future editions of a book or newspaper or magazine alters its existence as a new *fact,* which Norman Mailer aptly labeled a *factoid.* Factoids abound in advertising. Trade journals employ many writers who are not only untutored in advertising but are also not very experienced reporters or researchers. They rewrite advertising history based on imperfect information and commit their "facts" to print, thus creating a factoid, which becomes an established source for other writers. In a recent book I came upon the subject of Xerox, which contains this astounding claim:

> For decades the chief impetus for sales and rentals was simply seeing the near-miracle of a 914 in action. Only in the early 1980s, when the competitors finally became a threat, did Xerox really begin to advertise, and their All-time Greatest campaign was the devout monk reminding us what a miracle the original invention had been.

A new factoid has been created and a new generation of students, scholars and trade press reporters will use the factoid again and again. For the rest of my life I could send letters to publishers and editors pointing out that I used a monkey to sell the Xerox 914 on television at least *twenty years* earlier, and because of that advertising and our television campaigns that followed in a series of classic CBS specials ("Death of a Salesman," "The Kremlin," "Mark Twain Tonight")—"Xerox culture" became an integral aspect of American business life and made anyone who bought Xerox stock rich.

The ego factor finds corrupting expression in the awards madness that afflicts the advertising world. With so many competitions out there, some of the least talented agencies are able to flaunt framed certificates of excellence on their walls. When I entered advertising there were just a couple of award competitions that attracted all the attention: the New York Art Directors Club awards was the primary competition, and the second was the AIGA competition (American Institute of Graphic Arts). Subsequently, all kinds of award competitions were created for copywriters (the ANDYs), for work on television (the Clio awards), and for "creative" performance by industry, by state, by nation, by continent, by universe, by galaxy. To cut down this time-gobbling and expensive activity (the cost of my tux rentals alone would have put me out of business), Ed McCabe, then president of the Copy Club, and I combined the major award competitions in 1974 into just one event, which we called The One Show. I had the clout to bring about this radical consolidation during my stint as president of the New York Art Directors Club, but in bringing sanity to chaos I stirred up opposition from all quarters. Heads of agencies and many creative people were furious at the thought of cutting down the number of awards, and those aggressive entrepreneurs of awards seminars wanted me castrated. I was not a very popular guy and my reforms were short-lived.

Despite my efforts, award competitions have continued to proliferate as agencies try to prove how creative they are by touting their awards. Awards, after all, are big business. It costs big bucks to enter a competition (while the paperwork ties up many good people for an unconscionable amount of time), not to mention the cost of the formal dinner when the winners receive their statuettes.

I've had a standing rule for decades not to enter any award competition. Clients are often surprised that no framed certificates can be found on my agency's walls. I may have been the biggest award winner of all time in the ad agency business, but I haven't entered a competition in over twenty years because I believe awards have cheapened advertising —you could be the ultimate schlock shop and collect dozens of certificates of excellence. Award entrepreneurs pander to the egos of Madison Avenue, while the trade press dutifully reports on who won what where.

Imagine if there were thirty Oscar-style shows, all devoted to achievements in filmmaking! That single Oscar, which encompasses so many categories in the film industry offers breathtaking proof that less *is* more. There are only two awards in advertising that put a lump in my throat and fill me with pride: the lifetime achievement awards that richly deserve to be coveted. The most important in our industry are the Art Directors Hall of Fame (for art directors) and the Creative Hall of Fame (for copywriters and art directors). These two recognitions of a life's creative work can bring tears to the eyes of the most rabid award-haters.

Occasionally a client will suggest that we enter a certain competition to give recognition to the people in their company who might not otherwise receive credit, but most clients look for sales, not awards. Amen.

I can shake off creative applicants who include my work in their portfolios and I can laugh at all those silly awards, but I can't forgive phony claims to authorship of a genuinely big idea. *New York* magazine was just such an idea. In 1962 my agency was appointed to do the advertising for the *New York Herald Tribune*—which led to the still memorable campaign theme, "Who says a good newspaper has to be dull?" As a result of this campaign, weekday sales shot up and gave the paper a new lease on life, but the *Trib*'s Sunday edition was a disaster. My partner Fred Papert and I came up with a plan to build readership on Sundays by creating a great new magazine section that we estimated would get 100,000 more people in Manhattan to buy the *Trib*. The *Times'* Sunday magazine section was bursting with ads but could put you to sleep, while the *Trib* carried a skimpy syndicated insert. We saw a terrific opportunity to do something exciting, while offering dramatic proof that a good newspaper did not have to be dull. We met with Jock Whitney, the *Trib*'s owner, and Jim Bellows, its new editor, to show them a prototype of a new magazine we had created, a combination *New Yorker* and *Cue,* with articles that would appeal directly to people who lived and worked in New York City, especially Manhattan. No such magazine existed. *The New Yorker* was for highbrows and college kids, more a national magazine, and while the *Times'* magazine was Sunday's drawing card, it was dull and deadly (and still is).

Our Sunday magazine for the *Trib* was called *New York, New York,* out of my love for this wonderful town. Jimmy Breslin and other *Trib* staffers had pitched in with articles for my prototype, which I created with my colleague (and school chum) Tom Courtos, one of the world's most superb designers. Whitney listened carefully to every word we said. But he clammed up completely and finally walked out. I was baffled. A few days later Bellows called me to say that Whitney had okayed it. "Only one thing, George," said Bellows. "Jock Whitney doesn't want to call it *New York, New York*. He thinks it should be called just plain *New York.*"

"Not half bad," I said. *New York* was born.

I made a special point of urging Bellows to set aside a hefty piece of his budget for a top-flight art director, and I recommended a tasteful pro, Peter Palazzo. When I mentioned the salary that a guy like Palazzo would command, Bellows thought it didn't make sense to pay New York's art director more than its editor. "It's about time it happened," I told Bellows. Palazzo was hired, he gave the magazine a special graphic class, and *New York* was on its way. But the sixties was a rough decade for newspapers in our town. The 114-day strike of 1962–63 hurt the *Trib* badly. Before the strike, its circulation had climbed steadily. After the strike, its price had to be raised, circulation slipped, and in 1966, after a second strike, Jock Whitney closed its doors. All of us who had helped the new *Trib* grow shared Gentleman Jock's obvious sorrow in shutting it down after his spunky fight. But its new magazine section, *New York,* was later revived by Clay Felker and converted into an independent weekly. *New York* magazine is now a thriving publication—the fruit of one of my most cherished concepts.

As the years went by since the inception of *New York,* new factoids were created in the trade press on who conceived this magazine idea. For a long time it was (and still is) regarded as Clay Felker's invention, and with each new statement from me describing my role in the creation of *New York,* I've become a public nuisance. Finally, when I had it up to here, *Spy* magazine began snooping around, and in a telephone interview, I made my definitive statement:

"Let me say right now, with my hand on the Bible, I, George Lois, created New York *magazine. I wanted to call it* New York, New York *and make it a combination of* The New Yorker *and* Cue. *I went to Jim Bellows with the idea . . . We took the idea to Whitney . . . later Bellows came back and said he liked it but wanted to call it* New York. *But they didn't want to hire an art director. I said, You got to. I knew Palazzo and convinced Bellows to hire him. I got Palazzo the fucking job after we had the name decided. Twenty years later, what does he tell everybody? 'I designed* New York *magazine.' The problem started after a seminar about eight years ago. [Former* New York *art director] Milton Glaser was speaking, and he credited Felker with starting the magazine. Dougherty [Phil, the late* New York Times *ad columnist] reported it and started a big hoo-ha. Then Bellows started taking credit for it. They [Palazzo and Bellows] will burn in hell for this . . . Mistake I made is, I gave Bellows the comp. Who knows where it is. He probably burned it. Now here I am telling the truth and I feel like a man who has to defend himself, saying that he doesn't fuck pigs."*

And that's my last word on the subject.

As we go to press I am in the midst of a lawsuit in which the plaintiff is yours truly against the defendant, the Honda Tri-State Dealers (New York, New Jersey, Connecticut) for having filched my agency's campaign, *"Honda. The car that sells itself."* Such contretemps will always go on because our business is populated by bristling egos. But once in a while, you must act on your anger and get litigious. My suit against Honda is a legal first, of sorts, and I'll see it to its conclusion. No more Mister Nice Guy. Anybody steals from me from now on, I'll see you in court.

Section Three

Execute the Big Idea

1

Advertising
That Adds Value
to the Product

If you don't agree it's possible, stop reading

In his important work on advertising, *Madison Avenue, U.S.A.* (1953), Martin Mayer concluded that advertising conferred "added value" on a product. In other words, advertising, in and of itself, can become a benefit of the product—but only if the advertising is vivid and memorable. By conferring that "added value" on a product, great advertising makes food taste better, makes clothes feel smarter, makes cars ride smoother, makes beer taste richer.

This is a fundamental dynamic of our free market culture, of *capitalism*. Brands in all product categories are ultimately similar or identical. Our marketplace is inundated by parity products. In my entire career, only one product—Xerox—was undeniably unique. Yet even revolutionary Xerox eventually lost its market edge as others, such as Canon,

Kodak and the Japanese, developed variations of the Xerox duplicating method and brought product parity to this huge category.

Most new businesses are new *enterprises,* but their *products* are not new. They are variations or direct knockoffs of market leaders. What differentiates these parity products from one another is how they are *perceived* by consumers: their *image.* Advertising shapes image. Advertising gives one parity product the *appearance* of being superior to its peer brands. Appearance, however, often becomes the product's reality as the brand strives to catch up with its advertising image, to close the gap between perception and reality. A quality product with a richly defined, *appealing* image enables a brand to be *experienced* as superior by advertising-receptive American consumers.

Critics of advertising become righteously moralistic in any discussion of product imagery and appearances, the smoking guns of their argument against our profession. Advertising, they claim, creates artificial wants and needs. Not so. Advertising is the spark plug of our economic machine. It enables parity products of quality to survive and prosper in the marketplace through appealing *imagery* that confers "added value." Note carefully: we're talking about parity products of *quality.* The free market shakes out most lousy products, regardless of how much advertising is invested toward their success. The magic of advertising—its ability to make food taste better, cars ride smoother and beer taste richer—works *only* if it is employed to promote quality products. Great advertising for a quality product lifts that product out of the soup of parity and gives it appealing definition.

After delivering a speech on this subject several years ago, I was criticized by one of the ad trades for being more interested in the advertising than the product. I make no apologies for my obsession with the magic of advertising; I confess proudly to an almost religious belief in the power of advertising, in its awesome ability to move mountains and make miracles. Most advertising moguls do not share my faith. Most advertising agency presidents do not really believe that their work can lead to dramatic results, but they are determined to build billings. Alas, most people in advertising are more impressed by the size of a brand's budget than by the content of its creative campaign.

This dollar dependency obscures and minimizes what should be seen and accepted as the primary "product" of our business: the *advertising.* In Madison Avenue's large marketing agencies, big budgets provide persuasive rationales for creating pedestrian work. "Risky" advertising can endanger hefty billings, but by playing it very safe, *parity advertising* is created for parity products. Great advertising, a rarity in the advertising world, can make a one million dollar budget look like ten million; most advertising makes ten million look like one. Here is a true story, drawn from the abundant annals of advertising foolishness, that perfectly exemplifies the traditional dependence among so many major advertisers on dollar tonnage rather than creative resourcefulness:

In 1979 *Advertising Age* selected as its marketing man of the year the president of Burger King, whose advertising budget that year was a big, whopping $80 million. Acknowledging this honor, the Burger King president protested that he could have done an even more impressive job with a *bigger* budget: "We [Burger King] only have $80 million to advertise with. McDonald's has $200 million. You can't talk to everybody in America with only $80 million."

It must be tough to get by on just $80 million. If I had that kind of budget I would personally travel to every town and hamlet in America and I would visit with each and every family. I would break bread and rub elbows with all these people and personally convince every one of them to eat at Burger King. It would take longer than the present method of communicating, but after visiting every family in all fifty states, I would still have about $40 million left over for a posh retirement.

It's good to be rich, but the clue to an advertising campaign that can enable a parity product to compete effectively can only be found in its *advertising,* not in its budget. In and of itself, great advertising *can* become a benefit of the product. That benefit is its "added value" that distinguishes one parity brand from its peers. That benefit is what makes the free market work. That benefit is what makes capitalism, to me, exciting, vital *theater.*

Dear Dick Tiger:

Here's why I think
I deserve
a crack at your
middleweight crown:
The last time we fought,
I beat you!

          Respectfully,
          Joey Archer

A Coty Cremestick turned Alice Pearce...into Joey Heatherton.

Dear Dick Tiger:

The Middleweight
Champion should meet
the best middleweight
(not a welterweight).
I'm a middleweight,
and I licked every man
I ever fought, including you.

          Respectfully,
          Joey Archer
P.S.
(How about a fight, Dick?
I'm going broke
on these ads.)

2

The Impact
of Being
"Seemingly Outrageous"

Between the initial shock and the recovery,
you capture your audience

The late Alexey Brodovitch, the pioneering art director of *Harper's Bazaar* in the forties, would tell his students, "Surprise me." To me, that's not enough. Some good and *bad* advertising is full of surprises. I prefer to say *stun* me . . . *flabbergast* me . . . make my head spin . . . knock me down. I prefer the "seemingly outrageous." The operative word is *seemingly.* Advertising should stun *momentarily* . . . it should *seem* to be outrageous. In that swift interval between the initial shock and the realization that what you are showing is not as outrageous as it seems, you capture the audience.

To be seemingly outrageous is to ride your motorcycle in a drag race toward the edge of a cliff and stop as close to the edge as possible. Go too far and you fall to a fiery end. Stop too soon and you've chickened out. Screech to a halt right at the rim and you cause gasps of tension, but you have survived the challenge and you're on the cutting edge. The phrase "seemingly outrageous" usually comes as a strange and unfamiliar locution to my clients. Only when they experience the jolt of exposure to that kind of idea can they grasp what I have in mind.

How a seemingly inconsequential product
can take the town by storm by extreme self-mockery.

In 1960, shortly after I started my first advertising agency, I was contacted by two New Jersey housewives who had created a gourmet specialty called Dilly Beans—strips of raw string beans pickled in vinegar and dill. With a total kitty of $30,000 (for *everything*), they were hoping we could somehow bring their delicacy to the attention of people who bought gourmet foods in a town drowning in gourmet foods. We had to make thirty grand look like a million bucks. Here's how we did it:

We created a variety of messages, beginning with small space print ads and radio spots. The common denominator of these ads and commercials was a sassy, self-mocking, tongue-in-cheek irreverence. Our ad showed a woman "smoking" a Dilly Bean as though it were a cigarette. The copy said, "Break the smoking habit, eat Dilly Beans." When we learned that Dilly Beans had 1.2 calories compared to 7.2 in an olive, we put our secretary on a crash weight-gain diet of Dilly Beans and announced the results in a tiny ad: "Diane Shugrue ate 3,925 Dilly Beans last month. She didn't gain an ounce. Is she tired of Dilly Beans!" Another wiseass small space print ad (one column by eight inches) asked the ominous question, "Is the Dilly Bean a threat to the peanut and the pretzel?"

In a radio commercial we said: "If your friendly neighborhood grocer doesn't have a jar of Dilly Beans, *knock something off the shelf on the way out.*" That spot fired up a lot of otherwise well-behaved East Side ladies to stampede their supermarkets, shoving cans and jars off the shelves where no Dilly Beans were to be found. (At times like these I shudder at the power of tongue-in-cheek advertising; everyone knew we were having fun—and everyone wanted to join the party!) Many grocers protested angrily to New York's radio stations and we were compelled to tone down the message to *"move to another neighborhood."*

Our small space messages (an excellent media device for attention-getting firecrackers that explode off the page) were so strong that solely on the strength of these modest ads, Dilly Beans was becoming famous. Radio converted the Dilly Beans madness into riotous behavior in the stores. With the addition of spot television, Dilly Beans became the most famous food product in New York. Our first spot was a video version of *"Break the smoking habit, eat Dilly Beans"*—a screwball 10 second message as we showed an attractive young woman "smoking" a Dilly Bean, then crunching off its end. In another 10 second television spot, we showed a beautiful woman jamming Dilly Beans into her mouth as the voice-over announcer asked solemnly, *"Is it vulgar to put more than one Dilly Bean in your mouth?"*

In as many bars as we could canvass, we buttonholed bartenders to place tent cards on their tables for a new cocktail, the Dillatini—a martini plus a Dilly Bean. You stirred the drink with the Dilly Bean and ate the stirrer. The tent card copy said, *"Ask the waiter to bring you one, and warn him to leave that damn Dilly Bean alone."*

The onrush of these downright outrageous messages caused New York to go dilly for Dilly Beans as many stores jacked up the retail price by 20 percent. New York's highbrow radio station WQXR gave our agency a special award (wholly unsolicited) for "unusual, imaginative and effective use of radio advertising on behalf of Dilly Beans," the third such award in their low-keyed, twenty-five year history. Fittingly, *Time* magazine had the last word by declaring, "The Dilly Bean's success is a tribute to the power of advertising." And the two New Jersey housewives asked us to please ease up on the advertising until their supply caught up with demand.

The astonishing success of Dilly Beans, generated entirely by seemingly outrageous advertising for an absolutely outrageous product, became the talk of Madison Avenue. Our fledgling shop became known as "the Dilly Bean agency" and went on to attract new clients with much bigger beans.

How to sell a beauty product by spoofing advertising that sells beauty products.

The cosmetics category, enslaved by the notion that women respond only to images of sublime beauty, invariably rejected any approach that strayed from this fantasy formula. When Coty came out with its Cremestick line of lipsticks in 1966, it wanted a promotion to catch a woman's eye on retail store counters flowing over with lipstick brands, all promising instant beauty.

On the assumption that most women saw most lipstick ads as the usual cosmetics con job, I did a Coty campaign that spoofed instant glamour in a *totally* outrageous way. In a four-color spread, the left-hand page said "Before" with a closeup photo of comedienne Alice Pearce applying Cremestick. Alice Pearce was a lovely, funny lady, but no looker (she made a living playing a bow-wow) and her tortured face caught the comic pathos of all the desperate women of the world, yearning to be beautiful. Alongside Alice Pearce on the right-hand "After" page was a closeup photo of a young, sensual Joey Heatherton. The copy across both pages declared, without adornment or apology, *"A Coty Cremestick turned Alice Pearce . . . into Joey Heatherton."* ("Truth in advertising" took a battering.)

Would women respond to cosmetics advertising that spoofed instant glamour? Yes, if done without a heavy hand—if done with the kind of respectful wit that says *you* know and *we* know that there's no such thing as instant glamour, so let's not kid ourselves, but on with the fun! As an ad and a counter display, this gigantic spoof sold a lot of Coty.

Before I could proceed with photographer Richard Avedon on the television version, Alice Pearce died. Finding a replacement for a beautiful woman would have been a piece of cake, but there was only one Alice Pearce. I finally hit upon Alice Ghostley, another beautifully talented non-beauty. In millions of living rooms her homely face was physically transformed into luscious Joey Heatherton. Cremestick became a cosmetic winner of that season.

If beauty is only skin deep, the myths about transforming oneself from a wallflower into a sexpot are transparent. The subject of beauty in advertising has always been treated with a reverence that deserves to be punctured. That's what I did. My approach said beauty advertising is transparent, as everyone knows—but who said we can't pull your chain, baby! (And they call *me* a male chauvinist?)

*How ingenuity (budget or ad size notwithstanding)
can cause mass impact. The secret is to seem outrageous
when you're just having a lot of fun.*

Here is the first of the two tiny ads, a *pro bono* effort in 1966 on behalf of a struggling boxer. Ad size: twenty agate lines. Total cost, net: $203.

Dear Dick Tiger:
Here's why I think I deserve a crack at your middleweight crown:
The last time we fought, I beat you!
Respectfully,
Joey Archer

And now, a marketing overview on this possibly cryptic message:

In 1966 Joey Archer, a lesser ranked middleweight contender, thought he deserved a shot at the crown. The champion, the Nigerian Dick Tiger, who was planning a title match with former champion Emile Griffith, wanted nothing to do with Archer, a good boxer, with a history as a spoiler.

Ed Rohan, my agency's production manager, happened to be a Bronx buddy of Joey Archer and mentioned to me that Archer was going nuts running up against a stone wall, trying to force a title shot. I figured what the hell—let's challenge the bum in an ad. So we ran an itsy-bitsy ad, the size of a large postage stamp, in the sports section of the *New York Daily News*—and boy, did it cause an explosion! The gabby sports media and fans throughout the city made this Topic Number One. Sports columns and letters to the editor poured in to New York's newspapers, demanding a fight between Joey Archer and Dick Tiger. I felt like a kingmaker, until Joey Archer's brother Jimmy came to my agency with a tale of woe.

"Dat was a helluva ad, George," he said, sounding slightly punch-drunk. "Joey's getting calls from all his buddies and from big-name fight reporters, and every goddam cabbie in town is talking about Joey Archer's challenge to Tiger. Dat's all terrific. So far so good. What's happening out dere is unfuckinbelievable. But we still ain't got a fight. What can we do, Lois? We gotta cage this guy Tiger."

"Goddam right, Jimmy," I said. "What we need is another ad—another challenge to Tiger. Listen, pal, you got another two hundred bucks on ya?"

"Holy shit—whaddayuh think, Joey's loaded? When he whips Tiger he'll be loaded. Right now two hundred bucks is a lotta bread."

"Joey, I'm talking two hundred *dollars,* not two *grand.* That's pea-nuts." After a hat was passed around in a Bronx bar, Jimmy came back the next day with two hundred singles, and I placed the next ad in the Joey Archer campaign:

Dear Dick Tiger:
The Middleweight Champion should meet the best middleweight
(not a welterweight). I'm a middleweight, and I licked every man
I ever fought, including you.
Respectfully,
Joey Archer

P.S. (How about a fight, Dick?
I'm going broke
on these ads.)

If the first ad caused a commotion among the media and sports fans, the second ad escalated the commotion to a furor. The sports world was now completely ensnared by Archer's Irish chutzpah. The *New York Daily News* put Joey on its front page, challenging a snarling tiger through the bars at the Bronx Zoo. Archer became a hot property on the talk show circuit as sportswriters attacked the nonplussed Dick Tiger. The pressure on Tiger mounted. Before long, before my disbelieving eyes, Joey Archer was given his chance to win the title by having an immediate big money elimination bout with Emile Griffith, who now had to prove his mettle by fighting Archer instead of Tiger. The Griffith–Archer match was set for Madison Square Garden. Here are the results of my two ads:

1. The fight was a sellout.
2. I wasn't able to get free tickets.
3. I had to buy them through
   a scalper and I paid through the nose.
4. I bet a bundle on Joey Archer.
5. Archer lost.

In retrospect, these two ads may not have been seemingly outrageous—they were just plain *ridiculous!*

Here's how a shocking visual image can help a brand become a raging success. (With some "low-interest" products, you have to jolt people into paying attention.)

When I was the rookie art director at Doyle Dane Bernbach in 1959, my first assignment was to create a campaign for a new product, Kerid ear drops. I was the new kid (just twenty-seven) at the world's first and only creative ad agency, and I wanted to hit the ball out of the park. In burrowing through Kerid's research I learned that most people cleaned their ears by poking around with pencils and bobby pins. I pushed that finding to its graphic brink by showing a colossal closeup of an ear, sprouting pencils and pins and assorted hardware. The warning could not have been clearer: don't tinker with your ears, use Kerid ear drops.

Bill Bernbach knew it was a startling way to get attention and to sell Kerid, but a posse of DDB art directors and writers galloped up to Bernbach's office to protest this "disgusting" campaign. (In those days the buzzword at DDB was "tasteful." Taste, schmaste, my ear! I've always felt that tasteful was anything I thought I could get away with.) Bernbach listened, then he patted his outraged creative people on the tush and herded them out the door. Bernbach and I presented the campaign to Kerid, the ads ran, Kerid sold a lot of ear drops, and a lot of people quit sticking bobby pins in the wrong places.

I was fortunate to have a perceptive and pioneering boss like Bill Bernbach. He was the first person in the ad game who readily understood the power of *imagery*—vivid verbal themes and/or vivid visual symbols. He also clearly understood the distinction between imagery that would shock people for shock's sake—and imagery that could attract and hold attention because of a meaningful and powerful message. Everyone who looked at that ad was reminded of their having poked around in their ears with a foreign object. More than thirty years later, the concept of imagery is better understood in the advertising world, but the distinctions that Bernbach grasped intuitively are still perceived with difficulty.

How to push through a naughty ad.
(The best time to do your dirty work and bust taboos
is when the boss is out of town.)

Listen to the lesson of the leotard:

After the Kerid campaign had been put to bed, I became the recipient of an emergency assignment at Doyle Dane Bernbach. A crash campaign was under way to unload a big inventory of leotards made of Chemstrand Nylon. The hour was late and I was the only art director in sight. (Another piece of advice on how to succeed: work hard, work late, work joyously!) A double-page ad was needed for *Women's Wear Daily* to announce Chemstrand's blitz. DDB's traffic manager, searching desperately for an art director, found me at my drawing table. "Thank God you're here," he said. "We gotta push leotards." As he said these words he *wrote* the ad. I sketched a man's hand pushing against the snug behind of a girl in a leotard. The headline said, *"We're pushing leotards."*

The account man phoned the Chemstrand client at home and got an on-the-spot okay. My photographer picked out a woman at a local gym, but it was too late at night to find a hand model, so I volunteered my sensitive right hand (heh-heh). We shot the photo, I set the type, designed the ad and by early morning it was completed. Mission accomplished. The ad ran, and orders for leotards poured in. Chemstrand reported that it was its most successful trade ad ever. Boy, was I proud!

Bill Bernbach was out of town while all this happened and was unable to pass judgment. He saw the ad shortly after it ran and called me to his office. First Kerid, now Chemstrand! I was sure he was going to give me a medal (or at the very least, a raise). I entered his office beaming. He was holding the ad aloft. He looked angry.

"Disgusting," he said. "George, is this your handiwork? If so, think twice before you ever do an ad again with this flavor." For a moment, I was stunned. Then I came back at this wonderful boss and mentor: "Hey, Bill, you're completely wrong. First, the ad was exactly right for the marketing problem. Second, it was a big success. Third, it's a provocative approach. Fourth, I love it. Fifth, everyone else loves it, including Chemstrand. And sixth, the only thing wrong with you, Bill, is you're a *prude."* (He was.) I retreated from his office before he could call me a dirty young man. (I was.)

Bill Bernbach had been outraged by my work and I had been outraged by his failure to perceive, as he had so readily with Kerid, that I was being *seemingly* outrageous. Sexual prudery has diminished in the decades since Bernbach's humorless reaction. Interestingly, Chemstrand was much too determined to sell their leotards than to indulge nineteenth century biases.

When corporations learn to laugh at themselves, customers will laugh with them.

How's this for a corporate moniker: Warner Amex Cable Communications, Inc. This was the company that owned cable systems in Dallas, Houston and Cincinnati. It had many subscribers, but a flood of cancellations was plaguing the company because of bad service, which it was trying to correct. Feelings against Warner Amex Cable Communications,

Inc., were approaching lynch levels. (Cincinnati's Pete Rose refused to appear in a TV spot we were preparing—he felt he might damage his image! On the day of the shoot, I betcha he went to the track.)

A tough assignment: We had to increase cable subscribers in markets that already had high penetration levels. We had to overcome and correct Warner's poor reputation in these markets. We had to defuse its angry subscribers' *hatred* and convert these dark feelings into love!

Every problem has a solution, even impossible problems. We found our answer in the acronym for Warner Amex Cable Communications, Inc.: WACCI. By replacing that cumbersome corporate name with this unlikely acronym, we were able to communicate a self-mocking, humanized television message, urging everyone to *"Go WACCI!"* in a succession of double entendre vignettes: A bride suggests to her new husband as they leave the church, *"John, now that we're married, let's go WACCI!"* A teacher tells her students, *"Class, your homework tonight is to go WACCI!"* A conspicuously rich man asks his conspicuously rich wife, *"Cynthia, what shall we do for our holiday?"* In a snobbish, looking-down-her-nose voice, she answers, *"This year let's go WACCI!"* The vignettes are interspersed with short bursts of announcer copy describing the advantages of WACCI cable.

When we showed the campaign to Warner's board, they reacted as though it was poison gas. I looked up and four guys were on the floor— but their business was in such bad shape they finally gave in. This audacious concept went on to attract fresh, favorable attention from all the company's wired homes while projecting a human, appealing, self-mocking image to *prospective* subscribers. WACCI also gave to Warner Amex Cable Communications, Inc., an immediate, unforgettable identity and a likable personality.

When you're up against taboos that seem
to be insurmountable, disregard everyone's fears
and joke them into submission.

As AIDS became rampant in 1989, the condom industry expected sales to explode. Sales rose, of course, and quite sharply, but decidedly short of the industry's expectations. Something had to be done. Any advertising of condoms on television had previously sent a grim message: condoms or die—and because of the networks' incredible squeamishness about accepting any condom advertising, it was impossible to put across a human, interesting message. To get clearance, condom commercials had to be developed as anti–AIDS messages, with a public service flavor—and with minimal emphasis on the condom brand that was paying for the advertising.

Ansell–Americas manufactured and marketed LifeStyle condoms. Exasperated and stymied by the networks' stiffass parameters, the company wanted a breakthrough approach that would get LifeStyle on television with a message that did not look like a warning against AIDS. It was also beset by a social bugaboo that made it difficult, if not impossible, for many people who wanted condoms to use that taboo word with store clerks. (It's tough to ask a clerk for condoms if you can't say what you want—sign language is worse.)

In a survey of condom marketing, *The New York Times* (August 8, 1988) noted: "Many marketing people think the dark tone of the condom ads that first hit mainstream publications and local television stations in early 1987 may have repelled consumers. In large part, this approach was dictated by the publishing companies and television stations, which required a public health theme and prohibited advertising condoms as contraceptive devices."

Something totally different from all that had gone before was the only direction to take. Our approach could not be a change in degree—this challenge cried out for a radical solution. We had to break down social fears against buying condoms. *Humor* was a must. For the first time in any advertising for condoms, we would have *fun* with the subject of sex. It would have to be audacious and memorable. Working with my talented copywriter Elaine Kremnitz, we created a theme that set the tone: *"It's a matter of condom sense."*

We created three 15 second television commercials that cast highly recognizable personalities from the theater, the movies, history and legend as users of LifeStyle condoms. Our first condom consumer was Phantom of the Opera, who tells a store clerk, *"I could use some LifeStyles."* The store clerk tells him with a straight face, *"Oh . . . but you didn't have to wear that mask to ask for them!"*

In a second spot, the announcer introduces us to a primal sexy creature, Azania, whom he describes as *"The Queen of the Jungle, shopping for LifeStyle Condoms!"* Azania reels off her shopping list to the store clerk: *"I need sunscreen, hair mousse and a year's supply of LifeStyles."* Unfazed, the store clerk congratulates his customer: *"Good thinking, Azania—'cause it's a jungle out there!"*

And in our third spot, the customer is Robin Hood. In a cunning allusion to our vulnerable gay brothers, he tells the clerk, *"Shampoo for the fair Marion, and LifeStyles for all my merry men!"* All three vignettes come to a climax with the announcer popping our theme: *"LifeStyles. It's a matter of condom sense!"*

Not surprisingly, the commercial networks said no, no, no. And not surprisingly a few cable networks said, uh, why not. Several other cable networks needed considerable convincing, and thanks to an authoritative argument by our agency's top marketing strategist, Mark Rothman, whose smart planning helped bring this campaign to life, they kept an open mind and quickly came to the correct conclusion that these three spots were not as outrageous as they seemed at first viewing. Six cable networks agreed to take the spots. A historic breakthrough!

This was a milestone campaign that changed the fear of dying to the love of living. It helped make "safe sex" not just essential but pleasurable—while boosting sales and market share of LifeStyle Condoms. In her weekly *Adweek* column, "Adweek Critique" (August 15, 1988), Barbara Lippert made this incisive observation: "These have to be the unsexiest condom commercials around. They take a taboo subject and make terrible, hokey jokes, to our great relief. Unafraid, unashamed, they allow everybody access to the message. In that, they're so dumb, they're smart. Nah, they're so unabashedly idiotic, they're brilliant."

How a high-ticket high-tech product can be marketed like takeout pizza.

Advertising campaigns for business computers are usually mumbo jumbo that only a few "techies" can understand. They have no uniqueness or special character and are so dense in computerese they make a normal person feel stupid.

Data General asked us to create a campaign for their new, compact AViiON computer system. It had the power of a mainframe and could process tens of millions of bits of information—while needing far less space than conventional computers. Data General's director of corporate communications Peter Lange knew he had a great product, but he also knew his company had an image problem and its advertising was invisible. "We're technology rich," he said when we met, "but we've been marketing poor."

We did our own research among business executives and found

that awareness of the Data General name was perilously low, and the odds were heavily stacked against inviting Data General to pitch for a customer's business. But now, with their new AViiON, Data General could compete aggressively against other computer brands (IBM, Digital, Hewlett–Packard, Sun, NCR, Unisys).

As my alert copy chief Neil Brownlee and I were being oriented by our new client, what caught our eyes immediately was AViiON's flat shape and surprisingly small size—compact enough to fit under your arm or to slide onto the backseat of your car. In fact, it looked disarmingly *un*-computerlike. The Data General people told us that work station computers like AViiON, because of their size and shape, had been referred to in the industry as "pizza boxes."

Here was a situation where computer technocrats themselves were describing a high-tech product in human, household language. But who would *ever* think of actually using a pizza box to describe and sell a computer system, especially one with a price tag that started around $100,000? Not IBM. Not NCR. Not Hewlett–Packard. But Neil and I sure would—and we *did!* We grabbed this mass, universal image and built our campaign around the pizza box. (Another example of my almost mystical notion that you don't create big ideas, you *discover* them as they float by.)

I began by designing the pizza box that would become the selling focus for Data General. As part of their circular logo (which was actually shaped like a pizza pie), the name Data General sat over a pizza slice— where I added our slogan, *"Life just got a whole lot easier!"* We then condensed our selling message into two simple lines at the bottom of our pizza box package:

WE FIT 117 MIPS OF MAINFRAME POWER IN A PIZZA BOX!
CALL 1-800-DATA GEN (WE DELIVER)

In an industry that is known to make seemingly startling announcements of new products with regularity, followed by a swift letdown as everyone quickly sees that the news is less memorable than it seemed, we had to take Data General's *genuinely* startling announcement and make it stick. We had to make sure that the AViiON system would not be one more go-nowhere announcement. We did this by using a pizza box to show the system's compact size—and to tell the business world that Data General is a company run by human beings who talk like human beings and can make the lives of business executives "a whole lot easier!" The pizza box was a perfect symbol for Data General—and by distilling their marvelous product to this intensely human image, we boggle the mind so that you'll *never* forget it.

The *Times'* ad columnist Kim Foltz cleverly headlined the story on our campaign as a "Tasty Approach to High Tech." Carried away by our imagery, he described our pizza box with a flash of takeout passion: "Inside, it turns out, is a $100,000 computer, without anchovies."

Under the dynamic leadership of new CEO Ron Skates and his motivated sales force (armed with their trusty pizza boxes when they make sales calls), a virtual renaissance has occurred at Data General.

Look again.

Everything I've described here is really not outrageous—but all are *seemingly* so. The "strategy" is to get people's attention by *seeming* to shock. They then realize quickly that all is not as outrageous as it seems —and they're ensnared by the unforgettable Big Idea.

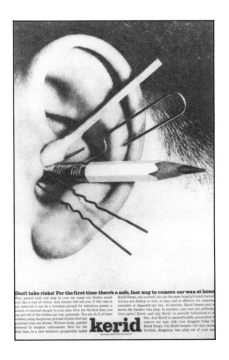

A lot of media people are saying USA TODAY is neither fish nor fowl.

They're right!

THE ADVERTISING MIGHT OF

USA TODAY

Call Valerie Salembier at (212) 715-5380

To our readers, we're a newspaper—bold, exciting, colorful and unique. To many of our advertisers, we're a newsmagazine—bold, exciting, colorful and unique. The truth is, we don't much care what you call us. Just as long as you call us.

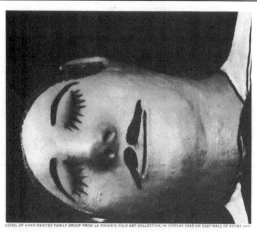

DETAIL OF HAND-PAINTED FAMILY GROUP FROM LA FONDA'S FOLK ART COLLECTION, IN DISPLAY CASE ON EAST WALL OF ADOBE BAR.

No, No, Stupido, we said <u>Fiesta</u> at La Fonda del Sol, not <u>Siesta</u>.

Every Sunday, from one o'clock on, La Fonda has Fiesta. We have the Canela Trio. A Mariache band. The Jose Montalvo Trio. Mexican Hat Dancers. Jose Bettencourt's Marimba Band. A flamenco guitarist. Free granizados (ices) for the kids. And food! Well, you know those La Fonda portions. La Fonda del Sol, 123 W. 50th St., PLaza 7-8800

3

How to
Make Tough Clients
Fall in Love
with You

...and still respect you in the morning

The best client is the entrepreneur who comes to you for fresh, break-through work because he wants to go places fast. The other great client is burdened by a brand in deep trouble. Clients like these feel they have to take a "chance" and must get an agency that will swing for a homer rather than lay down sacrifice bunts.

The most *interesting* experience for anyone in the ad agency busi-ness is to work for self-made entrepreneurs who have seized opportuni-ties and have risked their necks in pursuit of impossible dreams that became realities. Whether they made their fortunes and left their marks in booze or cosmetics or publishing or broadcasting, they all have one admirable human trait in common: they have survived the perils of venturing out alone into the unknown, and they are all the stronger for it.

"I Did It My Way" is their theme song, and their egos seep out of every pore. With this unmistakable power they become, in the eyes of so many people who work for and with them, superhuman—and they are accorded a deference and respect more suitable for the court of Henry VIII or the bunker of Saddam Hussein. Surrounded by flatterers and corporate yes-men, these modern monarchs fall in love with anyone who talks straight and goes nose-to-nose with them.

I don't mean to be egotistical, but I happen to be on the same wavelength as these lovable tyrants who have become the power elite of my advertising life, beginning with Samuel Bronfman, the former Canadian bootlegger and fabled boss of Joseph E. Seagram & Sons, Inc. I am about to take you into hazardous territory. This is largely a personal survival chapter on how to duel with the top guns of American capitalism. Mine is a risky way to pursue a career in advertising and selling and is not recommended for anyone with high blood pressure or weak knees —but for me, there is nothing quite as thrilling as earning the respect of genuinely tough clients.

How to sell independent thinking to a corporate tyrant.

They called him "Mister Sam." I called him *"Massa* Sam." In my roster of client-tyrants, Massa Sam rates a special laurel because he was a disarmingly sweet tyrant, but a crafty wizard like Bronfman could detect anxiety like a bad smell—especially the aroma of fear from nervous advertising jerks. He would let them go through their bullshit, and if his staff said yes while he slept (he loved to snooze during advertising presentations), he would say no when he woke up—because it was such a pleasure to rough up Madison Avenue's con artists. In dealing with Bronfman you had to grab his interest and hold it, even if it meant slapping the conference table while he snoozed (which I did) or addressing him slightly off key. My way was to address him as *"Massa* Sam."

After a while he seemed to catch the ring of it, even if he may have thought he was hearing me wrong when I first said it. As I became a familiar face in his conference room (in the early 1960s), he began to squint at me with a devilish, searching look that seemed to say: "Hmmmm—*Massa* Sam. It does sound more obedient than *Mister* Sam. You're up to something, but I'll figure it out."

He was a short, nondescript man, neatly tailored, about seventy, and actually meek in his outward appearance, but you couldn't tell Massa

Sam's book by its modest cover, even though he was richer than many countries and more powerful than kings. When something caught his personal interest, no matter how small, he jumped in with all his ballbusting power.

One day one of Seagram's brand managers asked me if I would do him a favor and take a look at some new labels for Leroux cordials, a lesser Seagram brand. I thought they were a mess, so he asked me to do him another favor and design new labels. He loved my designs. "Let's show these beauties to Massa Sam," he said. I didn't like the idea of his picking up my "Massa"—that was *my* phrase that gave me special status as his favorite slave—but when we met with Bronfman, the ad manager said, "Mister Sam, here are some new Leroux label designs that Lois *volunteered* to do for us."

The old man looked suspicious. "The labels you have are fine," I began, "but I think these new designs have more style." He grunted and grimaced. I went through a no-nonsense, no-wisecrack explanation, but in a flash I realized that Bronfman himself had probably supervised the design of the old labels and these were his babies. Bronfman peered up at the brand manager and asked for *his* opinion. "Well, Mister Sam," he said, "I think I agree with the agency on this." Bronfman leaned forward and drilled the ad manager with his eyes. "Who do you work for," he growled, "me . . . or this *pig-fucking agency?*"

I fell to the floor, doubled over with laughter. "Why are you laughing?" Bronfman asked me as I rolled on his luxurious carpet, at the foot of a sculpture of Balzac by Rodin, guffawing uncontrollably. "I just insulted you." But the lovable old tyrant enjoyed my slapstick groveling, aware in the recesses of his heart that I genuinely respected him, and was expressing affection by not taking his excesses seriously.

"Oh, Massa Sam," was all I could mumble, rocking in convulsive laughter at his feet. The mighty Bronfman stared at me, looking slightly confused, then he leaned toward me and said, *"You* I like." Not long after that encounter, the labels that were designed by my Massa Sam were replaced by the new designs from his pig-fucking advertising agency.

One day I was in the conference room with his staff, but there was no point in reviewing our advertising until Bronfman arrived. When he walked in, a bunch of guys fell over themselves trying to seat their leader. He plunked into the nearest chair and was ready to get on with the meeting, when someone blurted out, "No, *no*—Mister Sam—sit here at the *head* of the table."

"Young man," Bronfman said humorlessly, *"wherever* I sit is the head of the table."[1]

Bronfman's son and heir Edgar was especially proud of our agency's work, and surely much of our success for Seagram was largely due to our refusal—and Edgar's—to be intimidated by this domineering authority figure. We had won Sam Bronfman over to our irreverent advertising style, an accurate reflection of our irreverent *personal* style. That cocksure, happy attitude toward life and work enabled us to create the legendary talking bottle campaign that staggered the parochial world of booze advertising.

The only way to win with certain irascible clients is to let them chase you until you catch them.

One day in 1978 I received a call from Joe Baum, restaurateur and cultured tyrant, informing me that somebody wanted to work with me. "Really?" I said. "That's terrific. Who?"

"The Riese brothers," he said.

"The Riese brothers," I shouted. "You gotta be kidding, Joe. Those guys are the biggest goniffs in New York."

"George, George," Baum persisted. "They're the best marketing people in the world. You could learn a lot working for them." In our Manhattan argot, Joe Baum was telling me these guys were smart and considerably more than colorful bandits.

Thus among my most picturesque clients were those Runyonesque brothers, Irving and Murray Riese, the Manhattan restaurateurs/real estate moguls. At one time or another they owned the Steak & Brew chain, Toots Shor, the Steer Palace, Lindy's, Ma Bell's, the BOSS chain, Charley O's, and fast food franchised eateries (Pizza Hut, Kentucky Fried Chicken, Nathan's, Burger King) in addition to major holdings in Beefsteak Charlie's and the Arby's chain in the New York area. In midtown Manhattan alone they owned a restaurant on damn near every block.

Despite their omnivorous penetration of the New York restaurant scene, and despite their extensive real estate holdings, their shabby, tiny office near Pennsylvania Station looked like the product of a government entitlement. A spare wooden desk sat in the middle of the room. Irving

---

[1] This is the source of what is becoming an almost apocryphal anecdote that has been told many times, substituting the names of other tyrants for Bronfman. This is the way it happened originally—in 1960!

sat on the edge of the desk while Murray crouched low on a wooden chair behind it so that any visitor could see on the wall behind him a cluster of citations from Catholic organizations and a photo with Terence Cardinal Cooke, all attesting to the Jewish brothers' chumminess with the Catholic power elite.

Our copy chief at that time, Richard Lynne, spent most of his time writing furiously at meetings with the Rieses. I once asked him what he could possibly be noting down so doggedly. "The sayings of Irving and Murray," he said. Here are two vintage quotes that shed some light on these shrewd schnorrers: Murray Riese, describing the customers of his salad days:"They used to ask: 'With the roast beef—instead of string beans, can I make a telephone call?' "

When we presented a concept for a new chain of restaurants to be called BOSS, an acronym for Beer, Onions, Steak, Salad—with these four words in the logo, Irving asked if anyone would know it's a restaurant. Murray snapped back: "Irving—beer, onions, steak, salad. What are we selling, SHOES?!"

My relationship with the Riese brothers evolved quite differently from the way I had insinuated myself into Sam Bronfman's favor. As New York originals, they felt naturally at ease with a fellow New Yorker whose accent was worse than theirs, and who could appreciate their comic banditry. One of Murray's vital aphorisms: "I'm gonna let that guy chase me until I catch him." He once reminisced about his early days in the restaurant business as the owner of a coffee shop near Grand Central Station. To save money on garbage disposal, he would surreptitiously stash their nightly load on the Twentieth Century Limited. "We kept New York *clean*," he boasted. "All our garbage was unloaded in *Chicago!*"

At our meetings, Murray, the younger Riese, played prosecutor and defense attorney. Irving, older and statesmanlike, played the avuncular judge who would step in before Murray overkilled. Murray once told me, "George, people you really like and work with, you fire"—eloquently (if obscurely) expressing the Riese philosophy that nobody who worked for them must ever be made to feel secure. Recognizing the totality of his younger sibling's remark, Irving added, "Not necessarily all the time. George, we like you and we wanted to talk to you about that markup on what you call 'production.' How come it has to be 17.65%[2] that you agency people always charge? Why can't we round it down to 10%?"

---

[2] The customary agency markup on production bills is 17.65% to yield a gross profit of 15%. A production charge of $100, for example, would be billed with a markup of $17.65 —which comes to 15% of the gross bill of $117.65.

"Why do we need it *at all?*" added Murray.

Early in our relationship with the brothers Riese, a considerable number of production bills had gone unpaid until our business manager blew the whistle and began the agonizing process of begging the brothers for payment before we proceeded with any further work. The Rieses told us they were unhappy with the whole idea of production bills, and wanted us to knock down the total drastically. To cut through our pleading for payment while the Rieses pleaded poverty, I wrote a three-page letter to Murray, which ended like this: "No one here wants to plunge in and work for you since they heard you're trying to "beat us" on production. Our people are disappointed, to say the least, that friends of ours, who we thought believed in us and trusted us, are trying to hurt us. Our relationship should be good for both of us. We know damn well we've been good for you. But we're being hurt—and Murray, you and Irving have got to stop trying to 'hondle' us down. We give you, and will continue to give you, a gung-ho attitude and brilliant work, *but don't treat us like dishwashers.*"

Within *minutes* after my letter was hand-delivered to their neo-welfare office, I received a call from Murray. A moving emotional experience ensued as Murray Riese wept crocodile tears over the phone. He was deeply embarrassed to receive my letter, he said, sobbing mightily, and never meant to treat anyone at our agency like a dishwasher. He promised to clear up the payment situation as soon as humanly possible. I thanked him, we kissed and made up over the phone, and waited four more months before we were paid (not in full, you bet) while new assignments multiplied.

With their double financial unpredictabilities—in real estate and the restaurant business—the Rieses were a perennial in-and-out client, with sudden demands for names and campaigns for new restaurants, followed by heart-rending pleas of poverty when we submitted our fee proposals, and the inevitable third act: the agony of getting paid.

When I met the Rieses originally, we happened to be looking for larger quarters. When Murray Riese heard we were a prospect for real estate, he came up with a small, ancient building near midtown. To renovate would have cost more than rebuilding Kuwait. "If you take it," said Murray, "we'll call it the George Lois Building." I never took the bait, for aesthetic reasons and because of the dread possibility of having these vintage goniffs as our landlord. But I will always look back fondly at the Rieses, who paid some of their bills some of the time.

How to sell a big idea to the tyrant of them all
by working in cahoots with his nervous right-hand men.

Like many of the great tyrants of American business, Charles Revson had a keen understanding of power. He also understood mass preferences. Back in the 1960s he sponsored the TV quiz show "$64,000 Question" and made Revlon a household name. He knew what national taste was all about. He understood women (in his *advertising).* And characteristic of the many lovable tyrants with whom I've worked, Revson couldn't and wouldn't mince words. His marketing executives—impressive professionals with big salaries and a lot to lose if they fell into their boss's disfavor—were not inclined, however, to rock any boats, a not unusual situation.

In 1974 we launched a new shampoo for Revlon named Milk Plus Six, a name designed to reassure women that health-giving milk was a dominant ingredient. Our concept for this new shampoo was: *"Like my hair? Meet my hairdresser."* Then the commercial took an unexpected turn: when the charming (model and later actress) Susan Blakely uttered that simple invitation, *"Meet my hairdresser,"* the camera pulled back to reveal a *cow.* As a serious friend of animals, I allowed the cow to have her Warhol seconds in the celebrity sun. She delivered a mellifluous *"Moooooooo!"*

When I showed the commercial in storyboard form to Charles Revson's marketing and advertising executives, I realized I was causing big trouble for these nattily dressed commuters who wanted to get through life alive. They knew my concept was udderly stunning, but they wanted no part of showing it to the mighty Charles. Instead they agreed, reluctantly, to allow *me* to show it to him, but with the clear understanding that all of us would pretend that nobody had the faintest idea of what Crazy George was going to show. I understood: if Charles chewed *me* out (and he was the fiercest chewer-outer since Hitler), I would be the only fall guy.

I laid the idea on Charles, complete with a resounding but not excessive *"Moooooo!"* He frowned at me incredulously, a look of admiring exasperation I have come to recognize among the many benevolent tyrants for whom I have worked, and said, without affectation or qualification: "I like it, Lois. Let's milk it."

I heard a collective sigh of relief from his staff, an audible exhaling of tension, followed by a robust, "We knew you'd love it, Charles"—and the campaign ran. In the overcrowded shampoo category, Milk Plus Six took off and remained a strong brand many years later. But not too long after the premiere of that inspired commercial, the cow was slaughtered. I learned that some male hairdressers had put up such a *fuss* that even the mighty Charles knuckled under. That's what I meant when I spoke of advertising having relevance to its contemporary social situation. (Easy, fellas: I gave my blood and guts to help organize and promote the 1990 fundraiser for the Gay Men's Health Crisis. Why should a cow come between friends?)

One afternoon, in the last year of his imperial life, Revson summoned a marathon meeting with his four advertising agencies—on Christmas *Eve,* for chrissakes! He herded all of us into his private office, where we sat and fumed while he made long-distance calls to his top men at home as they were trimming their trees, wishing them interminable greetings of the season. One of these calls dragged on with the most syrupy praise I've ever heard a tyrant pour on a subject. Then, after gushing compliments for a great year's effort, Charles paused, looked coldly into his gold phone *(gold—*I kid you not) and said without a trace of humor, "But fuck up *once* next year, and *out* you go!"

Don't get them to love you; get them to fall in love with you.

Harding Lawrence, the boss of Braniff Airways in Dallas, had an insightful grasp of the power of seemingly outrageous advertising and enthusiastically approved *"When you got it, flaunt it!"* When the local vigilantes in Dallas raised hell because Braniff was using an underground oddball (Andy Warhol) and a surly *nigger* (Sonny Liston) in one of our television commercials, Harding reassured us, "Sheeet, Lois, I *love* it."

The year 1968 was an extraordinarily eventful one for airline advertising, with major account shifts that rocked Madison Avenue. The Braniff shift was probably the most colorful: in 1966 Mary Wells started her own agency—Wells, Rich, Greene—with Braniff as her first client. Harding Lawrence fell in love with Mary and married her. In 1968 Mary Wells Lawrence resigned Braniff and picked up the much larger TWA account. Braniff then chose my agency to succeed the woman Harding Lawrence loved.

Lawrence was one of those clients who genuinely understood advertising (many don't), often responding with a "nifty." He bombarded us with new facts as his nose jutted forward while he grunted, *"Huh! Huh?"*—always expecting a *yeah, yeah.* He was rough on his staff, but they could always beat it out of Dallas on any flight they picked at any hour, which they did, because when Harding Lawrence chewed you out, he chewed you *up.*

In December 1968, *Fortune* wrote a long article on the shuffling of airline accounts. Everyone at Braniff wondered how that Texas buccaneer Harding Lawrence, cut in the mold of Lyndon Johnson and John Connally, would react to the article's first paragraph:

> Imagine a corner table at Manhattan's elegant Four Seasons restaurant, $9.75 steaks on the plate [that was 1968!!], a fine red wine alongside, and George Lois, as always, talking. George Lois is a man who is making a career out of starting advertising agencies. Listening to him talk is a little like getting a taste of pure garlic—pretty great if you happen to like garlic. Lois eats at this table every day he is in town, only the conversation and the menu varying. Today the subject is Braniff Airways, a big, juicy account that has just landed at Lois's agency. How, he is asked, did you happen to get Braniff? "Well," he says, spreading his hands, "Harding Lawrence fell in love with me."

Surprisingly, he never said a word about "Harding Lawrence fell in love with me" until more than a year after *Fortune* quoted me. When he raised the subject, he did it obliquely. "Goddam you, Lois," he growled one day when telling me how hard he worked, "you and your goddam Four Seasons lunches. I don't go out for lunch. I work through the day. I never stop." I goddammed him back and said, "I come in at six, and seven hours later I talk work at the Seasons, then I make ads until late at night. You come in at ten, work through lunch, but you go home to piss at *four."*

In the waning days of President Lyndon Johnson's reign, Harding Lawrence had become a man possessed, determined to extend Braniff's routes to the corners of the globe. The coveted Hawaiian route was almost in the bag, and he asked me to announce this momentous news with an ad campaign that would finally and firmly establish Braniff for the rest of the century as a big-league airline. The bravura style of Braniff, with its theatrical innovations, prompted me to proudly show Lawrence a campaign with a slogan that was so perfect, I was certain it would cement our relationship:

"Braniff and Hawaii. A marriage made in heaven."

To my astonishment, the devilishly handsome, bushy-browed, gun-slinging Texan plainly and simply lost his cookies. He roared at me with a frightening incoherence, his fierce eyes blazing with rage as froth actually began to bubble from the corner of his mouth. I was totally baffled at first, but as his raging and storming settled into coherent shouting, I somehow got the drift of his fury.

I had touched a raw nerve. Harding's many competitors and the Civil Aeronautics Board and his enemies (he had a few), but most of all his friends, with knowing winks, had assumed from the start that Harding's ol' cowboy buddy Lyndon would give Braniff the Hawaiian route as a going away gift. And there I was, celebrating this allegation of Texas cronyism in banner headlines in Braniff ads! But what did I know about Texas political shenanigans, I protested sincerely to this Dallas slicker like the big-city hick I swore I was.

In the 1980s, the Braniff bubble burst and it became apparent, finally, that the airline's expansion to Latin America and Hawaii was the first big step on its road to ruin. Not too long after Harding's Hawaiian war dance, even after I came through with a beautiful Hawaii campaign for Braniff without a whiff of political nuance, Harding Lawrence fired my agency. I took a lot of heat from my critics and got roasted in the trades, but I rolled with the punches. What the hell, I figured—when you got it, flaunt it!

If you have to work with tyrants, pick perfectionists.
You'll always stay on your toes.

Restaurant Associates was a network of classy restaurants, including The Four Seasons, Forum of the Twelve Caesars, the Brasserie, Tower Suite, La Fonda del Sol, and other stylish eateries. Their boss, Joseph H. Baum, was leading a personal crusade to convert eating into a theatrical and aesthetic experience. Baum was the most cultured tyrant I've ever known. (He later created all the dining facilities at the World Trade Center, including that popular tourist attraction, Windows on the World. He then went on to create the elegant Aurora restaurant in midtown and breathed exciting new life to the Rainbow Room atop Rockefeller Plaza.)

The word *perfection* is almost inadequate in describing this demanding entrepreneur. Nothing was ever exactly right for Baum and he hated to praise anything because praise might imply that perfection had been attained. The first time I asked him to comment on a proposed campaign for one of his restaurants, I knew I was ahead when Joe said, "I don't care, run the shit."

Joe was a Commandeur of the elite French gourmet order, the Confrerie des Chevaliers du Tastevin. One night he hosted a dinner for a hundred Chevaliers at The Four Seasons and budgeted ten thousand extra dollars to be sure the evening met his stratospheric standards. The night before, as I watched in awe, the restaurant's entire staff rehearsed the exact meal, and the real event went off perfectly, even by Baum's standards. The Chevaliers left The Four Seasons with stars in their eyes. The next morning Baum asked his public relations man what their reaction was to that grand event. "Well, Joe," he said proudly, "let me read their telegram: 'We resolve unanimously that your dinner was the finest meal ever served *in the history of the world.*' "

Baum reflected for a full thirty seconds, then blurted out, "Goddammit, *that's not good enough!!!*"

Restaurant Associates was the sort of account that scares off most advertising people. The work never ended and you never did any full-page, portfolio-puffing ads. (We did 1,200 ads a year, all small space.) I relished Restaurant Associates because it needed gutsy work for a growing string of restaurants, many of which I helped create, each with a distinct personality, each requiring a special creative solution, and all stretching your talent beyond its apparent limits. La Fonda del Sol in the Time–Life Building was a classic example of Baum's sweeping vision. Its South American flavor was so real you could almost believe Montezuma was the doorman. Unfortunately, Baum's Peruvian paintings and South American folk art scared away all those secretaries who swarmed through the concrete canyons of midtown. Since La Fonda looked like a museum, they were certain its tab was for art collectors. We had to sell a restaurant that looked like El Prado to typists from Hackensack.

One of Baum's imported folk treasures was a puppet's head with a pencil-line mustache. I put him in a prone position and closed his eyelids to show him lying down on the job. By christening him Stupido, we converted the museum into a fun place. *"No, no, Stupido,"* said our ad, *"we said* Fiesta *at La Fonda del Sol, not* Siesta." And surely no gallery would say in its ad, *"Will the lady who lost her composure during Fiesta at La Fonda del Sol please come back every Sunday?"* When New York's reservoirs were drying up we announced, *"Water shortage or no, we'll turn the hoses on the next group of dowagers who break into a fandango during Sunday Fiesta."*

Baum was a Renaissance man with clairvoyant taste. He personally transformed America's concept of a "restaurant," whatever its price or menu, into an *experience*. To dine at a Baum restaurant meant more than a meal—it was a promise of being transported to another age or another stage. He chose the main floor of Mies van der Rohe's Seagram Building for his incomparable Four Seasons when this startlingly modern international-style building was having trouble renting space. Later, when the Pan Am Building was going up, we created three restaurants for its main lobby: Trattoria for Italian food; Zum Zum, a Bavarian snack bar; and Charlie Brown's Ale & Chop House. Emery Roth & Sons, the architectural firm that executed the designs of Pan Am—designs that were supervised by the great Bauhaus pioneer Walter Gropius—watched over the graphic integrity of that grotesque erection. Any signs or designs for Joe Baum's restaurants had to fit in with the bland atmosphere of Pan Am's lobby. Not surprisingly, they vetoed my designs for Trattoria, Zum Zum, and Charlie Brown's; their lobby was not to be botched by expressive logos. But I was convinced that each design was true to the flavor of Baum's new restaurants and we were given an audience with Emery Roth & Sons to plead our case.

My reverence for Gropius and my irreverence toward the Pan Am Building was summed up in a speech I gave at a designers' seminar in 1964: "If I were an architect or an industrial designer, I would owe everything to Gropius. Not only because he was the great educator, but also because he showed in actual work what could be done. He was a better modernist as early as 1911—and certainly in 1925, when he did the Bauhaus Building in Dessau—than most "modern" architects are today. But I am not an architect. All I can do is sink to my knees to him. His leadership has directly and indirectly inspired teaching, industrial design, pottery, weaving, stage design, painting, typography, layout, and, of course, architecture. *I forgive him the Pan Am Building.*"

Emery Roth & Sons would not relent. My designs, they insisted, were not in keeping with their lobby. While Joe Baum chewed on a Havana cigar, a lookalike for Edward G. Robinson in *Little Caesar,* I blew my stack royally: "You guys have the nerve to talk about taste after putting up this monstrosity and fucking up the look of New York City for a hundred years to come? You have the nerve to sit there and criticize *my* designs?" The Roth boys weren't about to take that kind of crap and they showed me to the door. As it turned out, while I was talking, the great Gropius had been walking past the conference room and heard every word. I was later told by one of the guys from Restaurant Associates that Gropius walked into the room after we left and said, "I think his designs are good." They gaped at Gropius in disbelief but the lights, colors and graphics came to life in Pan Am's antiseptic lobby, pulling in paying guests to Baum's warm, bubbling new bistros.

Two years later I met Walter Gropius for the first time at an Art Directors Club reception in his honor. "Mr. Gropius," I said, shaking the great man's hand, "my name is George Lois." I said my name very slowly to trigger an association with my "forgiving him the Pan Am Building." He turned over my name in his mind, smiled in recognition, and said, "Ah yes, yes—verry lovely, verry lovely—*Trrattoria . . . Zoom Zoom . . . Charrlie Brrown . . .*" The trace of a Bauhaus accent flavored that lovely moment.

Baum respected my belligerence toward the Roth vulgarians because he was witnessing a fellow madman in pursuit of perfection, and he welcomed the comradeship of this crazy Greek. I was also his perfect audience. One evening at the bar of the Forum of the Twelve Caesars, Baum checked to see if I was watching his every move as he ordered a Bloody Mary. Before sipping his drink, he asked the bartender, "Is this the *best* Bloody Mary you can make?"

"Yes, Mr. Baum," the bartender answered with assurance.

"Taste it," Baum ordered. The bartender sipped and reflected.

"It's pretty good," he decided.

"Can you make a better one?" asked Baum. The bartender mixed a new Bloody Mary. "Now taste it and tell me what you think," said Baum. His lips had not yet touched either drink. The bartender took a sip.

"This is very good, Mr. Baum. It's *perfect.*" The magic word was finally dropped.

"Then why the fuck didn't you make it that way in the *first* place?" asked Baum.

The tougher they are, the straighter they talk— and they won't take waffling for an answer.

One of the most important innovations in modern journalism was the creation in 1982 of the first national newspaper, *USA TODAY*. It was the brainchild of Gannett's gutsy chairman, Al Neuharth, and readers took to it immediately, with circulation over 1.1 million by mid–1984. But advertisers were staying away, despite the dramatic ascent of *USA TODAY* to third place in circulation (behind *The Wall Street Journal* and the *New York Daily News).*

Unhappy with his agency, giant Young & Rubicam, Neuharth talked it over with his new president, Cathie Black, who was responsible for advertising sales. In his best-selling biography, *Confessions of an S.O.B.* (Doubleday, 1989), Neuharth recalls that turning point for his break-through newspaper:

> When Cathie Black met with Lois [to sell me and my agency's clients on choosing *USA TODAY* for their media buy], he had a simple message for her. "Your product is better than the competition's," he said, "but you're not communicating that to the advertiser. The truth is your advertising sucks."
>
> To see if Lois could improve things, we arranged a competition for the *USA TODAY* account. First Y&R made its presentation. Then George Lois came into a room of poker-faced Gannett executives—many of them skeptical journalists—to hype his ideas.
>
> One proposed print ad Lois prepared tackled the question of *USA TODAY*'s identity head-on. Was it a newspaper or a news magazine? The ad showed a drawing of a creature that had a body of a rooster but the tail of a fish.
>
> "A lot of media people are saying *USA TODAY* is neither fish nor fowl," his copy said. "They're right. The truth is . . . we don't care what you call us. Just as long as you call us."
>
> I liked Lois's bright new approach. But it left us with a dilemma—it wasn't easy for a new product to ditch the country's largest ad agency. And we would be switching from the largest to one of the smallest . . .
>
> I asked Lois what people would say if we did that. "They'd probably say you're finally getting your heads screwed on straight," Lois replied. "You're doing pussy advertising now. You ought to be doing triumphant fucking advertising." The man spoke my language.
>
> I decided to give Lois part of the advertising—the part aimed at the trade press. It worked. Combined with continuing circulation gains, *USA TODAY*'s advertising linage began to pick up. Within a short time, Lois had won the entire *USA TODAY* and Gannett account.

Right from the start, I understood Neuharth's newspaper as a big new marketing idea—and Neuharth understood that I brought talent and genuine enthusiasm to the advertising for his newspaper.

In a testimonial campaign on TV to fix clearly in people's minds the various sections of *USA TODAY,* we lined up Senate Majority Leader

Howard Baker to talk about the News section, Joe and Deborah Namath to talk about the Sports section, hotel executive Bill Marriott, Jr., to talk about Business, British sexpot Joan Collins for Entertainment and basketball giant Wilt Chamberlain for Weather (so tall, he was in the clouds).

We later produced a second television campaign to promote daily readership starring former Chicago Mayor Jane Byrne (News), discount broker Charles Schwab (Business), Willie Mays and Mickey Mantle (Sports), Diahann Carroll (Entertainment)—all crooning (with varying degrees of talent), *"I read it every day."* These campaigns put *USA TODAY* in the front of mind of millions of Americans. Three years after our advertising began, *USA TODAY* moved into the black.

My most unforgettable lesson from this Dakota country boy who became one of the world's mightiest media tyrants involved pride and brand integrity. (He was also one of those rare clients whose grasp of obscenities was *almost* as great as mine, and our meetings were usually punctuated by a duel of cusswords.) More than anything, it seemed, he was obsessed with preserving the purity of the *USA TODAY* brand. At one of our first meetings with Neuharth and his staff to present new ads, I read aloud a headline that said, "Why *USA TODAY* is gaining advertisers from all over America." Neuharth exploded. "Goddammit, Lois," he said, in deadly earnestness, "when are you going to learn that *there is no America.*" He had banished America from the language as long as there was a *USA TODAY!*

The S.O.B. once called me in the middle of the night. "I'm here in Lincoln, Nebraska," he boomed over the phone. "I gave a speech to five hundred people and I was talking about my good pal George Lois. I described you as the most legendary creative wizard in the U.S.A., and the most amazing thing happened . . ."

"What's that, Al?" I asked.

"Not *one* person out of the five hundred who came to hear *me* talk knows who the fuck you are!"

*How to spot the worst kind of client: He has bad taste—
that's bad enough. But when you have
to sue him to get paid, that's outrageous!*

When the Trump Organization switched its advertising account for Trump's Castle from McCann Erickson to my agency, the *Times* (January 26, 1987) reported that estimated billings, based on assurances to us from the Trump staff, would be about $5 million. *Ho ho ho.* Trump's Castle was handled by his then non-estranged wife Ivana, for sure no Mary Wells. While she was the titular boss of Trump's Castle, her beloved Donald made the big decisions. At meetings with our client Ivana, her husband often appeared and cooed at her without flinching (the rest of us did), "And how's my little CEO today?"

Trump liked the great campaign we had done for Harrah's, his competitor in Atlantic City. Before we started to work for Harrah's it was a minor league, virtually unknown name in Atlantic City, with its rankings for casino awareness, advertising awareness and slogan awareness among the lowest in town. We created the campaign, *"I'm just wild about Harrah's!"* with long-legged Susan Anton breezing through Harrah's glitzy gaming rooms, hotel suites and many eateries, while belting out our instantly recognizable theme song, *"I'm just wild about Harrah's . . . and Harrah's wild about you!"*—based on the classic American song, "I'm Just Wild About Harry!" This campaign was quickly recognized as the reason for the miraculous reversal of Harrah's, rising so dramatically from the cellar to the top. Harrah's no-nonsense head honcho, Dave Hanlon, told me, "Lois, I never really thought advertising worked—and I always thought you ad guys were just slick hustlers. But I gotta confess I'm just wild about your work."

We were then invited to work for the Trump organization in Atlantic City. The original campaign for Trump's Castle by another agency had done a credible job of telling people that you get treated like a king, complete with a Henry VIII lookalike in its television spots—a slovenly, unshaven monarch who drove up in a horse-drawn carriage to Trump's flashy hotel casino. The campaign's theme, *"You're the king of the Castle,"* had been heavily promoted on television and radio and had become one of the more familiar Atlantic City campaigns, but after relentless exposure, it had become abrasive. Consumer research showed that many people *hated* the slob king, while more than a few women were offended by the campaign's emphasis on a male monarch. A token queen was brought into the campaign, a wonderful example of bad art imitating life—Donald and Ivana Trump were the Louis XVI and Marie Antoinette of Atlantic City.

By the time I found myself in their orbit, *"You're the king of the Castle"* had achieved a high level of loathing. I told the Trumps to kill the king and go with a new approach we had developed, *"Live the Trump life!"* Donald and Ivana were so taken by our concept, they spoke of using it for Trump Plaza on the boardwalk in addition to Trump's Castle (on the bay side of Atlantic City), and as the thematic framework for an ambitious licensing venture they were considering. They responded to *"Live the Trump life!"* as the perfect theme for their lifestyle, indeed as their raison d'être, and authorized us to run several ads in Atlantic City media. But despite their apparent affection, they wanted to wait before replacing *"king of the Castle,"* despite the flaws (and fleas) uncovered by research. We tried to dissuade them from this self-defeating course, but it was always very difficult to get through to these two narcissists. After months of trying to get their attention, then trying to persuade them to run our campaign, Donald and Ivana had grown weary of *"Live the Trump life!"*, a campaign that never ran!

Or maybe they were smarter than all of us—maybe they knew that *"the Trump life!"* would eventually go down the tube with all the other excesses of the Reagan eighties. Or maybe they wanted to save a few bucks on production by continuing to run Henry VIII. Meanwhile, we had to deal directly with Donald Trump's little CEO, who had as much talent for marketing and advertising as a poodle. It was always extremely difficult to get Ivana to focus on advertising. Her concerns were always cosmetic. In her $20,000 LaCroix dresses she would send home teary secretaries whose working ensembles were not up to her lavish standards. When we showed any ads with women, she focused on their heels (she wanted them higher), on their nails (she wanted them longer and redder), on their dresses (she wanted LaCroix). Any dramatic bread-and-butter ads aimed at attracting gamblers were met with vacant stares. One afternoon, as we were explaining the extensive applications of *"Live the Trump life!"*, supported by blowups and illustrations and enough visual crutches to sell Helen Keller, Ivana took over the meeting to tell her startled staff how she planned to spend thousands of dollars on hideous rococo ashtrays in the lobby of Trump's Castle. One day, in an ecstasy of confusion and pique, the little CEO asked aloud, "Why doesn't this agency *do* anything for me?"

It was a no-win situation. Meanwhile, back at the Trump treasury, no funds were forthcoming for all our work. Collecting money from Donald Trump was a high-risk gamble. When we worked for him he was unrelenting in his attempts to knock down our fee, but what can you expect—the guy has the ingrained attitude of a landlord: he made sure he collected the rent without giving you enough heat. When we pleaded for payment he tried to cut us down, and when we finally said no dice, pay us what you owe us or we'll sue, he offered us thirty cents on the dollar. We took our lumps from the Trumps. We learned later (too late!) that this was the way Trump treated many of his contractors, suppliers and vendors—never pay 100 cents on the dollar. So after a lot of skirmishing, we settled for less than 50 cents on the dollar. (I pity the many poor guys who got stiffed by him at Taj Mahal.)

Donald Trump has several afflictions. First, I believe he has flamboyant, dreadful taste, buoyed and buttressed (when they were still basking in connubial togetherness) by the equally tasteless Ivana. Second, he's also cheap—a deadly combination. Everything Donald Trump touches turns to brass.

Predictably, his Taj Mahal is the ultimate vulgarity of Atlantic City, while his Trump Tower in Manhattan, with its landlord's glitz, marble waterfalls and pretentious shops, has turned Manhattan's Fifth Avenue into a carnival. Tourists come to town believing *this* is New York, when New York is really the Chrysler and Seagram buildings.

The landlord Trump would never understand.

You must get tyrants to respect you— not just your work, but your backbone.

I relish working with benevolent tyrants because they value what they respect—and I have an intuitive sense of what has to be achieved to get them to respect *me*.

After I returned from combat duty in Korea, I went to work for CBS in its television advertising and promotion unit, an elite atelier of brilliant designers. Bill Golden, a totally fearless, uncompromising perfectionist, was our boss. To a young designer like me (I was twenty-one, but wanting to sound more mature, I pretended to be twenty-two), he was an icon of integrity, taste and courage. Breaking the ice with Golden was another story. Two days after I joined CBS I went to his office and asked his secretary if I could see him to show my first ad—for a new television series called "Gunsmoke." She looked up at me from a massive dictionary and smiled nervously. Golden was at work at the far end of a long room. I walked to within four feet of his drawing table and waited for him to look up, but he continued working. I began to feel like a fool, standing there without even being acknowledged. After almost thirty seconds—an eternity to a supplicant—I cleared my throat, but he continued working, ignoring me. I leaned forward and held my layout almost in front of my knees to catch his eye, but he kept working, his left shoulder jerking with a slight tic. I knew he would never look up.

I walked back to his secretary, lifted the massive dictionary from her desk, and returned to Golden's desk. I held the dictionary chest-high and opened my hands. It fell to the floor with an ear-splitting crash. The pencil flew from Bill Golden's hand and his face jerked up.

"Oh, George—can I help you?" he asked. His tic had stopped.

"Uh, yes. I'd like to show you this ad." I handed him the layout and he looked at it briefly. "Good. Very good," was all he said.

In that symbolic act I was telling Golden that I would not only do what it takes to get his attention, I would do it in a slightly physical way. It was my way of warning him not to treat me lightly. Although I was only twenty-one, I clearly understood that I could never let the business world's tyrants, admirable as they may be in many ways, lose respect for me for one second. If you let that happen, you're dead. By expressing myself with an act that also suggested my pent-up physicality, tough cookies like Golden knew I would never kneel.

Thirty years later I had a similar experience with Al Neuharth, at our first meeting. I was presenting our trade campaign to Neuharth and all the top executives from Gannett and *USA TODAY.* That first encounter is accurately recalled in *The Making of McPaper* by Peter Prichard (Doubleday, 1987).

> Lois finished his spiel. He was standing there, surrounded by a profusion of ads, and no one said a word. The Gannett executives just sat there, stone-faced. "George put on an Academy Award presentation," Cathie Black says. "And of course what you would expect from any normal company with normal people is that everybody would have clapped. Not here. And I am sitting there thinking, 'I can't believe this. What is wrong with all these fuckers?'
>
> "For twenty seconds, no one said anything. Lois knew what was going on. 'People are afraid to react,' he says. 'They're trying to figure out what the top guy is thinking.' Neuharth was silent, wearing shades —no one could read his eyes . . .
>
> "Lois finally said to an aide, 'Okay, let's go,' and started to pack.
>
> " 'Hold it a minute,' Neuharth said, breaking the ice. 'I think we've seen some pretty good stuff here.' "

Neuharth saw exactly what was going on. In that act of defiance against his omnipotence and his staff's timidity, in that assertion of my manliness, tinged with an edge of physicality, Neuharth saw me as at least his *equal.* By refusing to plead for approval and by my willingness to kiss off the Gannett "jury," and especially Al Neuharth, I gained this powerful man's respect.

Strong leaders like Neuharth and Golden, Revson and Bronfman, Harding Lawrence and Joe Baum are equipped by God with a destruct button. If they see you're weakening, they push the button, like Goldfinger, and you go down the chute to be ground up alive.

But don't get me wrong—sometimes you *have* to kiss ass. At a meeting to review one of our campaigns, the apoplectic Joe Baum and my extraordinarily talented copywriter-partner Ron Holland went at each other's throats, cursing and screaming. Ron finally shouted at Baum, "Joe, *I hope you die.*"

"*—a rich man,*" I added.

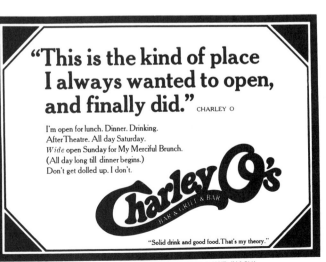

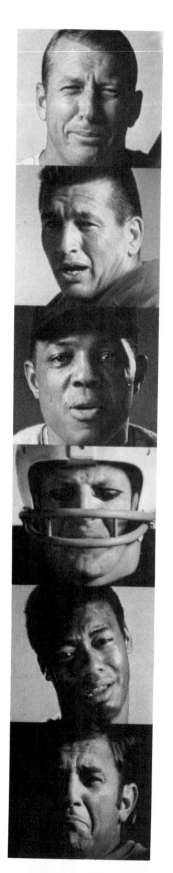

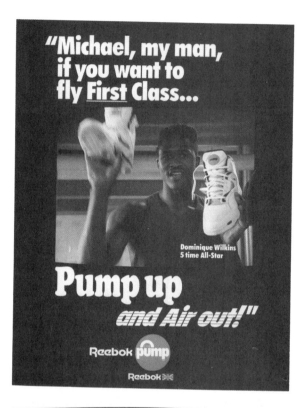

"Michael, my man, if you want to fly **First** Class...

Dominique Wilkins
5 time All-Star

Pump up *and Air out!*"

Reebok **pump**

Reebok

4

Celebrities

The art of choosing and using
famous personalities

We're all suckers for a famous face. A celebrity can add an almost *instant* style, atmosphere, feeling and/or meaning to any place, product or situation—unlike any other advertising "symbol." Unfortunately, celebrities are too often used in belittling and demeaning ways (belittling to them, demeaning to the product). Too often they end up looking like mercenaries, doing the spot *only* for money (such as Bill Cosby for E. F. Hutton). Moreover, the traditional idea of having celebrities say they use products insults our intelligence. (Who cares if Linda Ellerbee loves Maxwell House coffee?)

I use celebrities for the pleasant shock of their *seeming* irrelevance to the product, for unexpected juxtapositions, for certain connotations and implications, for a marriage between myth and the marketplace, for a subtle but deep credibility.

Using celebrities can be a daunting experience because everything is magnified: money problems, image concerns, schedules, shootings, credits, direction, legalities, egos, ambitions, fears. (I happen to like working with people who ain't entirely normal.) It's worth all these magnified problems if the results are fresh, exciting, memorable and effective on the tube and in the marketplace.

Getting the big names to laugh at themselves.

The famous campaign of the sixties, *"I want my Maypo!"* (see page 54), caused some confusion at the time among a few advertising folks, but not among ordinary kids. More than a few Establishment stiffasses wondered if Lois had lost his mind—imagine using awesome jocks like Johnny Unitas, Ray Nitschke, Oscar Robertson, Mickey Mantle, Wilt Chamberlain, Willie Mays and Don Meredith to sell a breakfast cereal to kids by weeping on camera and moaning, *"I want my Maypo!"*

The Maypo campaign was a colossal put-on. I knew *kids* would understand that. The idea of getting the greatest superstars of that era to weep on camera—all of them in *one* commercial, no less—was an extraordinary tour de force. The athletes were so taken by its disarming wackiness, they did it for zilch (only after I begged and cajoled; that's the usual process in lining up athletes—and when they see a commercial that's right for them, they'll play ball with you). The kids—even those who were too young to know Wilt the Stilt or Dandy Don—saw *adults* actually *crying* for Maypo, and they understood that those adults must mean it *because they were making fun of themselves.* Our message got through to the kids, and their rallying cry at breakfast became, *"I want my Maypo—or else!"*

Celebrities should not look like mercenaries.
To make them believable, show them in a human way by downplaying their celebrity.

A commercial has little credibility if we think its spokespersons are hustling a buck. We may *know* this is almost always true, but we recoil from the commercial that rings false by parading out a platoon of celebs. In *"When you got it, flaunt it!"* for Braniff (see page 61), our juxtaposition of unlikely couples was unprecedented. Pop guru Andy Warhol tried (but failed) to engage the sullen former heavyweight champ Sonny Liston . . . Whitey Ford talked baseball to Salvador Dali . . . black baseball legend Satchel Paige talked about fame with neophyte Dean Martin, Jr. . . . poet Marianne Moore discussed writing with crime novelist Mickey Spillane . . . British comedienne Hermione Gingold trumped film legend George Raft at cards whilst inundating him with pretentious palaver. Sounds slightly whacky on the face of it, but we see these celebrities as passengers on a Braniff flight, and by eavesdropping on these odd couples trying to out-flaunt each other, we hear everything that has to be said about Braniff International. (We also imply that you might bump into a celebrity on a Braniff flight.)

In the ultimate celebrity commercial, we assembled a parade of stars boarding a Braniff plane: A stewardess greets a procession of celebrity passengers as they enter the plane. *"Welcome on board, Mr. Namath,"* she begins, followed by *"So nice to see you, Miss Lollobrigida . . . Welcome, Mr. Dali . . . Good to have you with us, Mr. Warhol . . . Hello, Mr. Pucci."* Etcetera.

These spots were not perceived as celebrity "testimonials," but as the musings of interesting, credible people who flew on Braniff regularly, trying to out-bullshit one another. These are not idealized celebrities— they are a mini-cavalcade of famous people who are portrayed as lovable spotlight hustlers. All these factors combined to radiate a *surreal* kind of believability.

Creating profound believability (and building swift brand awareness) by using the most unlikely celebrities.

In preparing our television campaign for one of the least known Wall Street brokerage firms, Edwards & Hanly, we needed celebrities to make a small budget seem large and confident. We also needed *unlikely* celebrities, whose presence in the firm's advertising would swiftly suggest that here was a smart, sharp bunch of brokers, unlike all the traditional Wall Street houses.

Why should any investor turn to Edwards & Hanly, one of the most invisible brokerage houses on the New York Stock Exchange? Only if they sensed a certain trustworthiness, honesty and intelligence that people look for in an investment broker. Our selection of Joe Louis, who lost all his money and ended his years living off the kindness of friends, was a powerfully subtle way of telling the world that Edwards & Hanly brokers were not hip shooters—and were tuned in to the real world. By saying, *"Edwards & Hanly—where were you when I needed you?"*, he was declaring that Edwards & Hanly was an honest, thoughtful broker who understood the perils of flashy advice. Because Joe Louis was a thorn on America's conscience, by using him in its advertising, Edwards & Hanly was signaling America that brokers must *care* about their clients' money as though it were their own.

Bill Cosby doing serious standups for E. F. Hutton was patently unbelievable. Joe Louis for Edwards & Hanly was *profoundly* believable. The beneficiary of such honest advertising was Edwards & Hanly. And when the world's original fan dancer Sally Rand said, *"Edwards & Hanly —fan-tastic brokers"*, we were tooting our client's horn in a patently self-mocking way. Despite the Stock Exchange's decision to kill this spot because it was a "testimonial" (not allowed in financial advertising), Sally Rand's presence in this television campaign added to its disarming wit—particularly when paired with the soulful Joe Louis message, which was also quickly killed by the Exchange a few weeks after the campaign began. But the damage was done: the TV spots had taken the town by storm and our client's business exploded.

In 1967, the year this campaign ran, Mickey Mantle was one of the most famous personalities in New York. To allay many people's fears of dealing with a stockbroker, and to sell investors on switching to a different broker, we put Mickey Mantle on television. Like Joe Louis, Mantle's fame was no guarantee of financial security; he was known to have lost a bundle investing in lousy business ventures. We made no attempt to portray an idealized Mantle. Instead, The Mick delivered these vulnerable lines:

> *Boy, I'm telling you,*
> *when I came up to the big leagues,*
> *I was a shuffling, grinning, head-ducking country boy.*
> *But I know a man down at Edwards & Hanly.*
> *I'm learning, I'm learning.*

Mantle's honesty in admitting his mistakes further enhanced the image of Edwards & Hanly as *honest* brokers. (This had to be as powerful a "testimonial" as the Sally Rand spot, but the New York Stock Exchange okayed it.) *"I'm learning, I'm learning"* became an au courant phrase among talk show denizens and stand-up comics.

This campaign proved that megacelebrities are often unnecessary.

Aging celebrities (Joe Louis, Sally Rand) or a retired jock (Mantle) can have a strong impact on sales if they create the kind of ambience that consumers look for and respect—a crucial consideration in choosing an investment broker.

How to attract big celebrities with a small budget.

With smart advertising you can attract big entertainers who are more interested in promoting their shows—through your advertising—than in collecting endorsement money. Our Off-Track Betting campaign in 1973 (see page 62) had to attract far more than hard-core bettors; we had to convert OTB into a *sport* that interested everyone. Our "New York Bets" approach needed prestigious celebrities who were admired by a broad spectrum of New Yorkers so that our advertising could attract all population segments to Off-Track Betting. Our first spokesperson was Carol Channing, starring in the Broadway musical hit, *Lorelei.* She kicked off our campaign in a full-page newspaper ad, followed up by a vivid four-color bus poster, showing her bedecked in diamonds and wearing a New York Bets T-shirt. *"Next to diamonds,"* she said, *"my best friends are the N.Y. Bets."*

Carol Channing plugged OTB free—in return for our plugging her show. The formula was a natural to attract the biggest celebrities in America to do OTB ads for nothing. Word got around fast among entertainers and their agents, and as celebrities came to town, they came to us without even sniffing for any "tradeout." Many simply wanted to be in OTB's popular, well-liked advertising—and because most of them felt a special affection for New York that ran very deep and wanted to help our city. Superstars such as Rodney Dangerfield, Bob Hope, Jackie Gleason and Frank Sinatra "joined" OTB and appeared in a New York Bets T-shirt, each plugging OTB as something beyond *betting.* (Sinatra: *"Some of my favorite performers are horses."*)

Unlikely celebrities can be doubly effective in unexpected roles.

For Puss'n Boots cat food, I proposed to our client that we film a conversation between a beautiful tabby and a warm, recognizable man. The cat's voice would be familiar and would have some connection to the warm, recognizable man. My client thought I was hallucinating, but he let me go out on my limb. The voice of the cat would be (the obviously versatile) Whitey Ford, with his Long Island Irish twang—and I cast Yankee catching great Yogi Berra as the warm, recognizable man. (Berra had caught Ford during his greatest years with the Yankees.)

He began to warm to the concept, but was concerned that Whitey Ford might be an expensive voice-over. "Naaah," I said. "I already got Whitey signed up. When he heard he'd be feeding stuff to Yogi again, he lapped it up."

He was also worried, understandably, about Yogi Berra's recognizability. "What about women?" he asked. "They buy most of the cat food. Are you sure they know Yogi Berra, a ballplayer?"

The fact that my wife knew who Yogi was did not convince him. We therefore researched a cross-sectional sample of women, and it was no surprise to us to find that Yogi Berra was very well known to most of them (because of his distinctive name, obviously). We created a 60 second television commercial featuring Yogi the conversationalist and the voice of Whitey Ford as the cat, while Yogi and the cat engaged in a serious dialogue. Yogi told the cat he looked in great shape, followed by a lot of banter between the cat and Yogi about how the cat kept fit. *("I work out every day. Gym, roadwork, you know.")* After another question by Yogi on the source of the cat's energy, he gets a long answer from the cat on Puss'n Boots, winding up with this charming line: *"Yogi, you know I was once a five-pound weakling. Then I started eating Puss'n Boots. Now look at me."*—followed by a windup tag line for Puss'n Boots by Yogi.

In this charming juxtaposition of the bearish Yogi Berra engaged in a dialogue with a pussycat, the viewer never saw the cat mouthing its words—there was none of the predictable lip-synching when commercials show talking animals. Instead I shot the cat from the back of its head, with the camera focused on Yogi's face, showing him riveted on every word the cat spoke. The cat was filmed from the back, showing his head bobbing and weaving, punctuating each point as a voice-over delivered the cat's lines. It was a mesmerizing thirty seconds: watching the cat's head movements as his lines were spoken, and watching Yogi's entranced reactions to the cat's verbal wisdoms convinced people that a real dialogue was taking place.

It was a radical switcheroo from the customary animal commercial genre, and our client wanted to be entirely satisfied that the effect came through—that viewers would believe a conversation was taking place. We therefore did the commercial for a research test, with an eyeball-to-eyeball discussion about Puss'n Boots between a cat and an interviewer à la David Frost or Dick Cavett—in other words, a serious dialogue in which the professional interviewer would give the impression that he was determined to draw out the cat's life story. For the role of the interviewer I did extensive casting and selected a talented young actor who lived up to my expectations by performing brilliantly.

Our client then tested audience reaction to the spot, and he found to his delight (and to ours) that people loved it. The conversation projected enormous believability. We then went ahead and shot the final commercial, using that veteran thespian, the distinguished Lawrence Berra as the interviewer—and our original choice, Whitey Ford, as the voice of the pussycat. (The young actor we had used in our test commercial as the interviewer was the then-unknown aspiring actor, Alan Alda.)

When the product's name
suggests a certain kind of celebrity . . .

In 1989 Alan Pottasch, the marketing/advertising impresario of Pepsi–Cola, who had engineered the famous campaigns, "The Pepsi Generation" and "The Pepsi Challenge," appointed us as Pepsi's second agency for its Mug root beer brand, to do "guerrilla warfare"—that tough, market-by-market attack to make a brand famous against entrenched competition. We had to expand Mug's distribution and consumer acceptance beyond its limited base in California. My copy chief, Neil Brownlee, and I saw great power in the name Mug. It was an all–American moniker with a sunny, funny association that everyone could remember. Our advertising was based on the intensely human, all–American theme, bursting with tongue-in-cheek vanity: *"I love my Mug!"*

We created two 30 second commercials in which an off-camera voice sings in answer to the announcer's question, *"What do you love?"* Cyrano answers, *"I love my nose."* A ballerina chants, *"I love my toes."* A bride in a wedding portrait chimes in with *"I love my pose,"* etcetera—winding up with a mug of all time, Phyllis Diller, singing, *"I love my Mug . . . root beer!"* In a second commercial we followed the same pattern, winding up with the unforgettable mug of Richard Kiel, the steel-toothed giant of James Bond fame. In his three seconds at the end of the spot, his steel-toothed smile made it impossible *ever* to forget Mug.

In a few months, our bright young account guy, Andy Brief, (with one of the prize-winning mugs at the agency) reported that Mug root beer was now number two in America.

How to compete against a competitor's strong image by needling their superstar celebrities.

Toward the end of 1990, our agency was contacted by David Ropes, with whom I had worked on Mug Root Beer at Pepsi. Ropes had been a helicopter pilot in Vietnam and was no stranger to combat—but now as the new vice president of marketing services at Reebok, the famous sports performing shoe company, he was at the heart of the action in a mercilessly competitive category. Searching about for tough allies, he called us to come up with a promotion for the many malls across America to attract customers to buy the Reebok "Pump"—an athletic shoe that could be inflated to provide support, protection and a custom fit. And he was dying to go to war against the category's number one brand, Nike.

If ever there was a product that was put on earth to be promoted by my agency (where I'm surrounded by sports perverts), it was a basketball sneaker. And the Reebok Pump was heaven-sent for us to apply our talents. No heavy research was needed to tell copywriter Neil Brownlee and me that the Pump was a great product—but was not as "respected" as it deserved to be. I knew that its "technology" was dimly understood or even poo-pooed by millions of people who bought athletic shoes. I also knew its strong sales were due largely to its "hot" look.

On the first Saturday morning after Ropes had contacted me, after my full-court basketball game at the 23rd Street "Y" in Manhattan, I questioned my fellow jocks in the shower and learned that (1) almost all of them thought that Nike, not Reebok, made the Pump; and (2) they all regarded the Pump as a gimmick made for youngsters trying to look sharp. And they had no understanding of how it supported and protected the feet of serious athletes.

We told Ropes that before we did a promotion to attract mall shoppers we literally had to reintroduce the Pump to the American people, almost as a *new* product. We had to prove that its unique technology made it the greatest sports performance shoe in the world— for basketball, cross-training, golf, running, aerobics, and so forth. It offered a custom fit that no other could possibly provide.

Over the years Nike had created an image based on two superstars,

Michael "Air" Jordan and Bo "Bo knows" Jackson, both larger than life. We decided we couldn't out-dazzle them, but we could talk sense to the public. Don't get me wrong—the athletes in Reebok's stable were no slouches. Reebok had signed up famous athletes in every major sport— big names such as the NBA basketball great Dominique Wilkins, football superstar Boomer Esiason, Davis Cup tennis champion Michael Chang, U.S. decathalon champion Dave Johnson and The Great White Shark of golf, Greg Norman.

"Let's get these sports heroes talking directly to the audience in a human way," I said. "Our superstars can deliver their thoughts in straight, simple language to explain why they wear the Pump. But let's wind up with a delicious hot shit ending and kid, wiseguy style, Nike's imagery. Let's poke fun at Michael and Bo."

And I insisted, "Let's have a coup de grace *slogan* that tells people the next time they buy sneakers to nix Nike and Pump up! Let's have an in-your-face slogan—*'Pump up and Air out!'*"

That was the strategy: Reebok jocks talking up the Pump, comparing it to Nike's "Air" products. And we wanted the jibes at Nike's jocks to be almost esoteric—you had to be a sports fan to understand them. Boomer says, *". . . Boomer knows something that Bo don't know . . . Pump up and air out!"* Dominique stabs Nike's imagery with *"Michael, my man, if you want to fly first-class . . . Pump up and Air out!"* And Michael Chang takes a volley at Andre Agassi's brash "rock 'n' roll tennis" spot with, *"If you want to beat those rock 'n' roll tennis guys . . . Pump up and Air out!"*

We presented the campaign to Reebok's boss, the commanding Paul Fireman, in Boston. He saw its power immediately and told us not only to go ahead but to produce the Boomer and Dominique spots in time for the upcoming Super Bowl, even though our original assignment was limited to a mall promotion.

On Super Bowl night, America knew for the first time that (1) Reebok made the Pump, not Nike . . . and (2) the Pump was not a Mickey Mouse toy for kids, but a marvel of technology that was clearly believed by some of America's greatest athletes to be superior to Nike. The warmth and locker room camaraderie of our approach let us get away with this audacious, intrusive rallying cry. Sports fans loved these spots because they challenged Nike symbolism while the Reebok athletes charmingly delivered their straight-on lines without jumping through hoops. So when Boomer Esiason threw away a Nike shoe while promoting the Pump, he touched a sensitive nerve among sports fans who respond to honest, human talk by their sports idols.

"Pump up and Air out" became the rallying cry that carried over into every demographic group and into every retail store that sold athletic shoes. (Reebok had been a strong brand with women, but not with serious athletes. Our warm, believable campaign—with its theatrical tossing away of the Nike shoe as Boomer needles Bo Jackson, as Dominique jabs at Michael Jordan, and as Michael Chang tweeks Andre Agassi's rock 'n' roll tennis . . . all powerfully summed up by our slogan, *"Pump up and Air out"*—expanded the world's understanding of the Pump as a serious athletic shoe that was created by Reebok and a must-use favorite of the world's top athletes.)

The morning after our spots ran in the Super Bowl, in gyms, locker rooms and conference rooms all over the U.S.A., people were repeating, *"Boomer knows something"* and *"Michael, my man . . ."* And after this relatively modest exposure in the Super Bowl and with additional advertising during their NCAA basketball tournament—a small period of exposure, limited to just two sporting events—*"Pump up and Air out"* captured the public imagination and became a rallying cry for shoppers of athletic shoes. From sales of $100 million the previous year, the Reebok Pump will soar to an unbelievable $500 million, thanks to that big idea: *"Pump up and Air out."*

An analyst for Kidder, Peabody & Co. observed in an interview with *The Wall Street Journal's* advertising columnist Joanne Lipman that "Reebok's most recent, hard-hitting ads stressing performance are 'back on track. Their advertising strategy had been in a state of disarray, and now they finally got their act together.' " In a very short time period, with our three spots in the Super Bowl and then some exposure in the NCAA basketball tournament, we were able to change the way the public in general and athletes in particular regarded the Pump. As a result of this campaign, if the Pump were a separate company, it would be the third largest sports performance shoe company in the world!

If you can't afford the super celebrity, the unknown celebrity may even be better.

Two million people live on Long Island, but its native-born celebrities are scarce. Our client, Central Federal Savings, a Long Island bank, needed identification as a distinctly and unmistakably Long Island bank—but its generic sounding name was a source of confusion, while its identity as a Long Island enterprise was dim. We created this theme: "Central Federal Savings—The Island Bank!"

We produced four 15 second television spots that featured native-born celebrities from Long Island, which turned out to be tough detective work. The most famous Long Island celebrity is pop singer/writer Billy Joel. His price, if we were willing to do it, would have been one million smackers. That was a touch too much in view of Central Federal's total budget of $800,000. Instead, we pinpointed four celebrities who were not quite as spectacular as Billy Joel, but famous enough to add strong credibility to our message. Comedian Alan King is a Long Islander, but like Billy Joel, his tab was in the hefty range. But his wife was a heaven-sent spokesperson. She delivered this honest, straightforward pitch: *"My husband Alan King may know funny, but I know money . . . He makes it, I invest it . . . In fact, he's so big-hearted that if it weren't for me and Central Federal Savings, where would we be? Forget it!"* The announcer then winds up with our simple theme line, *"Central Federal Savings. The Island bank."*

Jeanette King, a spunky, attractive lady, was a *better* choice than her husband. She was the ultimate Long Island wife—smart, shrewd, funny, tough, *believable.*

In addition to Jeanette King, we lined up several quite famous Long Islanders. Boomer Esiason (our Reebok star), quarterback for the 1989 Super Bowl losers, the Cincinnati Bengals, delivered these lines: *"So what, the other team got lucky! But this Long Island boy will be back! Because with all the misfortunes in life, all the dropped and intercepted opportunities . . . I'll never lose my interest!* (Holds up bank book.) *Thanks, Central Federal Savings!"*

Basketball buffs like us knew that Bob Cousy, the legendary Boston Celtic, was originally from Long Island. Our copy plugged in to Cousy like this: *"Back when I played basketball, I made peanuts—people thought I was rich! But if I was on the court today . . . I'd own the bank! And instead of calling your bank Central Federal, you'd call it Bob Cousy Federal."*

Our last spot starred Long Island born and bred baseball Hall of Famer Whitey Ford of the New York Yankees reacting skeptically to Cousy's "hometown" spiel: *"Bob Cousy in a Central Federal commercial? He's from Long Island, but he went to Boston! I never left Long*

Island . . . my heart's *in Long Island, and my* mortgage . . . *my* CDs . . . *my* checking."

This campaign attracted immediate new business to Central Federal and made it an important, front-of-mind bank.

Long Islanders (and the Long Island press) loved it.

How surprising celebrities can expand the national audience for a major sporting event.

Seth Abraham, former top gun of HBO Sports, created Time Warner Sports after Time, Inc., and Warner merged, seeing a great opportunity to synergize their strengths with the sports world. To take advantage of the powerful distribution, clout and entertainment resourcefulness resulting from this corporate marriage, Abraham embarked on an ambitious program to expand sports viewership—and revenues—through the pay-per-view facilities of cable television.

As bona-fide sports freaks, our agency worked with Time Warner Sports on a new pay-per-view venture that would offer the paying public important monthly fights on Friday nights, as a kind of successor to Gillette's "Friday Night Fights" decades ago. We created the name TVKO, designed its logo (as well as the logo for Time Warner Sports) and helped define its marketing possibilities. The first bout TVKO signed was the April 19, 1991 fight between the heavyweight champion Evander Holyfield and aging ex-champion George Foreman. The contest was winningly dubbed "The Battle of the Ages."

We wanted to attract a broad audience that went far beyond the usual fight fans. We wanted this bout to enter popular culture, above and beyond the sports world. This would be a pay-per-view event that would cost each household about $36—which meant that the entire family, not just the fight-loving father, might have to participate in the decision. We therefore created a strong human interest rivalry between the younger Holyfield and the aging Foreman, using a variety of celebrities to stir up attention and get America excited.

We began our campaign with forty-two-year-old George Foreman in a rocking chair, saying, "Some folks think I'm too old to be fighting for the world heavyweight title. I'm just a big old baby boomer—and I'm going to lower the boom on that baby, Evander Holyfield." The young Holyfield counterpunches by saying: "My momma taught me to always respect my elders. But Mr. Foreman, if you think you're going to beat me, you're off your rocker!"

Sports Illustrated swimsuit cover girl Ashley Montana taunts Foreman (who proclaims himself spokesman for "the senior citizen crowd"), "George, shape up"—only to be outdone by comedian Billy Crystal, who advises Holyfield that it's all over because "You never fought a man who has prostate problems."

In young Holyfield's corner, basketball great Patrick Ewing says to George, "Evander's gonna stuff you, old man!" Billy Crystal, rooting for Foreman, fires back: "Patrick, you made a mistake. You should never say 'stuffed' to George—because George translates that to 'stuffing,' which means he's gonna eat this kid."

Bart Simpson tells his man Evander to "do the Bart-man on the old geezer!" And fifty-year-old Bugs Bunny gets into the act for his aging hero George Foreman, by declaring, "Oh, brudder . . . George'll pulverize the kid."

By popularizing the fight for a mass audience, we were able to attract the highest percentage ever of cable homes with pay-per-view access and a record $60 million in revenues. This fight is now considered a bellwether occasion for future sporting events. America's sports and entertainment planners are now all flirting with pay-per-view for major sporting events. (Could the World Series and the Super Bowl be far behind?)

P.S. By the end of the Holyfield–Foreman brawl, everybody in America, young and old, including all our celebrities, were rooting for George. The old man fought valiantly, and in a helluva battle, lost on points. But the first event produced by TVKO was a *knockout!*

Dear Gael Greene,

After all those wonderful meals we've had together.

Restaurant Associates

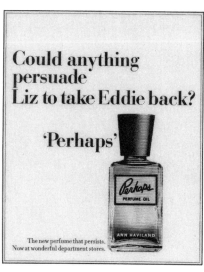

Could anything persuade Liz to take Eddie back?

'Perhaps'

Perhaps
PERFUME OIL

ANN HAVILAND

The new perfume that persists.
Now at wonderful department stores.

"Boy, what a bunch of Newsbreakers!"

The Channel 2 Newsbreakers. Concerned...Aggressive...
Street-smart...Street-tough. Ready to go anywhere to break news.
New York. New Jersey. Long Island. Westchester. Anywhere.
And ready to break any news. Whether it's big or small.
Join the Channel 2 Newsbreakers as they break news.
Twice a night. Seven nights a week. You won't find
a bigger bunch of Newsbreakers anywhere.

Channel ⊙2 Newsbreakers
6 & 11pm

5

When Humor
Should Be Anything
but Hilarious

We're talking serious comedy here!

Humor in advertising is like humor in life.

That frequently asked question, "Does humor work in advertising?" is stupid. Did anyone ever ask, "Does humor work in *life?*

If humor is appropriate and funny (if it ain't funny, we ain't talking humor), it should "work." The question should be, "How can you possibly create advertising *without* humor?" In advertising, humor is a natural way to win someone's heart. As that great sage *Anon.* has said, "Win their hearts and their balls are in reach."

In examining my work over the years, it's difficult to isolate "humor" as a category because it runs through almost everything I do—and through most of my waking hours. Humor disarms and makes one more accepting of certain thoughts and images that could be hard to take in serious discourse.

I'm often pigeonholed as someone who practices "street smart" or "wiseguy" advertising. I know what they're trying to say, but there's too much constipation out there to say it correctly. If my critics said I believe in "wiseass" advertising, this would at least show that someone has a sense of humor. When I rail against scientific fools, marketing windbags, stiffass bureaucrats, research fascists and pompous biggies, I'm crying out against a lack of humanity in advertising that kills communication, that makes it impossible to send a message. Most advertising is invisible because it is emotionless and humorless. Advertising communicates to large groups of people, one at a time. Whether the audience is a dozen or millions, people do not respond as "target consumers" or as "demographic cross sections," but as me, and you, and her and him.

Deflating a hot issue with gentle humor.

The letter (in and out of advertising) can be a deadly weapon in using humor. Back in 1970, *New York* magazine's restaurant critic, Gael Greene, wrote a withering review of Restaurant Associates, the chain of some of the most exciting and imaginative restaurants in the city. She was especially rough on The Four Seasons, (owned at that time by Restaurant Associates), probably the finest restaurant experience in New York, then and now. Her article, which I thought was unfairly critical, sent shock waves through Restaurant Associates as its stock took an immediate beating on the American Stock Exchange and business fell off ominously. RA panicked, then turned furious, and ordered us to cancel all their ads in *New York* magazine. I got them to calm down and instead of allowing them to vent their rage in a self-destructive way, I prepared an exquisitely simple full-page ad in the form of a one-sentence letter to Gael Greene, all in white type against a sea of black:

> **Dear Gael Greene,**
> **After all those wonderful meals we've had together.**
> **—Restaurant Associates**

The ad said very sweetly, *"We fed your face dozens of times, you ate it up—and now you bite the hand that feeds you?"* Fans of Restaurant Associates cheered when they saw this "rejoinder" in the very next issue of *New York* magazine, the stock rebounded and everything was soon hunky-dory again at Restaurant Associates. By being disarming, this "letter" turned a potential disaster to an advantage. (Later, I invited Gael Greene, disarmed, to lunch—at The Four Seasons, natch.)

Social change can be a rich source of humor.

What you are about to read describes the use of humor in advertising in the early seventies, when the feminist movement was just beginning to gather force. This genre of advertising humor would probably be impossible today—and may offend some of my female readers. But bear in mind, this approach reflected the mores of a generation ago—even though I still think it's very funny.

The beautifully designed Italian typewriter Olivetti was going nowhere in America. IBM had the market locked up. When we learned that purchasing agents of large companies would not consider Olivetti because secretaries insisted that an IBM gave them status, we conceived "the Olivetti girl," who would out-status everyone. We produced four-color magazine ads and television spots that showed the Olivetti girl as the star performer in her office, as the secretary who typed faster, neater and sharper, as the girl most likely to succeed. One of our headlines summed it up: *"When you want to do something right, give it to the Olivetti girl!"*

"Who is the Olivetti girl?" asked our kickoff color spread. *"And why are people saying such terribly nice things about her?"* Our ad showed a spirited secretary at her typewriter, symbolizing the kind of smart, sharp woman who types on an Olivetti. In a television spot we showed her tap dancing while she typed out: *"An Olivetti girl can really belt it out."* In another spot, a plain Jane confided, *"Would you believe, the men in the office never noticed me before I became an Olivetti girl?"* In a third spot, we asked *"Is it true blondes have more fun?"* as we showed a typist having a laughing jag while typing on her Olivetti. In *Cosmopolitan* we ran the tongue-in-cheek message: *"True confessions of an Olivetti girl (or, how a change in typewriters changed my life)."*

The campaign was a huge success in the typewriter marketplace as sales of Olivetti surged. On a local market basis we ran small space ads that listed the names of secretaries who had become Olivetti girls as their companies switched brands. This secretary-as-hero approach was clearly working, but it was no source of fun for the National Organization of Women (NOW), which attacked the campaign for stereotyping women as underlings. The organization was furious that only men were shown as bosses while only women were shown as secretaries. As bulletins poured in from Olivetti's sales staff reporting a jump in new orders, I found myself the object of a full-scale assault by NOW. I gotta tell you, it was scarier than fighting in Korea. Imagine—they called *me(!!)* a male chauvinist pig. They picketed Olivetti's corporate offices on Park Avenue. They even sent hecklers up to my office to un-n-n-nerve me. (Some were *very* attractive.) They demanded that we also show male secretaries in our advertising. Something had to be done. Sure, I'll do a male secretary, I said—and I'll also cast his boss as a woman. I'm for progress! The Olivetti people, classy northern Italians, who adored women in a Europ-ean sense, couldn't make heads or tails of any of this and seemed baffled when I cast a *male* secretary as an Olivetti girl and a *woman* executive as the boss. With trusting dismay, they told me to do what I thought was the right thing for these sexually primitive Americans.

I cast an actual woman executive, not an actress, as the boss. And I cast football superstar Joe Namath as the secretary! In addition to being such a famous, appealing guy, I knew that Namath knew how to type. Thus, in socially turbulent 1972, as women's movements were striking out for equality with men, we created a full-page ad—*"Joe Namath is an Olivetti girl!"*—and a timely television commercial in which secretary Joe Namath takes dictation from his lady boss, belting out her letter on his Olivetti as a voice-over describes the Olivetti Electric, winding up with the remark, *"But obviously, not all Olivetti girls are girls!"* Namath then hands the finished letter to his boss and she says, *"I'm very pleased with your work, Joseph. By the way . . .* [as she removes her glasses], *what are you doing for dinner tonight?"* Joe gives the camera a "here we go again" look.

When I showed the women of NOW the finished commercial, they knew they were checkmated, especially when I looked at them with great innocence and said, "You got your female boss in this commercial and I gave you your male underling. I'm just reflecting life. In your experience, doesn't the boss usually try to seduce the secretary?"

One of the Olivetti girls in our television advertising, a young red-head named Shere Hite, went on to become a major researcher of female orgasms. I often wondered if the author of *The Hite Report* had become radicalized while witnessing her militant sisters mount their offensive against little ole me.

Humor is not always hilarious . . .

Harvey Probber, a manufacturer of precision-built furniture, asked my agency to promote its luxurious chairs. My partner Julian Koenig and I visited the factory in Fall River, Massachusetts, to see the care that was taken and the fine workmanship in manufacturing these chairs. Each was placed on an electronic test platform to be sure that its four legs sat comfortably and perfectly on a floor. As I reflected on this extraordinary test procedure, I asked Koenig, a chain smoker, "Got a book of matches?" Koenig handed me a matchbook and I slid it under one leg of the chair on the test platform. "I got the ad," I said. *"If your Harvey Probber chair is crooked, straighten your floor."*

Koenig scowled and shot back, "Asshole—if your Harvey Probber chair *wobbles,* straighten your floor." I shot a red chair against a red wall on a brown parquet floor with a conspicuous white matchbook under one leg. Your eye was drawn directly to the white matchbook. And that's the way the ad ran: *"If your Harvey Probber chair wobbles, straighten your floor."* The body copy zestfully continued this droll approach: *"Every piece of furniture that Harvey Probber makes at Fall River, Mass., is placed on a test platform to make sure it's on the level. If you get it, it is. Mr. Probber loses a lot of furniture this way."*

Humor is not always hilarious. The most effective humor is insidious in its power to win your attention and persuade you—without your being aware that you have been seduced by funny imagery and language. The Harvey Probber ad, in headline and copy, was intensely clear and *charming.* And, on the level, it sold many chairs.

How humor can turn cheap into chic.

In 1968, Stevens Hosiery had produced an excellent new stocking that sold for 50 cents a pair, far less than other brands. It was such an unbelievably low price that many women wouldn't be caught dead buying them. We had to convert cheap into chic. We began with its name, by calling it "25¢ a leg." (Not half bad!) In a series of television spots using sophisticated slapstick, I showed a doctor's hand testing the knee reflexes of a woman's leg as an off-screen voice says: *"Any woman who pays more than 25¢ a leg for stockings ought to have her knees examined."* In another spot a woman stomps into view, wearing a full cast on one leg. Her one-liner: *"25¢ will buy you one beautiful leg. For another quarter we'll take care of the other one."* In a third spot a woman in a Rolls-Royce delivers this blue blood zinger: *"Though I'm filthy with money, why should I pay more than 25¢ a leg?"*

As a result of all this cute legwork, there was a run on Stevens stockings. Mass sales, especially in supermarkets, were huge. The campaign changed the way hosiery was priced, packaged and sold. "25¢ a leg," a smartass name for a product, became the basis for funky, funny television advertising, and turned an industry inside out.

How humor plus the daily headlines made a tiny budget look huge.

Perhaps was the name of a new fragrance that had been put on the market a few weeks before Christmas in 1967 by Ann Haviland Perfume. Coming out so late in the gift-giving season, the only way to make it a winner was by violating all the rules about fragrance advertising. The owner of Ann Haviland was a debonair aristocrat named Gaston de Havenon, who happened to be a fellow collector of African art. "It is late in the season for introducing our magnificent Perhaps," said Gaston in December. "Or would you say, Monsieur Lois, that it ees actually *trop tard* to advertise Perhaps?"

"How many francs you got to spend?" I asked him suavely.

His budget was only $16,000, but, believe it or not, I knew that in 1967, in just the New York market, it would be enough to do a strong job for Perhaps, despite the lateness of the hour. While it was too late to get into magazines, and with too little time to buy television spots, there was still enough time to convince the salesgirls at the perfume counters of Fifth Avenue stores to push Perhaps. We created a series of small newspaper ads aimed at the big Fifth Avenue stores and eleventh-hour Christmas shoppers. And because they ran in newspapers, we were able to turn on a dime with last-minute messages that connected with the day's headlines. All of our messages were set-up questions for the punchline—the perfume's name:

> **Have Chanel, Dior, de Givenchy and Arpege heard the news?**
> **Perhaps**
>
> **If you bought her a copy of that fake Greek horse,**
> **can you still save face?**
> **Perhaps**

(This ad ran the day after the Metropolitan Museum announced that one of its classical bronzes was a fake.)

Could anything persuade Liz to take Eddie back?
Perhaps

(A very timely message: as this was being set in type, Richard Burton was cuckolding Eddie Fisher, Liz Taylor's husband, again and again, on the set of *Cleopatra*.)

Can a perfume become famous overnight?
Perhaps

As these small space ads peppered the town, we lined up a brigade of models (our gung-ho secretaries) to "picket" Bonwit, Bergdorf and Bendel for the week before Christmas. They wore luxurious rented fur coats (during that pre-animal rights era), high heels and they were bedecked in sandwich sign blowups of our ads—an incongruous miniparade on Fifth Avenue. Suddenly, it became impossible for anyone shopping for a Christmas gift *not* to know about Perhaps. In just two weeks, on a petty cash budget, Perhaps sold as much as Revlon's Intimate, with its big-brand, seven-figure television budget. We were talking basically to men who bought a lot of perfume as gifts. To these shoppers the brand that stood out was the brand they chose. Through our ads and pickets we built awareness and consumer demand right at point-of-sale, enabling Perhaps to compete successfully against the big, heavily advertised fragrance brands. It was a campaign that assumed (correctly) that New Yorkers appreciated fresh, funny advertising.

When you have a chance to use ballbreaking humor that sells . . . do it!

The rating wars between news shows in major markets are fierce and endless. In 1979 we went to work for New York's drifting Channel 2 (WCBS–TV). Channel 7 (WABC–TV) had a power lock on the 6:00 and 11:00 o'clock news despite Channel 2's strengths in investigative reporting. Dislodging a leader from a news slot has always been extremely difficult. Here was a challenge that cried out for a big idea—for a campaign that would knock you down. We created "Newsbreakers":

> ### The Channel 2 Newsbreakers.
> ### Concerned . . . Aggressive . . . Street smart . . . Street tough.
> ### Ready to go anywhere to break news.

Join the Channel 2 Newsbreakers.
Twice a night. Seven nights a week.
You won't find a bigger bunch of Newsbreakers anywhere!

Our headline said, with thick tongue in cheek: *"Boy, what a bunch of Newsbreakers!"* I loved this ad because it was pure New Yorkese, with delicious wordplay. Any real New Yorker was able to read this correctly as "Boy, what a bunch of *ballbreakers!"*

"Newsbreakers" took over the town with print ads, jumbo bus posters, television and radio. The impact of this tough descriptive, with its street-funny double entendre, was extraordinary. Six weeks into the campaign an independent research study, commissioned by Channel 2, compared "Newsbreakers" with five long-running station campaigns and concluded that "Newsbreakers" was sweeping the city while there was little or no recall of the other campaigns. Better yet, Channel 2 moved ahead of Channel 7 in the 11:00 o'clock news race and narrowed the gap strongly in the 6:00 o'clock news.

A natural extension of "Newsbreakers" was "Newsbreaker Territory"—our name for every corner of the tri-state area. In one outrageous television commercial a hospital patient comes to after emergency room surgery and asks, *"Where am I?"* His nervous wife at his bedside says *"Yonkers."* The patient rears up from his bed and shouts exultantly, *"Yonkers? That's* Newsbreaker Territory!"

We created a pool of equally wacky spots. New Yorkers couldn't resist the boffo hilarity of our ballbreaking campaign and switched to the "Newsbreakers" on Channel 2.

The power of gentle wit.

Humor in advertising can be tremendously effective by being gentle and bright—particularly when you want to reach advertisers.

USA TODAY was preparing to celebrate its fifth birthday on September 15, 1987, marking a spectacular comeback from near extinction a few years earlier. Our savvy account manager Jim Feigenbaum told us the client wanted a "State of the Union" ad on *USA TODAY*'s accomplishments over the last five years—but we all knew this was a great chance to celebrate a birthday for a dramatically successful newspaper that media pundits and advertising gurus predicted would be dead years before. We wanted a joyous affirmation of the newspaper's vitality and success—not the expected self-congratulatory message inflated with corporate puffery.

Our surprise solution was a series of sweet and engaging messages based on the theme, *"Two of the most famous five-year-olds in history."* We drew attention to *USA TODAY*'s achievement by pairing *USA TODAY* in each announcement with *"another five-year old."* We showed E.T., who came from outer space five years before and won the hearts of the entire U.S.A . . . Michael Jackson, who became lead singer of the Jackson Five at age five . . . the great Kelso, named Horse of the Year at age five—the greatest five-year-old who ever ran . . . Shirley Temple, the child film star legend who made her debut at age five . . . Rin Tin Tin, the superhero dog who made his first film at age five . . . and the most talented five-year-old who ever lived, Wolfgang Amadeus Mozart.

Huge birthday party celebrations were held by *USA TODAY* in cities across the country, capped by a gala party in New York at the Museum of Modern Art. Our campaign, a gently humorous amplification of *USA TODAY*'s brilliant five-year history, turned a traditional backslapping event into a memorable, witty campaign *to advertisers* that said *USA TODAY* was not only a great success, but also had a lot of style.

Using humor to advertise humor.

When the advertised product is humor itself, you have to get funny in a serious kind of way. Home Box Office (HBO) had brought comedy to prominence on cable television, from stand-ups to specials—but this leadership was losing its perceived validity as other cable channels started to barge into the comedy club. We wanted everyone to know that HBO not only *had* comedy, but was its pioneer on cable, and was largely responsible for the explosion of comedy clubs on television. After HBO's agency (a giant marketing shop) was unable to come up with an effective theme for its powerful comedy programming, we were asked to try our hand at creating *the* theme that would say it all and say it memorably. This assignment was a natural for my agency's jokemeister, copywriter Shelly Isaacs, always the first to know the latest jokes from every corner of America (and if his inventory is low, he makes up his own jokes). Shelly worked with Jackie Mason early in both their careers—and he happens to look like Mel Brooks. With those comedic credits we went to work on HBO's fascinating assignment, and we came up with . . .

HBO. We're talking serious comedy here!

"Serious comedy" is obviously a contradiction in terms, an oxymoron—and that's the fun of it! We say comedy is funny, and HBO takes comedy seriously. Got that?

In a pool of television commercials we shot America's most popular comedians doing their schtick, using the oxymoronic "serious comedy" as their motif—Billy Crystal, Bob (Bobcat) Goldthwaite, Howie Mandel, Elayne Boosler, Paul Rodriguez, Louie Anderson, Robert Klein, Judy Tenuta, Gilbert Gottfried, Steven Wright, Jim Morris, Carol Leifer. Since its debut, *"We're talking serious comedy here!"* has come out of the mouths of the funniest people in the business and has entered the language as HBO continues to reign as the Cable King of Comedy.

Say something serious in a funny way and you can win over people every time. We're talking serious comedy here!

Sure you can put Pirelli fantastico
steel-belted radial tires on your car.
Pirelli has tires that fit
almost all American and imported cars.
Capish?!

PIRELLI

"Remember
darling—
Never
pay more than
25¢ a leg."

Spirit
by Stevens
25¢
a leg!

Sheer glamour:
25¢ a leg.
(Any woman who pays
more than 25¢ a leg
for stockings
ought to have her
knees examined.)

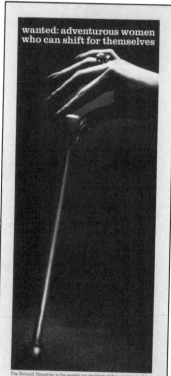

wanted: adventurous women who can shift for themselves

The Renault Dauphine is the easiest car we know of for a woman to drive.
  When parked, you turn the wheel with a finger. *Natural* power steering.
Its shift floats from gear to gear ("phenomenally simple and certain"
says one critic). Its Feriec clutch eliminates pedals.
  You park (and unpark) in tiny places with a single swing. You turn on a
franc. You do tight U-turns (the Renault runs rings inside other cars).
  You have a sense of pleasure and control that has almost been lost in a
push-button world. Driving is fun again.
  And the Dauphine is beautiful. The word means "Princess." Your hand-
some Renault dealer wants women like you.
  Suggested retail prices: the Renault Dauphine $1645; Renault 4CV $1345.

6

Sex in
Advertising

It's just a tool—but you gotta learn
how to use it right

Sex in advertising is overrated. For years advertisers and their agencies have been accused of using sex to seduce people into buying products through the cunning manipulation of erotic images. When Vance Packard wrote *The Hidden Persuaders* in 1957, he introduced the occult subject of subliminal advertising. The impact of that work in shaping how advertising was understood by Americans has been extraordinary. Here at last was a master clue to the mysterious powers of this new and inscrutable pseudo science that was becoming a major force in American life—a conspiracy of subliminal manipulators was at work, corrupting America with the virus of sex in advertising. For decades this idiocy has obscured the banal truth that sex in advertising is hardly what it's cracked up to be and may be more trouble than it's worth.

Sex in advertising should be handled with care. Despite the sexual revolution and the loosening of limits on sexual expression in mass media, particularly in movies, advertising is not a hospitable environment for sexual expression. Advertising seeks to command attention through inventive imagery; sex is a separate passion, a loose emotional cannon that has no clear direction—and it has a self-contained imagery that may not easily merge with that of an advertising campaign. Sex, however, is a potentially explosive force. It works best in advertising when leavened by humor, which makes it acceptable—and non-threatening. An ideal marriage between sex and humor can result in great advertising.

A classic example is my "talking bottles" campaign for Wolfschmidt vodka (see page 48). A vertical Wolfschmidt bottle saying, *"You're some tomato"* to a luscious red tomato is flagrantly sexy (if you like dirty pictures); it's also such good fun that the phallic horseplay becomes acceptable. When the Wolfschmidt bottle comes on with his pitch— *"You're some tomato. We could make beautiful Bloody Marys together. I'm different from the other fellows."*—sex becomes a convenient metaphor for selling Wolfschmidt. When the tomato answers, *"I like you, Wolfschmidt. You've got taste,"* the metaphor is complete. This was one of those rare campaigns where sex and humor merged effortlessly to create innovative imagery in a category that was cliché-ridden with scenes of beautiful, astringent people at cocktail parties in penthouses. When I showed Seagram's Sam Bronfman a follow-up Wolfschmidt poster with a blatant headline, *"Taste my screwdriver,"* the humor wasn't quite as charming as the talking bottle ads. Bronfman was confused. "This is for California," I explained. He seemed to accept what we said as he walked away, scratching his head.

This campaign said drinking booze, especially vodka, often means parties, men and women meeting . . . and fornicating. Our follow-up ads, week after week, showed a lemon, a lime, an onion, an olive, a swizzle stick and all of the sexually relevant paraphernalia seen on a bar, each talking a blue streak with the Wolfschmidt bottle, always in sexy double entendre. The joyful message of this advertising boiled down to: let's all drink and copulate.

With one conspicuous exception (which I'll cover later in this chapter), I have almost always found that sex in communications, to be effective, must be *funny*. When I was doing covers for *Esquire,* its ad sales people were always pressuring the magazine's editors to give them a "girlie cover." Once, when the pressure became intolerable, *Esquire*'s editor, Harold Hayes, threw in the towel and told me, "George, we *gotta* do a girlie cover." What was I expected to do—a *Playboy*–style cleavage cover? Never. My covers were visual commentaries on our life and times. Instead, I fastened onto an article that portrayed liberated American women as victims of changing values and competitive pressures. I did a cover on "The New American Woman: Through at [age] 21." I showed a nude young woman jackknifed in a garbage can, only her head and legs protruding. Her mournful face removed any possible erotica from the shot. This was sex turned upside down—and the visual was inspired by this ancient (forgive, therefore, its modern-day ethnic chauvinism) dirty joke: A young housewife is hanging laundry on the roof of her apartment house. She slips and falls off the roof, landing headfirst into a garbage pail. A Chinese laundryman walks by and spots her shapely legs protruding from the garbage pail. He spreads her ankles and peers down. "Amellicans velly funny people," he reflects aloud in his English patois. "In China, good for ten years yet."

The more I explore the subject of sex in advertising, the more I become convinced that I'm a prude. Even in my campaign for LifeStyle condoms (see page 154), sexy as its subject matter might be—Phantom of the Opera being told by a store clerk he doesn't have to wear his mask to order condoms . . . Azania, Queen of the Jungle, ordering a year's supply of condoms because "it's a jungle out there" . . . Robin Hood buying condoms for "all my merry men!" (a covert allusion to those amongst us who are gay)—nobody watches these commercials and gets sexually aroused. A consumer in heat runs for a partner, not to his (or her) local supermarket. But this campaign sold a mess of LifeStyle condoms. Sex in advertising sells only if it does not get in the way . . . or if it is put in its proper place through a bold coupling with humor.

In a full-page ad for Stevens Hosiery's "25¢ a leg!" I showed an overbearing mother giving last-minute advice to her just-married daughter as she heads for her honeymoon, groom in tow. In a pure non sequitur the mother says, *"Remember, darling—never pay more than 25¢ a leg."* The sweet sexuality of a honeymoon is deliberately shattered by this bizarre admonition, a joke out of the blue, but a joke all the same. Better to sell Stevens hosiery than to get all worked up about deflowering the virgin bride. An *informed* customer is worth much more than an *aroused* customer.

To be informed *and* aroused is even better. In 1973 the president of

Pirelli tires asked me if I could come up with a big idea to build sales. After many years and millions of dollars in advertising this superb steel-belted radial tire, only 3% of American car owners had ever heard of Pirelli. The company's dull advertising followed the industry's hoary formula: show tire cross sections and torture tests, preferably with a macho spokesman. Because Pirelli's budget was only about a million bucks a year when we became their agency, they put it all in magazines. We showed that for the same money they could be on television. And I insisted that our campaign should proudly emphasize their Italian origins (Pirelli in America had always hidden the fact that it was Italian). A tire with Italian pedigree was an integral aspect of Italy's great racing and car design tradition, and should not be sold in America without these rich image assets. Instead of the customary tread-directed machismo advertising, I chose a high fashion model with a voluptuous northern Italian dialect (and with the lyrical name Apollonia) to sell Pirelli on television. I designed a custom-made dress with Pirelli logos as its design, à la Pucci. Our spokeslady sensually rolled the name Pirelli over her sophisticated tongue, always caressing a Pirelli tire, even swinging in one.

In one television spot Apollonia struts into view, rolling a Pirelli tire toward a disabled car as she hums a passage from a Verdi opera. She jacks up the car, her body flawlessly outlined in her skin-tight dress, adorned with its ubiquitous Pirelli logos. As she removes the old tire she looks at us and says, *"Every Tomasso, Dick and Harry knows steel-belted radial tires is the molto fantastico tire."* As she replaces it with a Pirelli tire—*"ooofff!"*—she resumes her Milanese-accented pitch: *"And a molto fantastico tire is . . . Pirelli—a comfortable, steel-belted tire. So change into something comfortable . . . change into Pirelli."* As she lowers the car, she looks at us and asks, *"Capish?!"*

By today's standards, this campaign would be considered sexist. By the standards of any era it was certainly *sexy*. Here was a rare situation when sexist and sexy worked wonderfully well together. We were, after all, addressing macho-minded car freaks for whom a tire was more important than a wedding ring. The Italian manufacturer Pirelli was reaching its American audience in a way that traditional advertising could never accomplish, with an extraordinary confluence of messages (quality tire, Italian tradition, suitable for American cars) that attracted attention through a deliberately sexual metaphor, made acceptable through distinctly American tongue-in-cheek humor. Through this advertising, Pirelli became a well-known brand name in America.

If this campaign was sexy, Joe Namath as an Olivetti girl (see page 198) was even sexier. When his female boss asked him for a date, America burst out laughing. Many men have fantasies of being approached by women (and many women wish they could initiate a date with an attractive man). The steamiest X-rated movie has less sexuality than this 30 second television commercial, especially when the proper female boss removes her executive-looking glasses and says softly, with some uncertainty, *"By the way, Joseph, what are you doing for dinner tonight?"* This is also an intrinsically *funny* encounter, an inverted juxtaposition of sexist roles that commands attention and generates excitement. Humor makes its sexuality acceptable.

Back in the late sixties, old people were Wheatena's best customers, but we had to expand its customer base to younger people without losing the strong loyalty of seniors. When we learned that wheat germ was in Wheatena we were bowled over. (Wheat germ, one of the first "health" ingredients, was considered a source of energy and vigor.) We played up wheat germ on the package and we advertised it in a television commercial to young and old. Our theme became, *"Miraculous Wheatena, loaded with wheat germ!"* We created a 30 second television spot made up of three 10 second vignettes: a surfer *("I'm certain I feel better on days I eat Wheatena!")* . . . a young woman *("I know I feel meaner when I eat my Wheatena!")* . . . and an older lady having breakfast with an older gent. The last vignette correctly assumed that old people enjoy making love. It was one of the sexiest television scenes I've ever done:

OLD WOMAN: *To your health, my dear.*
OLD MAN: *To your health, baby!*
ANNOUNCER: *Miraculous Wheatena. Loaded with wheat germ!*

This vignette let the world know that sex is not the exclusive province of the young. An edge of humor and ambiguity (are they married? did they have a wild night?) gives this otherwise domestic scene an appealing credibility.

Our client was concerned that this might offend seniors. I told him to go ahead and risk it because I knew that old people weren't the prudes we made them out to be. Young or old, people are smart—especially when the subject is sex.

I recently tried, unsuccessfully, to penetrate the outer limits of sex in advertising. To promote mammography for the American Cancer Society, I wanted to create advertising that would go far beyond what any pro bono campaign is normally expected to accomplish. For early detection of breast cancer, enough years had gone by and enough cases had been recorded to convince American women that mammography could detect this dread malignancy at its earliest, most curable stages. Here was an ideal opportunity to save lives by getting attention—by being seemingly outrageous in a sexual way. In the 30 second television commercial I proposed, let me first show you the copy we wrote that explains the concept, to be delivered by a voice-over announcer:

> We asked eight of the most beautiful women in the world to bare their breasts . . . and they agreed. Why? To help us dramatically demonstrate the bare fact that early detection, through self-examination, regular medical checkups, and mammography, is essential in curing cancer . . . and preserving the remarkable beauty of a woman's breast. The American Cancer Society celebrates 75 years of life!

As the announcer's voice is heard saying these words, the camera dissolves from the bare breasts of one woman to the bare breasts of each of seven other women. A total of eight women—all celebrities— would appear voluntarily in this commercial, each allowing their uncovered breasts to be filmed. But we would see *only* their breasts as the announcer speaks, never their faces. At the end of the spot, we would show the logo of the American Cancer Society as the announcer concludes with, *"The American Cancer Society celebrates 75 years of life!"* At this point we suddenly cut just to the *faces* of the eight women celebrities whose breasts were shown.

In unison, all eight women say, *"Join us."*

That big idea would have ignited gigantic publicity and would have made every woman in America aware of the need for mammography— while everyone who saw the spot would have tried to guess whose breasts were whose. The people at the American Cancer Society were stunned at first, but they understood the powerful potential impact of this approach. When CBS saw the concept they blinked, but seemed enthusiastic; indeed, they were aroused enough to encourage us to produce a demo commercial. We shot this demo spot very tastefully (without celebrities), with fashion-style photography of the models' bare breasts, softly lit. This was not done in the blatant in-your-face *Playboy/*

Penthouse style. The CBS censors were astonished by our sensitive treatment—but, predictably, they came to their senses and chickened out. Too bad. It could have saved the lives of many women. What a paradox! Americans are the most breast-obsessed people in the world, but showing breasts in advertising—not to push products, but to save lives—is deemed bad taste. Who's crazy—me or our cultural custodians?

In an article on *Time* art critic John Hughes, "Shock of the Hughes" (*Vanity Fair,* November 1990), Martin Filler makes this interesting observation: "Hughes is always ready to explore the human element in art, and thus many of his reviews, short though they may be, delve into the artist's sexuality, whether straight (Rodin), gay (Marsden Hartley), monastic (Giorgio Morandi), syphilitic (Manet), or misogynist and probably impotent (Degas). In the case of Antoine Watteau, that peerless psychologist of courtly erotic melancholy, Hughes laments the fact that 'nothing is known about his . . . sexual life.' . . . 'I do think the sexuality of an artist is a very important component in the work,' Hughes insists. 'I've never presumed to conduct a psychoanalysis, but I think it's interesting in the general picture of character, and sometimes it's extremely relevant to the art, as with Picasso.' "

My sexuality, let the world know, is old-world, North Bronx straight, and my work apparently reflects an irresistible urge to flirt with women and to swap funny stories about sex, always the pluperfect subject for great jokes. Any advertising I create with sexual content, I confess, tends to be wiseass (with the conspicuous exception of the American Cancer Society spot), bordering on the sexist. I happen to be a simple, barefoot stickball player with uncomplicated sexual preferences: I love blondes and I regard women's high heel shoes as the world's greatest invention (as compared to panty hose, the worst). I also believe that the only sex of real value in advertising is working with an intelligent female client or co-worker. Gratuitous sex in advertising is like gratuitous sex in movies —it puts you to sleep. Sex in advertising, like humor in advertising, must be bound up in an *idea* to be effective (Namath as a secretary; the Pirelli spokeslady in a skintight dress; fan dancer Sally Rand doing a testimonial for a stockbroker). Even when no sexual message is intended, your unconscious mind can be judged guilty of prurience despite your conscious pleas of innocence: After my television spot ran for Dilly Beans (see page 146), *"Break the smoking habit—eat Dilly Beans,"* which

213

showed a profile closeup of a woman's lips, her hand holding a Dilly Bean like a cigarette, I was accused of playing with phallic symbols and making a statement on behalf of fellatio. In a print ad for Renault to persuade women that it was easy to drive a car with a manual transmission, I showed a woman's hand delicately working a stick shift, with this pre-feminist headline: *"Wanted: adventurous women who can shift for themselves."* Once again I was accused of creating a dirty ad; this time, they said I was really showing a woman's hand fondling a man's penis. Ah, the perils of advertising a French car.

Those notorious Calvin Klein jeans commercials that starred a very young Brooke Shields were widely criticized for exploiting sex; instead, I saw them as honest expressions of teenage rebelliousness. Advertising for perfumes and fragrances often meddles with sexual innuendo, an almost essential (and innocent) technique to clear a profit during the gift-giving holidays, their do-or-die selling season.

Sex in advertising simply happens to be one of *many* possible creative ingredients that should or should not be used. Creative people should keep *all* their options open. Nothing should be final. Everything should be considered.

I was once profiled in a television interview on the (now-defunct) CBS Cable by a highbrow, ad-hating interrogator. The interviewer asked for my opinion of sex in advertising. "It's good," I answered. "Sex is part of life. You breathe, you eat, you drink, you play—then sex. Sex is good." As the show was drawing to a close, having failed to work up my dander, he baited me one more time. "Answer me this—would you ever show *rape* in advertising?" he asked, quite stupidly.

"Of course not," I said reflexively. "Well . . . wait a minute . . . let me think about it . . ."—as the show faded to black.

Break
the smoking
habit –

eat
Dilly Beans

There are forty of these politely pickled fresh green-
beans in every jar, swimming in vinegar and dainty
dill. They are crisp, crunchy and absolutely the best
idea since the peanut and the pretzel. They have everything but calories. (Say, buddy, got a cigarette?)

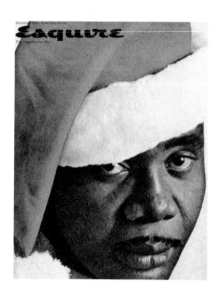

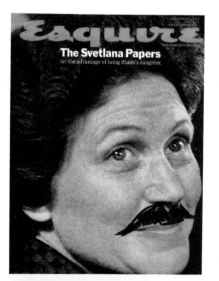

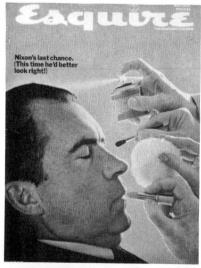

7

The Image
as Propaganda

**Those notorious *Esquire* covers that defined
an American decade**

The cover of a magazine—good, bad or indifferent—is a package design and a statement. The cover should give you the spirit and essence of its contents. It should say who you are. But most magazines don't have a clue as to how that should be done visually, so they express their existence by a mumbo jumbo listing of contents on the cover.

During the sixties, I created 92 covers for *Esquire* that raised hell, stirred up controversy, attracted new readers, and somehow defined that turbulent decade. Over 150 million copies carried my work. *Print* magazine made this observation in a retrospective article[1] on *Esquire*'s art direction over the years: "If any icons of America's graphic design are

---

[1] *Print,* February 1991, "Esquire and Its Art Directors: A Survivor's Tale," by Steven Heller.

worth preserving, George Lois's *Esquire* covers from the mid–1960s to the very early '70s are . . . they are considered among the most powerful propaganda imagery in any medium and certainly the most memorable magazine covers ever." These covers also cut the mustard financially: when I did my first cover in 1962, *Esquire* was in the red. Five years later its profits were well over $3 million. My front pages must have helped. (They sure didn't hoit.)

Esquire was a superb magazine, with brilliant contributors that included James Baldwin, Truman Capote, Gay Talese and Tom Wolfe—thanks to its brilliant editor, Harold Hayes. For years, however, *Esquire* had defined itself as a "man's magazine." Its symbol was a dirty old man with leering eyes known as "Esky," but with the rise of skin magazines, Esky had become a quaint anachronism—and some *Esquire* covers, although handsomely designed, had no connection with the contents.

Hayes asked my advice on how to create strong covers to attract more readers. "Show me the contents and I'll do the cover," I said. He sent me the advance contents of the October 1962 issue to see what the bigmouth would come up with. After that first cover, an implicit understanding evolved between Hayes and me that we would not be constipated by corporate taboos or restricted by group grope. Two smart minds were working exultantly to create messages of audacity and distinction. Two months before each issue Hayes sent me a rough roundup of its articles. In shorthand phone conversations or at quick breakfasts we "kind of" agreed on the subject for each cover, then I would call him and tell him what I was going to do.

I never showed him a rough layout or a comp. Communication between us was purely verbal—(if you can't describe the big idea in one short sentence, it ain't a big idea). Hayes also loved the idea that he could turn my ongoing "ultimatum" against his management when disputes arose about my covers—that if they meddled with my work, I would wash my hands of this project, however appealing it was to me.

My first cover (1962)

Amid the articles slated for this issue, I saw a short fictional piece on the pathos and isolation of losing a prize fight, and when I realized this issue would hit the newsstands a few days before the upcoming heavyweight title fight between the champion Floyd Patterson and the challenger Sonny Liston, I told Hayes I would show a flattened black fighter in an empty arena. I knew Liston would destroy the heavily favored but fragile Patterson. "Any way we can find out the color of Patterson's trunks?" I asked Hayes.

Harold Hayes was a midtown Mark Twain from North Carolina, stylishly decked out in a white suit when the weather was warm—(in apparel, he was Tom Wolfe before Tom Wolfe)—and usually waggling a handsome stogie, the skinny, elegant variety, in keeping with his white getup and poker-player eyes. He fingered his stogie and told me to do the cover—but he could not find out the color of Patterson's trunks because that was traditionally the champ's option. If his manager, Cus D'Amato, leaked it before a fight, that might put a whammy on the champ. I tried to extract this information from D'Amato, but he wouldn't reveal that guarded secret.

To cover my ass, I took a trim black model built like Floyd Patterson (he could never have been mistaken for Liston, who would later be described by Muhammad Ali as a "big ugly bear") to the empty, soon-to-be-razed St. Nicholas Arena with *two* pairs of Everlasts and we shot him on the canvas twice—in black trunks with white stripes, and vice versa. I prepared *two* mechanicals of the cover, one with white trunks, the other with black trunks. When I sent the two covers to Hayes, I told him I couldn't decide which to run. "Okay," I said, *"You* decide."

"Let's run the white trunks," Hayes decided.

"Naah," I said, "let's run the black ones."

"George, do you have trouble making decisions?" asked Hayes.

"Well, yes and no," I answered decisively.

We flipped a coin and ran the black trunks. On the night of the fight, a few days after the October issue hit the newsstands, when I saw the challenger Liston climb into the ring first, wearing white trunks, I knew Patterson was gone—and Liston demolished Patterson in the first round to become the new champ.

It took incredible chutzpah on my part to call the fight by showing a flattened Patterson in black trunks on a million covers of *Esquire*. When Patterson went down, Harold Hayes and his nail-biting brass at *Esquire* breathed a long, collective sigh of relief. This overt prediction became a news story as well, all to *Esquire*'s benefit.

My first cover for *Esquire* was almost mystical in its clairvoyance, as though the camera's lens had seen the future. That cover was a stopper on newsstands and sales went up. With that first cover we began a decade of visual editorials for *Esquire*.

The first black Santa (1963)

For the 1963 Christmas cover, after a year of unorthodox covers by the wild Greek, Hayes pleaded with me at lunch, fingering his pencil-thin stogie, "Ol' buddy, we gotta compromise this time. We're gonna need a Christmasy cover. Y'all gotta give me a goddamn *Santa Claus.*" Not one to disobey a command, I gave in and put a closeup face of Santa Claus on the cover. He happened to be a black Santa—the world heavyweight champion Sonny Liston, ex-con labor goon with a media-made image as the meanest man in the world. Harold was a southerner and many advertisers were not entirely thrilled about buying ad pages from "nig-gerlovers," but despite all this, and despite *Esquire*'s plea for a warm and cuddly fireside Christmas cover, Hayes was captured by the jolting symbolism of a black Santa at a time when America was being shaken by the black revolution.

Respirators were rushed to *Esquire*'s offices when my cover arrived featuring a dead-on full face closeup of this black, brooding Santa Claus under the white fleece. Liston had served time for armed robbery and didn't give a damn about his surly, sullen, menacing image at a time when the Freedom Rides, Martin Luther King and rising racial fever dominated the headlines of that era. Liston was the perfect baaaad actor. I was looking into the eyes of a changing America.

In a recollection of Liston eighteen years later, *Sports Illustrated* (February 4, 1991) recalled that astounding event, with its chillingly accurate anticipation of the black revolution: ". . . *Esquire* thumbed its nose at its white readers with an unforgettable cover . . . there was Liston, glowering out from under a tasseled red-and-white Santa Claus hat, looking like the last man on earth America wanted to see coming down its chimney." An explosion occurred when the issue ran—*Esquire* lost advertisers and received threatening phone calls and hate mail, although a professor of art history at Hunter College in New York praised the cover in a letter to *Esquire* as "one of the greatest social statements of the plastic arts since Picasso's *Guernica.*"

Portrait of a Native American (1964)

A few months later, a story was due on the American Indian. I had always believed that the Buffalo nickel that portrayed an American Indian was one of the greatest coins ever created, rivaling even the greatest of the Greek coins—and I had often wondered about the identity of the Indian who appeared on this magnificent piece. I called the Washington bureau in charge of Indian Affairs to find out if they had any idea as to who the Indian was and if he were still alive. I was lucky to speak with a young, gung-ho student of Indian affairs. Nary a week after he plunged into the problem I had posed, he called me breathlessly from Washington—he had discovered the identity of the Indian on the famous nickel and believed he might actually be alive! He learned that the Indian was one Chief Johnny Big Tree and there was reason to believe that he lived on the Onondaga Reservation outside of Syracuse.

Chief Johnny Big Tree had posed for the nickel in the early 1900s when he was in his thirties. I called my father-in-law, Joe Lewandowski, who lived in Syracuse, and asked him to drive out to the reservation to find out if the chief was still alive—and if so, to see if he was willing and able to pose, because he would be about ninety. Photographer Carl Fischer and I would then go to the reservation for the shot.

My father-in-law drove out to the reservation, to a ramshackle cabin without electricity. A few minutes later Chief Johnny Big Tree walked in, toting a bundle of twigs. He was eighty-seven years old and stood six feet two. I had given my father-in-law detailed instructions to work out the most convenient arrangements for a sitting at the reservation because if the chief was sick or senile, I wanted him to be treated like fragile ancient pottery. "Joe, what kind of shape is he in?" I asked my father-in-law on the phone. "He's in better shape than me," he answered. (Joe Lewandowski was a 200-average bowler and a scratch golfer.) The chief's dentures were the only thing giving him trouble. He insisted on flying to New York for the sitting.

In 1912 the great American sculptor James Earle Fraser spotted Chief John Big Tree in a Wild West show on Coney Island and asked him to pose for the Buffalo nickel. He was a Seneca, a descendant of the Iroquois Confederacy, dating back to the 1500s. He arrived at Carl Fischer's studio under the protective care of my father-in-law, wearing a business suit and sporting a crew cut. We dressed him in a black wig and started building up his mouth with cotton wads. He yanked out the cotton and waved his hand. "Nickel is only me from the bottom of my nose up," he explained. "I pose for forehead and nose. Other chiefs, a Sioux and a Cheyenne, they pose for chin and hair." Even with a mouthful of cotton, Chief John looked majestic. We shot his historic profile. Then he flew back to Syracuse on Mohawk Airline.

When the glorious face of Chief Johnny Big Tree hit the newsstands on the cover of *Esquire* a half century after he had posed for the Indian nickel, I was prouder than I had been of any other cover I had ever done for the magazine—it was authentic Americana. But the sales and advertising people at *Esquire* thought the cover was a loser because newsstand sales were not quite as high as on some of my previous ones—all far higher than any cover before I began with the October 1962 issue.

In my earlier book, *The Art of Advertising,* I included in a (predictably thin) chapter, "Stinkers," those scarce failures from my repertory, including this *Esquire* cover. But I keep asking myself: if this cover was a stinker, why am I so proud of it?

Going to the edge of Lyndon's knee (1966)

When HHH (Vice President Hubert Horatio Humphrey) was defending LBJ (President Lyndon Baines Johnson) for escalating the Vietnam War, Harold Hayes assigned a writer to do a major piece on the Vice President. I did a foldout cover that got rougher as it unfolded. I had a ventriloquist's dummy constructed to look like Humphrey. The cover showed him sitting on someone's knee. The HHH dummy said:

> "I have known for 16 years
> his courage, his wisdom, his tact, his persuasion, his judgment,
> and his leadership."

Pretty rough on the Veep, no? The cover didn't end there. It continued as a foldout, springing LBJ as the ventriloquist holding Hubert on his knee. *"You tell 'em, Hubert,"* said Lyndon the ventriloquist. (Lyndon Johnson was tied up at the time picking out mud huts to bomb in North Vietnam, so I never asked him to pose. The photograph was shot in a studio, using a model's body as large as LBJ playing the ventriloquist at work with the HHH dummy. I then did a composite shot of the model from the neck down with a swipe of Lyndon's imposing head—one of my notorious graphic transplants.)

Here's a case where I carried an idea to the edge of a President's knee at the expense of the Vice President, and nobody called me to chew me out. (God bless America!) Two years later, when I was in the Vice President's office for a meeting on political advertising, there was my cover, hanging on the wall of his anteroom. Embarrassed, I sucked my thumb and told Hubert Horatio Humphrey that I was the scoundrel who had done the dirty deed.

"You no good sonofabitch," he said.

"Well then, Mr. Vice President, why do you have it on the wall?" I asked, chastened.

"Because," he said, "it's a wonderful cover."

Warning Candidate Nixon (1968)

Before Richard Nixon was nominated to run for president, when he was thought of as a loser, I did a composite profile shot of him being made up prior to a television appearance. In the wire service archives I located a profile shot of Nixon snoozing on an airplane. We shot a separate photo of four hands working on the profile: one with an aerosol spray can to set his hair, a second with a makeup brush to paint out lines under his eyes, a third with a powder puff to dull the light bouncing off his nose—and a fourth hand with a lipstick to give his mouth definition. The four hands were lighted with surgical care to match the perspective and lighting on the Nixon profile photo. It was a masterful composite of a routine makeup job prior to a television appearance.

When that issue of *Esquire* hit America's newsstands I received an angry phone call from one of the numerous convicts-to-be on Nixon's staff, bitching about the cover, accusing me of portraying Nixon as a flaming queen. I explained, patiently, that it was a satirical comment on the 1960 television debates when his boss lost to John Kennedy by a shadow because he looked like hell in front of the cameras. In fact, I pointed out, the cover's title was "Nixon's last chance. *This time he'd better look right!*" I was flabbergasted—and I gave it to him straight. "It's a funny cover," I said. "You Nixon guys don't laugh too easy . . ." —but he hung up on me, too dumb to understand that I was doing his boss a huge favor. *Someone* in the Milhous camp must have gotten that message because new makeup artists made Richard Nixon look a lot better on television in 1968 than in 1960.

The drowning of Andy Warhol (1969)

The Pop Art movement in America was launched in 1962, with the works of Jasper Johns, Roy Lichtenstein, James Rosenquist, Robert Indiana— and Andy Warhol, whose image of a Campbell's soup can had become the symbol of the movement. Pop Art was the child of Dada (but not as

223

talented as its father). It used "popular" art: billboards, brand symbols, comic strips, type and you name it to make its "statements."

I've always regarded Andy as a bold innovator and a smart thinker, but a far cry from a Marcel Duchamp or a Man Ray. He lacked their extraordinary artistic *vision,* but there's no questioning Warhol's talent as a major league showman. Any guy who could parlay a Campbell's soup can and a Brillo box into personal superstardom may not fit my definition of a Rembrandt, but he's undeniably hot stuff. When *Esquire* scheduled an article, "The final decline and total collapse of the American avant garde," I decided to show Andy Warhol drowning in his own soup. He knew it was a friendly spoof of his original claim to fame, but he still enjoyed the fame enough to welcome a shot on a national magazine cover. When we dropped Andy into a giant can of his favorite soup, we almost lost him.

Lieutenant William Calley (1970)

While Army Lieutenant William Calley was awaiting trial for his role in the massacre of Vietnamese civilians at My Lai, *Esquire* scheduled an excerpt from John Sack's book, *The Confessions of Lieutenant Calley.*

"Tough subject for a cover," said Harold Hayes. "He's innocent until the army decides. Better lay off." But I persisted and asked if we could lure Calley to New York.

"Sack probably can," said Hayes, "but it depends on what in the world is running through your mind."

I explained the shot: "We'll show him with a bunch of Oriental kids —a group portrait with him in the center, smiling. He holds one kid, a baby, on his knee. One kid leans on his shoulder. The others seem to cling to him. Those who think he's innocent will say *that* proves it. Those who think he's guilty will say that *proves* it."

When the infamous lieutenant arrived at the photo studio, he looked us over very warily, still not sure he was going to pose. I relaxed him with macho banter about my Korean war experiences to make him think I was simpatico with any combat soldier having had to kill "gooks"—and I won him over. We went ahead with the shoot as Calley smiled obscenely, posing with the Oriental kids. When I sent the finished cover to Hayes, he called to let me know that the office staff was shook up. "Most *detest* it, but the smart ones love it," he said.

"You gonna chicken out?" I asked.

"Nope," said Hayes. "It's your most outrageous cover since Santa Claus. We'll lose advertisers and we'll lose subscribers, but I have no choice. I'll never sleep again if I don't run it. That cover is what *Esquire* is all about."

The cover ran. Those who thought Calley was innocent said *that* proves it. Those who thought he was guilty said that *proves* it. Many who thought he was guilty detested it with a vengeance. During a campus lecture, Hayes asked for reactions to the Calley cover. One student called it the statement of the century. Just one.

Artifacts of the sixties

It was a tumultuous decade, simmering and exploding with new trends, old idiocies, demographic upheavals and the overseasoned potpourri of new politics, new art, new youth, new narcissists, new women. *Esquire* was in the eye of this turbulence, and with Harold Hayes as my co-pilot, I loved every minute of it. Each month cried out for a new evisceration, a new outrage.

When I superimposed a movie marquee featuring *Easy Rider* on the front entrance to St. Patrick's Cathedral to dramatize an article called "Movies, the New Religion," Harold Hayes did the sign of the cross and took the heat.

When Senator Joseph McCarthy's former gofer, Roy Cohn, wrote a self-serving book on the Army–McCarthy hearings, which was excerpted in *Esquire,* my stomach turned over. Cohn was one of the most evil operatives of the McCarthy era, perhaps the most insidious period in the long, proud history of American democracy. Recalling the McCarthy aberration, when our country faced the real possibility of a choking fascism, I shot Cohn with a tinsel halo, visibly pinned to the back of his noggin by Carl Fischer. Oblivious to its slashing irony, Cohn posed most obligingly.

As he was leaving, he said, "I guess you'll pick the ugliest one."

"You bet your ass," I said.

Even though we made him look like a schmuck, Cohn was immensely pleased by the publicity. To the termite Cohn, ego was all.

During the Svetlana Stalin bender, *Esquire* ran a story on her weird religious hangups and the background of her hot manuscript about life with father. The American press had been transforming this pedestrian,

225

dowdy middle-aged nonentity into an icon. And all the women's magazines ran a cover photo of Stalin's little girl with the same sickly, saintly semi-smile that communicated weak character and an edited memory.

Many magazines used the identical cover photo of the deified Ms. Stalin. I managed to obtain an original print of that very photo, grabbed a grease pencil, and drew a graffiti mustache on Svetlana's face. She was instantly transformed into an image of her old man. (I don't care what her father did—and what he did defies the human imagination for evil— as far as I'm concerned, his daughter was a fink!) In visual terms I was shouting, "Your father's mustache!"—an upper-Bronx expletive.

For an issue with a feature on "The Pursuit of Happiness," I wanted *Esquire*'s readers to see what Aristotle Onassis, the man who had everything—except youth—would look like if he *really* had everything. I superimposed his head against the body of a muscleman. He looked like an aging Greek god. Good old Ari.

British feminist Germaine Greer took apart literary male chauvinist Norman Mailer in a 1971 issue. I superimposed Mailer's head over the body of a Kong-like monster, holding demure little Germaine, doll-like, in its claws. When Mailer saw that cover he called Hayes and challenged him to a brawl. Hayes chickened out and gave Mailer my phone number, explaining that *George Lois* was the author of the cover that he found so objectionable. Mailer called me, full of fury, and challenged me to a fist fight, which I readily accepted, with enthusiasm. We agreed to meet at the foot of the statues of Nike and General Sherman at the entrance to Central Park. Mailer never showed.

I did three covers on Muhammad Ali, all protesting his being punished for refusing to fight in an unjust war. . . . I also created an apparition of America's three martyrs in one composite shot—John Kennedy, Robert Kennedy and Martin Luther King—standing on the hallowed ground of Arlington National Cemetery. . . . A few days after aging Ed Sullivan introduced the Beatles to America on his television show, he posed for me wearing a Beatle wig with a lunatic grin.

In my own style, *Esquire*'s cover messages were uncensored commentaries on serious issues. Many covers used irreverent visual juxtapositions that were realer than real . . . indeed, *surreal.* "Pictorial Zola," Hayes used to say. The covers outraged the mighty, angered some advertisers, and infuriated more than a few readers—but this came with the territory. *Esquire*'s covers visualized the changes in America and pricked sharply at our hypocrisies. Some people carried their resentment with them for many moons. The ad director of *Esquire* from those halcyon days bitched in *Adweek* nineteen years later that the black Santa Claus cover lost the magazine $750,000 because some southern advertisers were outraged. In a rebuttal in *Adweek* (October 5, 1981), Hayes wrote: "Try as I might, I am unable to conceive of the *Esquire* of the '60s without George Lois. I suspect the same is true for others who remember it today. One might even go so far as to conclude, then, that with the loss of this inimitable element, *Esquire* could have ceased to be *Esquire*.

And if there had have been no *Esquire*, how could anything have been made or lost from it?"

Which of the
candidates for
the United States
Senate

has the better
chance of
becoming

a great
United States
Senator?

A great
United States
Senator.

8

Political
Advertising

The big idea attacks the human jugular

Great advertising must be wired into the world in which we live. My work over the years has tapped a reservoir of myths, legends and images that accumulate from the many streams and rivulets of our culture and society. Politics is a rich source of image and metaphor—but for many years, only Republican politics were acceptable in the advertising world because most clients and agency heads were WASPish Republicans. Most Democrats in advertising agencies kept a low political profile until the Creative Revolution opened Madison Avenue's doors to a world beyond the WASP community and politics came to be seen as more than a one-party activity. In addition, the size of political advertising billings from both parties has attracted many otherwise politically neutered agencies who would normally avoid political clients.

I've been working for political clients for more than twenty-five years. Most have been Democrats, but some have been Republicans who acted like Democrats. Before I start handing down opinions on how political advertising should be done, let me establish my credentials by summarizing my four (out of four) winning advertising campaigns in races for the U.S. Senate:

Jacob Javits (R) New York incumbent runs for reelection in 1962. His goal is a plurality of 500,000 to look good. He wins by a plurality of 979,000.

Robert F. Kennedy (D) versus incumbent Kenneth Keating (R) in 1964 in New York State, where Kennedy is attacked as a "carpet-bagger" from Massachusetts and "ruthless." Kennedy wins by 720,000 votes. (See pages 36–37.)

Warren G. Magnuson (D) runs for fourth term in state of Washington. Magnuson, seen as old and tired and even senile, is considered a sure loser against his young, attractive challenger. He wins 65% of the vote in 1968, the fourth-highest plurality of 32 Senate races.

Hugh Scott (R) runs for fifth term in Pennsylvania in 1970. He needs a decisive win, by at least 100,000, to remain Senate minority leader. After 32 years in the Senate, he has only 55% awareness. He wins by 220,000 votes while popular gubernatorial candidate Milton Shapp (D) wins by 900,000 votes—a turnaround of more than a million votes.

These four Senate victories reflect my belief that the best political advertising—like the best *product* advertising—is disarmingly *honest.* Jacob Javits, a fixture in New York politics, was getting old, was turning completely bald and was putting on weight. I shot a campaign photo of the senator to capture his Mount Rushmore strength without losing the warmth in his distinguished face and without attempting to conceal the real, aging Javits. Everyone liked the photo except Mrs. Javits, a tough, opinionated cookie. She detested it. "He looks *old,* he looks *bald,* he looks *fat,*" she told me with disgust. "Mrs. Javits," I said, "I got news for you. Your husband *is* kind of old, he *is* kind of bald and he *is* fat."

We were not "creating an image" or "selling a bar of soap." We showed the senator talking to people, answering their questions off the cuff. In 1962, showing a candidate as a believable person was unheard of—it had never been done. Javits was ideal for this approach. He was tough, he was tender and he was probably America's best informed senator. This was an age when a political television commercial consisted of a candidate at a desk, stiffly delivering a canned speech. An American flag stood conspicuously alongside his desk. In the Javits campaign we exploded onto the television screen with cinema verité—truth in film. In 1962 this idea, in and of itself, was a big idea!

Robert Kennedy was ambushed by attacks against his integrity and motives every step of the campaign, with some of the heaviest salvos from liberal Democrats who remembered him as the young pit bull lawyer for Senator Joe McCarthy's committee. And as in the Javits campaign we caught the real Bobby, videotaping give-and-take with commuters on the Staten Island ferry, with housewives in shopping centers, with blacks in a Harlem housing project. He was asked tough questions and he reached deep inside to find the answers, often in visible agony to avoid a phony comeback. We taped miles of Bobby taking-and-giving, all unrehearsed, and edited them down to television spots that showed the real man—bright, sympathetic, sensitive—a man who cared about people and brought new ideas to the electoral process.

He loved to quote Aeschylus, but he was no slouch on Archimedes. "One thing I learned when working with President Kennedy," he would say, "is that one man can make a difference. And as Archimedes once said, 'Give me a lever and I can move the world.'" Then he would thrust a thumbs-up fist at the crowd.

He once asked me, "How did Archimedes go over today?"

"I like the line," I said, "especially since my ancestors wrote it. But it could bomb out if the audience ain't right."

A few days later Bobby told me he was going to the black Brooklyn neighborhood, Bedford–Stuyvesant, and asked if I would like to come with him. "I'd love to come," I said. "I lived there, I played ball there." In the car I said to him, "Bobby, don't do that Archimedes shit in Bed–Sty." He was angered, and accused me of making an anti-black remark. "Your old man was a right-wing reactionary," I shot back, "and you bust *my* balls, accusing *me* of being prejudiced!" We stopped talking all the way to Brooklyn while his brother-in-law, Steve Smith (his campaign manager), sat in silence, stifling a chortle. At a major intersection in Bedford–Stuyvesant, a huge crowd awaited Bobby. A few minutes into his speech he dragged out the Archimedes line, and thrust a fist at his audience with a confident thumbs-up. The street crowd stared at him blankly. I was standing among them, the only Caucasian in a sea of black faces. Bobby scanned the crowd from the sound truck for a knowing nod, his fist stuck out with his thumb up. There was no reaction. As he spotted my white grin he slowly turned his thumb down. Steve Smith, who was standing on the platform, almost fell off.

During the closing hours of the campaign, when we ran that decisive twenty-second spot ("Which of the candidates for the United States Senate . . . has the better chance of becoming a great United States senator? . . . A great United States senator.") we asked voters to recognize the tenacious, even anguished, commitment of this rich man's son to the common good. They did.

In the reelection campaign of Senator Warren Magnuson in 1968, the press in Washington State was calling him old and fat and more than implied that he was stupid. They laughed at his baggy clothes and the food stains on his tie. And they latched on to his nickname, *Maggie,* using it derisively. Certain that he would be defeated, Magnuson had lined up a federal judgeship through the president, his old Senate drinking buddy, Lyndon Johnson. We gave this essentially decent and highly effective senator a new lease on life with a disarming campaign that turned his seeming liabilities into assets.

We knew we had to begin with an immediate, convincing message that Warren Magnuson was hardly a doddering idiot and had a lot between his ears. In our opening television spot we showed Magnuson —we called him Maggie proudly—facing the camera with a forlorn expression as a voice-over announcer says: *"Senator Magnuson, there comes a time when every young senator shows that he's putting on years . . ."* Maggie sits silently and juts his hands out as if to say, "What can I do about it?" The voice-over announcer keeps rubbing it in as he says, *"Senator Magnuson, there comes a time—sure as fate—when slim senators assume a more 'impressive stature.' "* This polite reference to his being overweight destroys Maggie as he ruefully glances down at his belly, looking very frustrated. The announcer moves in for the kill with these devastating words: *"So once youth is gone, once dash is gone, what can you offer the voters of Washington?"* Maggie reels back at this zinger, then he regains his poise, looks straight at the camera, points a finger to his head, and simply taps his noggin—once, twice, three times. The announcer then concludes: *"Let's keep Maggie in the Senate."*

The image of Maggie pointing a finger to his head became an instant mnemonic throughout the State of Washington. Wherever Maggie went, people pointed a finger to their heads, calling out affectionately, *"Hey, Maggie!"* And suddenly the overconfident Republicans were caught flatfooted, as the sure loser Maggie was miraculously transformed—by pointing his finger to his head—to a confident front-runner.

Flushed with the euphoria of having been raised from the dead, Magnuson became an enthusiastic contender—but he hit the bottle hard while on the road to corral votes. In his slurred voice during the escalating furor about our involvement in Vietnam, this distinguished United States senator referred, again and again, to the "Viennese" War.

Until we ran our finger-pointing spot, Warren Magnuson was straddled with a terrible image, and his own party expected him to withdraw. His young opponent, heady with confidence, was raising money like crazy, while Maggie couldn't raise a dime. By kicking off his campaign with this spot in early summer, months before the election, we made it clear that Maggie was emphatically in the campaign with all his vigor, appeal, and charm intact. Money poured in to Maggie while funds stopped flowing to his Republican challenger—but Maggie was shooting himself in the foot at every turn, his vision clouded by booze. One early morning he suggested we go to a Boeing aerospace plant to greet the workers, while his staffers desperately signaled me not to let him do it. I wanted to see Maggie in action, and as soon as he showed up at Boeing he was greeted warmly by hundreds of hard hats at the front gate. He was marvelous, pressing the flesh and hugging the workers—until one hard hat said to him, "We love you like a brother, Maggie, but there ain't a single guy at Boeing who ain't nuts about hunting. How could you possibly vote for *gun control?"*

"Why don't you go fuck yourself," Maggie replied.

From Boeing we went on to a women's breakfast, where the senator announced he planned to run for reelection. One of the ladies, a Maggie partisan, asked him in a friendly way, "Senator, could you tell us in your own words why the people of Washington should vote for you?"

"If you don't like me," he barked at her, "don't vote for me."

A few *days* into the campaign his distraught aides sent Maggie on a sabbatical, out of the state and out of range of any television cameras, while our *advertising* put his best foot forward. The senator was secreted away with a good supply of vodka, while a great advertising campaign did all the work in reelecting him.

Maggie was an early consumer advocate who went on to father major legislation during his subsequent terms in the Senate. Our advertising properly stressed his exemplary record as a pioneer in consumer protection with the theme, *"Let's keep the big boys honest!"* By following through with the strong issue of consumer advocacy, Warren Magnuson, despite his heavy drinking (not unlike Winston Churchill or Ulysses S. Grant) was truthfully portrayed to the voters of Washington—and they clasped him to their hearts. And by admitting that he may have had his faults—that he was growing older, getting fatter, and letting food stains dirty his ties—he was able to put across the more important truth that he had the right stuff between the ears, as people around the state mimicked our finger-pointing sign language with endearment. By underscoring his humanity, we told the voters in Washington that they had a helluva man representing them in Washington.

In 1970 Senator Hugh Scott of Pennsylvania, minority leader of the Senate, was in the doghouse with the Nixon White House because he had voted against confirming Nixon's Supreme Court nominee Clement Haynsworth. Political caveman Senator Roman Hruska of Nebraska, who later defended Nixon's second flop, Harrold Carswell, because he approved of his "mediocrity," was being groomed to replace Scott. We were contacted by Scott's staff because of our miracle for Maggie, and even though Scott was a Republican, if Nixon planned to dump him because he was no puppet, the fiercely independent Pennsylvanian deserved reelection. Nonetheless, the idea of voting for a real Republican stuck in my throat. After coolly turning down his people a few times, I got conned into having dinner with Scott, a man of formidable virtues. An intellectual, he collected Chinese art and had authored a first-rate book on that complex subject. He was surely the most intelligent politician I would ever have a chance to work for. "I've been a Democrat all my life," I told the senator at dinner. "How can I *possibly* explain to my grandchildren that during the Nixon administration I helped reelect the top *Republican* to the Senate!? Give me one reason a guy like me should work for you!!"

Scott put his trademark pipe in his mouth, chugged on it, looked me in the eye and said, "Tell them this. The only thing that separated

Richard Nixon from fascism . . . was Hugh Scott." I went to work for the Senate's top Republican.

Hugh Scott had worked with six presidents: Roosevelt, Truman, Eisenhower, Kennedy, Johnson and Nixon. He was a man of genuine national stature and he looked like a lovable country doctor. We caught those qualities through a series of television spots showing Scott with a young boy, talking about his role in the making of modern America. Scott's campaign occurred in the middle of the Vietnam War, which was going badly. With the young boy at his side, the senator was saying obliquely that we were going to get through this nasty war, that a new generation of young people faced a fine future, which Scott would help bring into being.

I filmed Scott and the young visitor in his Senate office where he had a marvelous grouping of photos with each of the six presidents. He spoke of his experience with them and ended with the line, "C'mon Billy, I'll buy you a Coke." We called him *"Scott of Pennsylvania,"* a heroic image in the genre of *Lincoln of Illinois* and *Charles of France* (de Gaulle).[1] And we described him as *"The most powerful senator Pennsylvania ever had."* This line was the big idea, and everything in our commercials led to it. We were telling the voters of Pennsylvania *don't lose this guy!*

These warm but assertive commercials made the senator real without resorting to schmaltz or hocus-pocus, and helped him overcome his dangerously low 55% awareness after 32 years as a Pennsylvania congressman and senator—and win the election decisively. P.S. He then went on to help torpedo Nixon.

We now live in a new political age, when attack and counterattack define political advertising. Here's an instructive story about a pre-emptive strike that could have changed presidential politics:

In the spring of 1988, as George Bush and Michael Dukakis were on the verge of clinching the presidential primaries, I received a telephone call from a Washington businessman, Herb Miller, a fat cat in the Democratic party, urging me to promote a concept called "Teamwork Economics"—a program from one of Washington's think tanks to strengthen the economy, but full of intellectual mumbo jumbo.

We decided the best way to focus on economics was in a tough

---

[1] I have labored for years to be called *George of the Bronx.*

advertising campaign that would spotlight the flip-flop of candidate George Bush, who had characterized Reaganomics as "voodoo economics" and was now its chief advocate.

Our campaign contrasted "Teamwork Economics" with "Voodoo Economics" to instantly remind everyone that Reagan's programs have led us into debt, deficits and social deprivation. Our theme was *"Voodoo Economics . . . or . . . Teamwork Economics"*—followed by a secondary theme: *"Veto the Voodoo."*

A sample television spot caught the essence of our message: *"Whoever the Democrats choose as their presidential nominee . . . will have to put an end to the voodoo economics that have created the largest deficit in our nation's history! What we need is Teamwork Economics—a coalition of capital, labor and technology to restructure our economy and create a permanent rising standard of living for all Americans! Veto the Voodoo!"*

Another spot, to the sound of voodoo drums, showed a witch doctor, who dissolves to George Bush. Its opening line: *"For eight years America has been bewitched by an economic policy the Republican nominee for president called Voodoo Economics!"*

We also presented this "Love Song to Vice President George Bush" for television and radio commercials, an adaptation of the Cole Porter classic, "You Do Something to Me": *"You did something to me, something that simply mystifies me. Tell me why it should be you have the power to hypnotize me. For our economy you'll do that voodoo that you named so well."*

The fat cats were thrilled, and a meeting was set up with Paul Kirk, chairman of the Democratic National Committee, at DNC headquarters. Kirk O'Donnell, who would soon be joining the Dukakis staff, was also present. My presentation was videotaped by Bob Squier (political consultant to the DNC) for distribution to Democratic Party fundraisers across the country. Kirk and O'Donnell praised my presentation, but as Dukakis moved toward the nomination, he had the final decision on advertising, and "Voodoo" was either vetoed or ignored.

Shortly after Dukakis was nominated, polls showed he had a 17 point lead over Bush. Resting on this deceptive margin, Dukakis did nothing about advertising. His people were not endeared by my comments to *Newsday* (July 24, 1988): " 'They should go for Bush's eyeballs the day after the convention ends,' " I was quoted as saying. " 'They're making a big point of lying low, and parrying [Bush ads] . . . I have strong ideas and strong images,' Lois said, expressing regret that he'll sit out this election, despite his Greek ancestry and his Democratic credentials. 'They're looking for something cushy. *So they'll pussyfoot around and run dull stuff, never touch anything powerful. They'll get blown out the way they're headed* [my italics],' he predicted."

The Dukakis people saw this as evidence that I would have gone for Bush's jugular, that I favored a fast, pre-emptive strike—and they wanted no part of me. Their strategy was to make Dukakis look majestic, a sure winner who would simply ignore Bush throughout the campaign. After his 17 point advantage evaporated, Dukakis took emergency advertising action and promptly shot himself in both feet when he allowed himself to be filmed driving a tank, a character out of "Peanuts."

"Voodoo" would have preserved much of that spread for Dukakis and would have psychologically wounded Bush and his campaign. Even the Willie Horton spot would have lost some of its insidious power against a battling, aggressive Dukakis who could have nailed Bush where he was most vulnerable from the moment he was nominated—and would have set the pace and momentum for the rest of the campaign. "Voodoo" would also have forced Dukakis to be aggressive, to show toughness. Instead, Dukakis stressed his Greek immigrant origins, oblivious to the reluctance of Americans to put an ethnic in the White House.

For better or worse, advertising happens to be the only way a candidate can project his or her virtues to attract voters, and if there's something wrong with selling a political candidate, there must be something wrong with selling a bar of soap. Maybe there's something wrong with selling *anything,* but I live in America, not on the moon. So let the process unfold.

On the creative level, most advertising people have never really understood politics, while those who have weren't able to move fast enough to get the job done. You have to understand the candidate's situation in your gut, then come up with talented and forceful answers—and you have to think and move *fast* to get your instincts on the air the next day.

Political advertising that works will simply put across to the voters the essence of a candidate's character—or the character of his or her opponent. ("Voodoo" captured the domestic philosophical aimlessness of George Bush, perfectly expressed later in his waffling on the deficit crisis.) If the advertising is truthful, you're betting on people's inner decency to like what they see and hear—or dislike what they see and hear about the opposing candidate. Political advertising must be truthful, clear as a bell, decisive—and fast. Here are my 10 secrets of political advertising that win elections:

1. Believe in your candidate. (If you think he or she is a bum but want the billings, *you're* a bum.)
2. Get to the essence of the candidate's character swiftly. (If you can't pull it off in 10 seconds, you won't do it in 5 minutes.)
3. Learn the difference between image and essence and don't confuse them. (If you think "creating an image" is the name of the game, you're in the wrong game.)
4. The entire campaign has to flow from an *idea* that must be stunning, even mind-boggling. (The *theme* is important, but if it doesn't reflect an arresting idea, you're wasting paper.)
5. Good ideas are directly connected to the way you define your candidate. (The truth about your candidate can only hurt his or her opponent.)
6. Truth is mightier than the cliché. (Use words that are human and get to the human being in your candidate.)
7. Don't deliver a discourse. (Advertising is not the place to run off at the mouth.)
8. Use TV. If the budget is too small, scream for dough. (You have to make your candidate a household name.)
9. Every piece of advertising material (from TV spot to newspaper ad to handbills to bumper stickers to buttons) should drive home your main idea.
10. Get paid for media up front. (When a campaign is over, even the winner has trouble raising dough.)

Counting today, I have sat in prison 3,135 days for a crime I did not commit.

If I don't get a retrial, I have 289 years to go. 6 months ago the "eye-witnesses," who testified they saw me leaving a bar in which 3 people had been killed, admitted they gave false testimony. Despite this, the judge who sentenced me won't give me a retrial. Why?

RUBIN "HURRICANE"
CARTER, NO. 45475
TRENTON STATE PRISON

"Oh my God —we hit a little girl."

The true story of M Company.
From Fort Dix to Vietnam.

The Passion of Muhammad Ali

1¼ Million unborn children will be born dead or have some gross defect because of Nuclear Bomb testing

SANE

9

The Selling
of Social
Causes

A maverick's perspective
on public service advertising

Advertising agencies love to brag about their work in that benevolent category known as public service advertising (PSA). Television and radio stations run PSA announcements gratis. There is no agency commission, no fee. Everyone, theoretically, works for the common good. The airwaves are thick with these messages on behalf of the Red Cross, United Fund, Drug Free America, the homeless, voting and other acceptable drives that buy respectability for advertising agencies without making waves. Causes such as these never disturb the status quo or right wrongs. Everyone agrees they're true blue, and no matter how competent or even imaginative their advertising, little of social consequence is ever achieved. (Some public service campaigns that attack a clear peril—the dangers of smoking—are exceptions to the rule because they can change public behavior.) Most public service advertising assignments are sought by advertising agencies for their own self-aggrandizement, to win so-called "creative" awards or to add a prestigious name to the agency account roster.

I'm too stupid to play that game. The causes I choose to support and work for have attracted me because I believe in my bones that by devoting my energy and talent, perhaps I can right a wrong or put a spotlight on a social evil. These causes are always unpopular and "controversial"—and assiduously avoided by all other agencies. Clients, after all, may hate the cause and fire the agency. It's much safer to shoot PSAs of Nancy Reagan delivering insipid "Just Say No" sermons to our youth so that you can stroke your conscience and sleep soundly.

I see advertising as a powerful weapon that can bring about social change. If I confront a situation where a profound wrong is being ignored, my blood boils at the injustice and I want to do something about it. I've worked for a sane nuclear policy, for democratic refugees from a fascist country, for a heroic protestor against an unjust war, for someone who is wrongfully imprisoned. And contrary to the conventional assumption, most clients have not objected to my passionate espousal of such causes; instead, they have admired their advertising agency for putting principle before profit. (I said "most"—one client ordered me to stop working for an unpopular cause or get fired. I kept on working and got fired. I'll tell you about it later in this chapter.)

Before the Atomic Test Ban Treaty in 1963, nuclear testing in the atmosphere by America and Russia was threatening the continuation of life on our planet. The Committee for Sane Nuclear Testing (SANE) was alerting the public in factual warnings by Nobel scientists that the fallout of radioactive materials would result in a growing number of birth defects. We created a subway poster that showed a conspicuously pregnant woman—my secretary at that time, Mrs. Diane Shugrue Gallagher—in a saintly silhouette pose,with this factual headline:

1 1/4 million unborn children will be born dead
or have some gross defect because of nuclear bomb testing.

One of SANE's leaders, Dr. Benjamin Spock, was rewarded for his warnings about the perils to unborn children by being called a Communist sympathizer. Although America was in its post–McCarthy period, with the enlightened John Kennedy as president, the Cold War was getting hotter and the country's mood was poisoned by hateful political passions. McCarthyism had left a legacy of paranoia and fear, and protests against nuclear testing were usually tarred as "peace propaganda." (The good old days!) In the subway poster, I used the silhouette photo of my pregnant secretary. It was a saintly portrait in the style of the fifteenth century Florentine painter Pollaiuolo that forced the reader to reflect on the horror of *this* woman's child being born with a birth defect because of the stupidity of those times.

For months after this poster appeared I received hate mail, mostly unsigned. Speaking out for SANE was like waving a red flag. Today, almost three decades after the Test Ban Treaty of 1963, it seems incomprehensible that protests against nuclear fallout could ever have caused such extreme reactions. In 1962, when the peril was real and malignant, not too many souls from Madison Avenue could be found on the barricades. (Diane Shugrue delivered a healthy baby and later, three more. After her four kids grew up, she joined the Peace Corps. What a woman!)

When the junta of colonels grabbed power in Greece in 1968, drowning that lovely land in the blood and muck of fascism for six years, Americans were largely unaware of and even indifferent to the tragedy. As the colonels imprisoned and tortured whoever opposed them, the numbers of political prisoners grew daily and concentration camps defiled the cradle of democracy.

During those dark years few in America would listen to the cries of pain coming from Greece, despite the documentation and condemnation of the torture, the concentration camps and the desecration of human rights by Amnesty International, the Council of Europe, the International Commission of Jurists and the parliaments of Norway, Denmark, Belgium, Italy, The Netherlands and Great Britain. The United States, lamentably, said nothing. It was business as usual as America's Vice President Spiro Agnew visited his ancestral village in Greece, and tourism from the United States flourished during the darkest years of the junta. Many Greek–Americans, like Agnew, ignored the cruelty and criminality of fascism in Greece, where more and more numbers of heroic Greeks who resisted the junta were being imprisoned.

I was asked by the North American Greek Relief Fund to help raise money to keep these prisoners and their families alive. I created a newspaper campaign to generate contributions for the support of families of political prisoners. Here are two of my heartfelt messages. My first ad: *"Weep for Greece. Poor betrayed Greece. Dead speech. Dead press. Dead liberty."* A second ad: *"Greece has torture, tyranny, concentration camps. What a lovely place for a vacation."*

During the last years of the junta I would occasionally meet affluent, influential Greeks visiting America, and all too often they asked why I persisted in "hurting" the land of my fathers. "Weep for Greece" had apparently dealt its intended side effect: in addition to raising money, it had begun to raise doubts about the morality of tourism. The junta nightmare ended in 1974 as democracy returned to Greece.

Why, I've often wondered, were there so few Americans who wept for Greece? And why, I've often wondered in sorrow, were there so few Greek–Americans, particularly in the advertising world, to volunteer their talent and energy to work for the victims of Greek fascism? Is advertising such a fragile, self-conscious community that everyone avoids doing the right thing for fear of nettling the mighty? The road to salvation is not paved with ads for United Fund campaigns. For six years I included on my client roster the North American Greek Relief Fund. To this day I'm prouder to have worked for this obscure "client" than for Xerox or Braniff or MTV.

How to become a pariah on Madison Avenue.

In 1966 black middleweight boxer Rubin "Hurricane" Carter was arrested for the murder of three whites in Paterson, New Jersey. During a period of intense racial acrimony, Carter was convicted and sentenced to 300 years in jail. Eight years later two key prosecution witnesses recanted, while new lawyers unearthed the suppression of vital evidence that would have helped Carter. I had read about the case like any fight fan and figured that the viciousness displayed in the ring by the shaven-headed, Fu Manchu–mustached Carter had somehow exploded into the streets. One day I received a call from a young fight fan who claimed Rubin Carter had been railroaded and begged me to read Carter's book, *The Sixteenth Round.* I read it, I talked to Carter's lawyers and I read the trial transcript. Then I got back to the young guy who had called me, Richard Solomon. "Let's get this guy out of jail," I told him.

I created a three-inch ad that ran on page two of *The New York Times* that shook up the public because Rubin Carter, the vicious fighter they thought was a mad-dog killer, might actually be innocent. Through that one small ad we were able to organize a committee of distinguished citizens (white and black, but mostly white). That was no piece of cake; I had to convince businessmen, politicians, athletes, writers, and entertainers (and their apprehensive lawyers) of Carter's innocence. It was a complicated case to explain, especially on the phone, but I was so imbued with Carter's cause I was hard to resist. Then I had to persuade them to lend their good names to the fight for a new trial. There was great reluctance—and fear—even when they were satisfied that Carter was a victim of miscarried justice. Nonetheless, many prominent citizens who listened to my plea for Carter and followed their gut feelings joined the committee of "The Hurricane Fund." Muhammad Ali became its chairman as soon as I convinced the world heavyweight champ that Carter was innocent. This immediately drew in Don King and other famous personalities. Our committee also included Hank Aaron, Jimmy Breslin, Ellen Burstyn, Johnny Cash, Pete Hamill, Congressman Edward Koch, Norman Mailer, George Plimpton, Burt Reynolds, Geraldo Rivera, Gay Talese, Dyan Cannon. (The young basketball player Bill Bradley, who believed in Rubin's innocence, did not join the committee but took on the role of "mole" among New Jersey's politicos.) We were then able to raise enough funds to publicize the plight of Rubin Carter.

This initial publicity inspired Bob Dylan to visit Carter in prison, learn his story and write "Hurricane." I convinced Dylan, who was on a tour with his Rolling Thunder troupe in small clubs, to commit to a "Night of the Hurricane" concert in Madison Square Garden as a fundraiser. He said he would only do it if it were a double-header: the Garden concert and a command performance in the prison where Carter was incarcerated. Dylan performed in both places.

The Rubin Carter case had become famous, particularly as Muhammad Ali spoke out at every occasion for a new trial, even dedicating his Las Vegas match with challenger Ron Lyle to Carter. The Hurricane cause was sweeping New Jersey. Publicized demonstrations led by Ali from the prison to the state house in Trenton elevated the case to a cause célèbre as New Jersey's Governor Byrne was deluged with letters from members of the Hurricane Fund Committee demanding a new trial. Before long the committee received overtures from the state for a pardon of sorts, but Carter insisted on being vindicated in a new trial.

In March 1976 the New Jersey Supreme Court ruled unanimously in favor of a second trial. With a new judge, a new jury, and the distance of a decade since the first trial, there was reason to hope that Carter would finally be exonerated. But with missing evidence, disappearing witnesses, and an obsession on the part of New Jersey prosecutors to nail this incorrigible black man, the verdict was the same. Rubin Carter was returned to prison, ending his nine-month interlude of freedom.

Despite this second conviction, my faith in Carter's innocence was unshaken, but I paid a price. As news stories about the Carter case escalated, I was told by my client Ed Horrigan at Cutty Sark, "Stop working for the nigger or I'll fire you." I didn't blink, I kept working for Carter, and a few weeks later we got fired. The loss of billings was devastating to my agency, while at home, on more than a few evenings, my family received death threats on the phone. Even some of my closest friends at work were convinced that Carter was guilty and thought I was nuts to give so much of myself to save him, but I believed in his innocence and would not turn my back on this victim of injustice. To compound my tsuris, a front page article in *The New York Times* on the Carter case implied that I was foraging for personal publicity.

Everything had been turned inside out. Rubin Carter went back to jail and I had to fight off a legion of critics who insisted I had been suckered into busting my gut and jeopardizing my agency for a baaad mother who was guilty in spite of everything, while the *Times* implied I was in it for ego and publicity.

In November 1985, citing "grave constitutional violations" by prosecutors, Judge Lee H. Sarokin of the Federal District Court in Newark threw out the second conviction. In 1988, the United States Supreme Court upheld Judge Sarokin's ruling that Carter had been unjustly convicted because the Passaic County prosecutor's office suppressed critical evidence about a lie detector test taken by a major prosecution witness. In 1990, the Passaic County prosecutor filed an application to dismiss all charges. After twenty-two years, Rubin Carter was freed.

An early warning on the war in Vietnam.

To me, the most worthy advertising actions ultimately become *political* statements. To protest the actions of one's government cannot be a bland pro bono campaign. Conversely, public service advertising can never be *protest* advertising—the networks run for cover if you make statements that have a whiff of advocacy. But in my role as "cover editorialist" for *Esquire,* I was able to express myself freely, particularly on the horrors of Vietnam. For me this was an insistent concern from the war's earliest days (I'm an expert on crummy wars, having fought in Korea), but it seemed to me that America was unconcerned. For the Christmas issue of 1963 I sent Harold Hayes a cover that showed a full-face photo of the war's 100th GI killed, with this caption: *The 100th American killed in Vietnam.*

The cover never ran because, in those days, the Vietnam business was still regarded as a fracas. There was also talk of a truce at Christmas that might end the shooting. The hundredth GI was never shown—and the vaunted Christmas truce never happened. When we finally evacuated Vietnam in 1974 with our tails between our legs, over 58,000 American GIs had been killed there or were missing in action.

On the killing of children in an unjust war.

In 1966 *Esquire* assigned the writer John Sack to report on the fate of an infantry company from training in Fort Dix through its combat cycle in Vietnam. In Sack's account of a search-and-destroy mission, he reported a GI's reaction when he found the body of a dead Vietnamese child. I put the GI's words on the cover of that issue, with no illustration and no visual—just the stark white words on a solid black page: *"Oh my God—we hit a little girl."*

Even the masthead was muted to give each word the power of a thousand pictures. (When I asked Harold Hayes if he thought I was going too far, he said, "If they don't like what's on the cover, they can always buy *Vogue,* sweetheart.") That was 1966, still a "premature" time for indicting that evil war.

Protesting the martyrdom of Muhammad Ali.

In 1967 Muhammad Ali, the world heavyweight champion, refused induction into the army in protest against the Vietnam War. He had converted to the Islamic faith, and under the tutelage of Elijah Muhammad had become a Black Muslim minister. Ali claimed this entitled him to conscientious objector status, but a federal jury sentenced him to five years in jail for draft evasion. Boxing commissions promptly joined in, stripping him of his title and denying him the right to fight. He was widely condemned as a draft dodger, even a traitor. In 1968, when *Esquire* planned an article on the martyrdom of Muhammad Ali, I decided to do a cover that would show Ali as Saint Sebastian.

I contacted Ali and explained my idea of photographing him full of arrows like a modern Saint Sebastian, the Roman soldier who survived execution by arrows for converting to Christianity and was then clubbed to death. At the photographer's studio I showed Ali a postcard reproduction of the fifteenth century Castagno painting of the martyred saint to visualize the stance I wanted him to strike—facing the camera, head high but weary, hands tied behind his back, feet pointing outward. He would be clad in his Everlast trunks and his boxing shoes. Five arrows would be affixed to his chest and one to his right thigh, as though they had pierced his skin, with simulated blood at each puncture.

Ali studied the Castagno with enormous concentration. Suddenly he blurted out, "George, this cat's a *Christian!*"

I blurted back, "Holy Moses, you're right, Champ!"

Before we could affix any arrows to Ali, he got on the phone with his manager and religious coach, Herbert Muhammad (son of Elijah). Ali was concerned about the propriety of using a Christian source in portraying his martyrdom as a Muslim. I held my breath during their involved theological discussion, then I grabbed the phone and got in a few Greek Orthodox licks. Herbert Muhammad finally gave us his okay—Allah be praised!—and we shot Ali as Saint Sebastian. When I saw the first transparency, I believe my exact words were, "Jesus Christ, it's a masterpiece."

In arousing concern about the abuse of a black man, "The Martyrdom of Muhammad Ali" drew attention to a terrible wrong that was righted in 1971 when the Supreme Court voted unanimously to throw out his conviction. That cover nailed down the plight of many Americans who took a principled stand against the Vietnam War and paid a heavy price for doing the right thing.

In dealing with social causes, act from the heart and commit yourself, expecting no rewards—or just say no. Doing the right thing does not necessarily mean carrying signs and manning picket lines—though I did my share during the McCarthy period. If you're in advertising and you have the opportunity to use your talents, remember that you don't need a big budget or big names (although these help!) to put across your message. What's most important is the imaginative use of words, visuals and media. (A tiny ad, with type set by the newspaper, can stir the heavens!) Remember Archimedes' inspiring call to action that Bobby Kennedy loved to use: "Give me a lever and I can move the world!"

Weep for Greece.

Poor betrayed Greece.
Dead speech.
Dead press.
Dead liberty.

The silence makes it worse.
Greece is so quiet today, that it's easy to forget.
Across that gentle land, a wicked government demands
allegiance, exacts obedience, destroys opposition.
The list of political prisoners grows every day.
The torture of "traitors" is refined, hour by hour.

"Fongool! I ordered *three* pizzas and *two* heroes!"

"Hello, is this the kindergarten teacher? Well, this is an obscene phone call: Ca-Ca. Stinky. Wee-Wee. Poo-Poo. Boom-Boom."

10

Big Ideas
on a
Small Budget

Even a tiny matchbook can pack a wallop

Don't conclude that big bucks are needed to create big ideas. A great concept has just as much power if it's an invitation or a package design or a promotion idea or a sales event or even a T-shirt. *Communication* is not limited to 30 second television spots or four-color magazine ads.

In 1981, New York's newly reelected Mayor Ed Koch had exceeded his campaign war chest by millions of dollars, was deeply in debt and needed to raise money badly. The guy was flat broke, and I was asked to design an invitation for a Gala Fundraising Roast to raise the needed bucks *after* he had won. My invitation was a small accordion folder that showed just the head and shoulders of a pleading Ed Koch, but when you opened the accordion you saw the whole picture: a coy Koch, his eyes with a pleading expression that told everyone he was broke and needed help, with his hands holding his completely empty pockets, sticking out from his pants. It was a small folder, five inches square, but it had the impact of a small bomb. The invitation drew a huge response and the vast banquet room in Sheraton Centre was packed with fatcats in tuxedos. To greet them as they entered the banquet room, I placed a lifesize cutout blowup of the mayor, showing his empty pockets. The big wheels from New York's power elite emptied their pockets and walked around all evening imitating Ed Koch.

The money was raised and the slate was wiped clean.

An editor of *Natural History* magazine asked me at lunch (in 1968) if I could think of an attractive premium for their subscribers for no more than 50 cents. They had been sending paperbacks but wanted something more interesting. As he was describing his gift problem a ravishing model swept into the restaurant, garbed in a wolf's coat. My guest, a dedicated naturalist, launched into an angry tirade against this visible extinction of yet another species, while revealing to me that he was a wolf freak with a collection of hundreds of wolf calls on tape in his office.

"Let's make a record of your wolf calls," I suggested, while digging into my delicious rabbit stew. "We'll have a commentary written, and I'll ask Robert Redford to narrate it." Redford, an old friend (who was originally planning to become an art director), was in the midst of shooting *Jeremiah Johnson* in the wilds of Utah. "I'm pretty sure he's doing a scene where he slaughters a pack of wolves," I said. "A record like this will help him purge his guilt." My guest was so thrilled, he almost choked on his venison.

A month later 250,000 records, "The Language and Music of the Wolves," narrated by Robert Redford, were produced and mailed, for the same 50 cents *Natural History* normally paid for a premium. Dogs in neighborhoods across America bounced off their masters' walls when they heard the calls of their ancestors, while *The New York Times'* distinguished music critic, Harold Schonberg, wrote a review of the wolves' sounds, beginning on the newspaper's front page! The rights to this "premium" were then sold to Columbia Records, with continuing income flowing to *Natural History* magazine. This big idea, on a budget of half a buck, was a howling success.

The poster, an early medium of communications in the evolution of modern advertising, will never go out of style as an opportunity to express a big idea. For the World Chess Championship series between the champion, Garry Kasparov, and his brilliant challenger, Anataly Karpov, that began at the Hudson Theater in Manhattan in October 1990, Tom Courtos and I created a poster announcing the event. The visual was a pair of silhouette profiles of Kasparov and Karpov confronting each other almost nose to nose. I did this to express the ultimate confrontation in the fierce combat of chess. Magically, in the white area between the profiles of Kasparov and Karpov on the poster, the shape of a chess piece emerged. When Kasparov saw the poster, the white chess piece between his profile and Karpov hit him like an emotional illumination, and he gasped in astonishment. "Tovarich," he said, "eet's ah vite kveen!" It's another example of my belief that ideas are there, floating around you. You have to learn how to smell 'em, see 'em, grab 'em. You don't create, you *discover.*

In 1960 a local distributor of Renaults called me frantically to help him unload dozens of cars to make way for the 1961 models. "I need a great idea for a sale—people respond to price-off deals, and I'm offering $300 off, but I gotta make it feel sexy." I told him we should do a "Scratch Sale of Wounded Renaults." I bought six cans of Johnson & Johnson Band–Aids and slapped at least three on each Renault—on scratches you could only see through a microscope. In our ad we described them as slight handling scratches that you wouldn't see if we didn't show you where.

The ad ran on a Friday. That weekend Renault's showrooms were jammed with people peeking under each Band–Aid to examine the "scratch," which was almost invisible—but when they saw they would get 100 bucks off for each Band–Aid—for as much as a $300 saving ($300 was a *huge* discount in 1960) for scratches they couldn't see, they began to grab up the Renaults, and we began to worry that some shoppers might start slapping their own Band–Aids on the Renaults. By Saturday night there wasn't a 1960 model left. Total cost of the campaign: six boxes of Band–Aids and one small two-column ad. Now that's a big idea.

Packaging, in particular, can send a spectacular message if it goes beyond design and embodies a selling idea. When Cutty Sark needed a Christmas wrap, we tied in our solution directly to our campaign, *"Don't give up the ship,"* in which the star of each ad was a blowup of the funky

Cutty Sark label, focusing on the tall sailing ship. (In the booze business, Christmas wraps are the most pretentious packages of them all, turning holiday shelves into a field of holly, wreaths, foil, ribbon and lots of green and red.) I not only blew up the label to become the Cutty Sark wrap, it was sized so that by placing four boxes side by side on a shelf or in a store window, a blazing poster of Cutty's standout yellow label was created—and it linked up directly with our advertising campaign.

This has become one of the most knocked off packaging ideas, and not just in the liquor business.

The Four Seasons restaurant became an official New York City landmark in 1990, the only Manhattan restaurant to earn this prestigious designation. One of the marvels of the intensely competitive luxury restaurant business in New York is the year-in, year-out vitality of The Four Seasons, now in its 32nd year—reflecting the imagination and receptiveness to new ideas by its owners, Tom Margittai and Paul Kovi, both emigres from their native Hungary in the aftermath of World War II, today among the most respected restaurateurs in the world. In the 1980s, as the public became increasingly sensitive to calories, cholesterol, fat and sodium, Tom Margittai asked us how to implement this timely idea.

We created the name "Spa Cuisine" to describe entrees (and appetizers) that are low in sodium, fat, and cholesterol and rich in minerals, while fully as delicious as any regular item on the restaurant's menu. We also proposed that Dr. Myron Winick of Columbia Physicians and Surgeons School of Nutrition direct Spa Cuisine's menu development. The Four Seasons' chef commuted regularly to Columbia, where recipes were created with Dr. Winick and his chief nutritionist. Spa Cuisine now accounts for a substantial share of The Four Seasons' business. And even though Spa Cuisine is a registered trademark of The Four Seasons, it has become a generic name for diet gourmet food. We have a legal right to sue anyone in the world for using our registered name, but we'd be in court five days a week.

Restaurants are a particularly fertile category for big ideas. In 1972 I made this proposal to Restaurant Associates: "Let's do a restaurant in Shubert Alley with a long, long bar opposite the theaters. We'll call the place Ma Bell's. Each table will have a 1930s telephone that works. Phone calls will be on the house. Businessmen will be able to make calls at lunch, mothers can phone their sitters at night. The floor will be tile, the furniture will be bentwood, the ceiling will have fans. We'll have a long-distance bar the length of Shubert Alley. Theatergoers will meet there before showtime, and anyone who needs a blast between acts will be able to run over for a quickie."

Ma Bell's came into being with its old-fashioned phones and its long-distance bar. Over the bar and covering its walls I hung a gallery of photo blowups of famous people on the phone making juicy remarks. (Fellow hoods beating up on a guy, with Jimmy Cagney on the phone saying, "No, this is not a gay bar . . ." . . . President Eisenhower coming out of a phone booth, saying to his chief of staff, Sherman Adams, "Shit Sherm, there's no nickel in this coin return either" . . . President Lyndon Johnson in the White House bellowing into a phone, "Now why would you call me, the leader of the Western world, to ask a chickenshit question like that?") Rarely advertised, Ma Bell's was a New York institution for more than fifteen years.

One recent client offers further proof that megabucks aren't needed to do the impossible. Chambers Development Corporation is in the landfill business—a tough way to earn a living in our environmentally sensitive society, where *landfill* has become one of the dirtiest words in the language. Chambers' president and CEO, John Rangos, has pioneered new, scientific methods for collecting garbage, hauling it away, recycling it and for creating ecologically safe landfills that go beyond the most stringent existing environmental standards. America creates 160 million tons of garbage a year, and despite the terrible connotations in the minds of most people (and all politicians) of the word *landfill,* someone has to deal with all that garbage. When Chambers came to us to get its story across, to defuse so much of the anti-landfill passions in every community in America, we saw our task as essentially a *political* campaign. We had to turn around people's attitudes by 180 degrees.

We learned that this was no ordinary landfill operation. Rangos was so environmentally conscious, we renamed his service the Chambers Eco–Landfill, accurately reflecting his company's worthy triumph of technology over trash.

We created four 15 second television commercials to run in markets where Chambers would be doing its vital work. The following message, narrated by John Rangos and accompanied by upbeat visuals of children and heartland American scenes, gives you the confident, almost idealistic style of our approach: *"America the beautiful creates 160 million tons of garbage each year! Cleaning it up is a dirty job, but somebody's got to protect our children's future. With recycling and the ecologically safe Chambers eco-landfills! At Chambers we do it right."*

By stressing "our children's future" and by replacing *landfill* with the phrases "ecologically safe" and "eco-landfills," we were able to gain public acceptance of a vital service that would otherwise frighten and enrage people. Through vivid visual and verbal imagery, we're tackling an explosive public attitude—people have actually taken to guns to stop landfilling—and are converting these intense feelings into enlightened acceptance by the public and by their nervous politicians. We're saying America must have landfills and Chambers does it right.

Chambers Eco-Landfills are among several clients for whom I've worked over the years that give me great pride in our profession. I've been able to work on cutting-edge products that somehow enrich or enhance or excite. I can look back with deep pride on my work for Xerox, which revolutionized duplicating technology and created the "Xerox culture" . . . on MTV, which revolutionized pop culture throughout the world . . . on *USA TODAY,* which has ushered in a new kind of journalism for the TV generation (that will be almost everybody in a few years) . . . on Lean Cuisine, which mass-marketed frozen gourmet diet meals and launched a new lifestyle of eating fast and eating healthily . . . on Jiffy Lube, a new concept in car care that ushered in a new, swift service, and is becoming a major industry throughout the world.

It's great to be on the cutting edge.

Advertising, a calling that I love, makes that possible.

Gala
Fundraising Roast for
Mayor Edward I. Koch

Roast:
Hon. Walter F. Mondale
Hon. William H. Mulligan

Rebuttal:
Ed Koch

Finance Committee
Chairman

Peter J. Solomon

Dinner Co-Chairs

Sol C. Chaikin
William M. Ellingham
Harold L. Fisher
Bess Myerson
Vitto J. Pitta
John Torres
Lloyd A. Williams

Tuesday
September 15
Sheraton Centre

Cocktails at 7:00 pm
Dinner at 8:00 pm

Dinner Co-ordinator

Ellin Delsener

New Yorkers for Koch '81
Matthew Nimetz, Treasurer

This committee was formed under the New York State
Election Law and files reports with the NYC Board
of Elections in compliance with the law. Individuals
may contribute up to $50,000 per election to a mayoral
campaign committee, subject to an overall limitation
of $150,000 in contributions to all candidates in New York
in a calendar year. A corporation may contribute up to
$5,000 a calendar year to all campaigns in the state.

Coda

11

The
Blood, Sweat, Tears—
and Joys—
of Advertising

If you don't work loosey-goosey,
you're a dead duck

Working hard demands that you laugh a lot or you turn into a drone and your work shows it. Advertising is a creative business, but to be creative, the vital juices must flow unimpeded. I like the phrase *loosey-goosey* to describe the kind of ambience so essential to me as I go about my work with gusto and pleasure. I like to have people around me who smile a lot and laugh at will and are smart enough to get my puns.

Working under pressure is another reason why having fun is not a luxury but a necessity. There is little logic to the way projects bombard you in the advertising business throughout the year. In the fall, most clients start thinking about the coming year and want to see something new, if only to feel they are on their toes. In the spring, clients want work created for the fall season. In the summer, campaigns are needed for the holidays. When Christmas approaches, all retail clients must have your total involvement. And there are always new products, grand openings, sales meetings, and pep talks to clients' sales staffs, special events, competitive skirmishes—all of which make it impossible to expect that work will be equally distributed over twelve months. The mayhem is continuous. In the advertising world, every month is the *only* month of the year, but I love that heat and pressure and intensity. At the end of each day I'm burned out—and I love that feeling of utter depletion; it is an ecstatic sense of having committed my talents to their absolute limit. I've always felt that at the end of each day, you should be totally burned out. I'm always infuriated when, for example, I go to New York Knicks basketball games where I'm forced to hear the shouting at the players from the well-dressed business stiffs in the corporate seats behind me. They want the players to kill themselves going for the ball. They hurl the worst obscenities at any jock for not giving 100%. But looking at these well-groomed, well-rested blowhards, you *know* that they spend more energy trying to avoid work than in giving 100% of themselves!

People watching me work ask me all the time why I'm not burned out, how I manage to keep going. The fact is, I'm totally burned out at the end of every day, because I've given myself totally to my work—mentally, psychologically, physically. When I head home at night I can't see straight. But with a little rest at night, I'm ready to start again the next morning—I'm ready to kill again. Isn't that what life is all about? If you're not burned out totally at the end of the day you've been holding back, you haven't committed yourself fully to your work—you're a bum! But to work each day on twelve cylinders makes it essential that the lubricant of *fun* always flows freely.

If creative work is your calling, beware of those button-down, low-voiced mausoleums that call themselves advertising agencies. Look for laughter and beards and jeans and Reeboks. Look for people who look happy and enthusiastic, but have a slightly crazed look in their eyes. Look for messengers who like their work and traffic people who come in early and leave late. Look for account people who dress well without looking like undertakers. Look for guys telling good jokes, preferably dirty. Look for women on the staff who stand up to the boss. And look for a boss who is always on the go, who is totally involved in creating great advertising, and who is probably a grouch (but can take a joke) because he has no time for bullshit unless it's very, very funny.

Fun in advertising is more than a corollary to work, more than an ameliorating force that transforms the furies of each day into productive actions. Fun in advertising is the fun of living, and should permeate and shape every aspect of working creatively with others. In so many ways, the love of life, the sublime joy of living and working, *must* intrude in the advertising life.

The sole of Walter Gropius.

A column I had written for *Adweek* in which I mentioned that the great Mies van der Rohe was the author of the classic phrase "less is more," drew an angry response from readers who insisted that the author was Walter Gropius. There had been some controversy over that priceless wisdom for a very long time, and at least fifteen years before I wrote that *Adweek* column, I had decided to go to the great Gropius himself. Walter Gropius, originator and director of the Bauhaus, was one of my heroes since I was in public school. I invited him to lunch at The Four Seasons, and to my eternal joy, he accepted. He knew of my work as the designer of the logos for the eateries in the Pan Am Building—and by that time he also knew of my reputation as an adman and art collector. At lunch the formidable Gropius glowered at me from under his dense eyebrows as he filled his mouth with a large portion of the Dover sole he was obviously relishing. *"Accch,"* he almost sputtered, "again zat question. So I will tell you. It vas Mies . . . yes, Mies, not me."

He went back to his sole, chewing a succulent chunk with unabashed pleasure. Suddenly he raised his eyebrows, set down his wineglass, leaned toward me, and said with a sweet twinkle, "But I tell you this, young man: more *tastes* better!"

Make sure you know the person you're rubbing knees with.

Unlike other careers, the advertising life offers everyone an opportunity to be seen and recognized for talent, style and brains—up to a point, because unless you make yourself known, you may lose your identity. That lesson was driven home to me in Rochester, New York, in 1961 when my agency was pitching Xerox (then known by its original name, Haloid–Xerox). We waited in the anteroom, cooling our young heels, knowing that a big-time marketing agency was inside, giving its pitch. Finally the conference room door swung open and a long gray line of admen paraded out, led by the famous Marion Harper, chairman and chief factotem of the Interpublic agency complex. We watched in awe, almost paralyzed by the presence of this tall, slim, suave agency impresario. Then we pulled ourselves together and waded in. As we described the credentials and philosophy of our young creative agency, we noticed that the staff of this prospective account, including the head man, Joe Wilson, was stifling laughter. While we were taken aback, we stuck to our guns and to our script—but soon the dam burst as a wave of guffaws swept the room. I looked around to see if one (or more) of our guys had his fly open. Wilson then apologized to us and took time out to explain what was going on:

He told us that Marion Harper had pounded away for an hour, reassuring this fledgling company that although McCann–Erickson was part of Interpublic, the biggest agency complex in the world, Haloid–Xerox would receive individual attention from him and his agency. Harper concentrated his drumfire on a young man at his immediate right. To underscore the intimate, familial attitude of his mega-agency ("Sure, we're big—in fact, we're the biggest—but we're also the most *involved . . .*"), he dwelled with pride on his personal closeness to his staff, reassuring his prospective new client that he worked shoulder-to-shoulder with every man and woman at his agency. He knew every employee at McCann, hundreds and hundreds of them—like the back of his hand, he insisted. On that intensely personal note, Marion Harper concluded his impressive presentation. All in his entourage then stood up and shook hands with the management group of Haloid–Xerox. Turning again to the young man on whom he had focused special attention throughout his persuasive spiel, Harper said, "And thank *you* so much for your hospitality." The young man blushed ever so slightly as he said, "Gee, Mr. Harper, my name is Joe Doakes. I'm an account executive at your agency."

In one of my columns for *Adweek* (September 15, 1980), I made this simple comment: "The ugliest woman I ever met in advertising was Marion Harper." *Adweek* received many letters from irate females.[1]

How to make sure the person you hire isn't a schmuck.

Hiring a new employee is always a risky experience. There's always the chance you'll be suckered by someone who interviews well. A bum is then added to your staff and you end up cursing under your breath for

---

[1] My editor pleaded with me to delete this remark because it might offend many female readers. I refused because Marion Harper *was* the ugliest woman I ever met in advertising.

months, even years, hoping the deadbeat will decide to leave. Not surprisingly, agency owners are always looking for a magic screening method that will detect talent and/or trouble in prospective employees. After years of searching for the perfect formula, I'm convinced the only way is to let the prospective staffer talk himself into or out of the job. When we meet, I just listen, saying very little. I let him do all the talking, and sooner or later he'll tell you everything you have to know (especially if he's a bum). I listen to his small talk, to his comments on love and marriage, to his large views on life, to his opinions on sports, politics, movies, television, literature, sex. I listen to see if he speaks English. I look for his sense of history. I watch his eyes, searching for traces of passion. This method works for me because assholes send signals.

You can also get a fix on the candidate by fitting him into one of these four categories of officers from the German Officers Manual of World War I:

1. **Very bright and industrious. (The dream officer.)**
2. **Very bright and lazy. (A damn shame, but no harm done.)**
3. **Stupid and lazy. (Won't do a thing, so it's a wash.)**
4. **Stupid and industrious. (Very dangerous.)**

Almost all agencies have an abundance of Category 2 types, a costly situation—causes a bloated payroll in relation to agency income. Category 3 types are hopeless—but easy to spot at a first interview. Category 4 types, treacherous people, have positions of authority at too many agencies. Being a Category 1 type, I always look for Category 1 types.

There's yet another way to evaluate job candidates: my partner Bill Pitts, an amateur graphologist, checks their handwriting. He once hired an account executive solely on the basis of his loops and crossed t's. After the kid was on our payroll, I took him to lunch and let him talk. Alarm bells went off as I beheld a classic Category 4 type: stupid/industrious. He turned out to be the disaster I had foreseen, but Bill, squirming, offered this limp explanation: he said it's not uncommon in judging handwriting to make a 180 degree mistake—which means a saint and a murderer can have the same scrawl. Fortunately, the account man quit before Bill fired him. He took a promising job on the client side and did well there, then went on to a better job at a package goods shop, and performed even more impressively there. Now he's a big man at one of New York's major marketing shops. He's still a schmuck.

How to dress on Madison Avenue.

In the early sixties, as my new agency, Papert Koenig Lois (PKL), was dazzling the advertising world with its innovative work, I had encouraged a deliberately relaxed atmosphere, hiring people who were creative, then giving them room to do what they wanted. Out of this remarkable universe, individual personalities flowered, a parallel blooming alongside the vivid advertising they created. One of our talented copywriters, Milt Trazenfeld, was a thrift shop addict. Always elegantly dressed, Trazenfeld never shelled out more than $2.50 for a suit *(circa* 1963), but for a tie he would go as high as $20. One morning he grabbed a fellow copywriter (and my partner-to-be), Ron Holland, and said, "Drop what you're doing and come with me—I'll explain later." Trazenfeld hailed a cab to LaGuardia and ran with Ron through the terminal onto a shuttle flight to Boston.

"This is the day for values," he explained on the plane. "It's the end of final exam week. All the students at Harvard and M.I.T. are trading in their wardrobes for cash to survive through summer." When the plane landed at Logan Airport, Trazenfeld shoved Holland into a cab and barked at the driver, "The thrift shop in Cambridge, *and step on it!"* He found a suit for $2 that was traded in by a Cabot. Back in Manhattan he bought an $18 tie. When he returned to the agency, Trazenfeld exchanged notes on tailoring with Monte Ghertler, one of the more cultured personalities on writers' row:

"The silhouette of your trousers is classic, Milt," said Ghertler. "Where did you purchase that remarkable wardrobe?"

"Only in those thrift shops, Monte, that most closely approximate the standards of Savile Row."

"Gentleman's Resale?"

"Thrift Shop off Harvard Yard. This suit cost two dollars."

"A reasonable value. The tailoring is brilliant."

"You do understand, Monte, the correct way to style trousers? At the waist, snug, yet ample. Lines descend to the knees in perfect parallels. Slight kick outward at the knees. Then a tapering toward the ankle, ever so minutely."

"Ah, yes," said Ghertler, "a good deal like the Parthenon."

(At work I wear torn T-shirts and Reeboks—Ralph Tuzzo, a superb art director, wears a surgeon's gown! However, when I go to The Four Seasons I become a vision of sartorial grace in my custom-made

Eyetalian suit. My clients understand my working nonstyle so well that when I show up in their offices in my first-class splendor, they get slightly pissed, assuming I'm putting on airs. They much prefer my longshoreman persona, which jibes so naturally with my Noo Yawk street elegance.)

But never judge a client—or a messenger—by his clothes.

Ever since he joined my agency years ago, I've always bragged about our messenger Jimmy Avalyiotis, often referred to as our "Greek in shipping." In addition to his professionalism in running our mailroom and in seeing to it that every letter and package reaches its destination promptly, Jimmy is one of the best dressed personalities in the advertising business and is known to spend two complete paychecks for a suit.

One day Jimmy was sent to the offices of our client, Jack Dreyfus of the Dreyfus Medical Foundation on Fifth Avenue in the upper fifties, a few blocks from our agency, to pick up a check. Jack Dreyfus, a probable billionaire, originally the founder of The Dreyfus Corporation and now involved in medical research, was a totally informal guy (and probably the fastest payer who ever lived). He wore loafers, golfer's slacks, and a polo shirt, and sported a two-day growth of gray stubble. When Jimmy the dude arrived, Jack Dreyfus greeted him warmly, addressing him as "James," and handed him the check, in payment for a media bill that we had sent to Jack by telefax a few minutes before. Jimmy thanked Jack Dreyfus, tucked the envelope into a pocket of his elegant double-breasted, chalk-striped suit, and headed for the door. "Oh, James," Dreyfus called after him, "can I give you a ride? I'm going downtown." Jimmy was flattered and accepted the offer.

When they got downstairs, Jack Dreyfus' deep green, four-door Bentley, with chauffeur, awaited them on Fifth Avenue. Jack guided Jimmy into the back seat, then slid onto the front seat alongside his chauffeur. Four minutes later the Bentley pulled up in front of our offices on 52nd Street, as I was walking out of our building, heading for lunch with another client. Jack Dreyfus, needing a shave and dressed like a golf bum, got out of the front seat and opened the rear door for his passenger. Jimmy Avalyiotis stepped out smartly, a vision of double-breasted splendour. "Hi George," he waved to me—and went into the building as Jack Dreyfus closed the Bentley door behind him. An extremely self-effacing man, Dreyfus nodded to me almost self-consciously, slid back onto the front seat, and drove off with his chauffeur.

"Who was *that?*" asked my client, still staring after fashionplate Jimmy, as he stepped briskly into an elevator.

"That was our messenger," I said. "And the guy in the front seat of the Bentley, the one who needed a shave, is a billionaire."

"Ahh, George," said my client, "you're full of shit—as usual."

Sex during working hours is healthy, but should not conflict with equally serious agency pursuits.

During the halcyon years of Papert Koenig Lois, the only ad agency in the world that gave athletic scholarships, ballplaying was serious business. PKL produced the best basketball team in the advertising world, but we lost by one point to the Bank League champs, led by basketball Hall of Famer Dick McGuire. We were thrown off balance in the final championship game by a true story in the locker room from a PKL account man on our team who had been schtupping a voluptuous movie star. (We did a lot of traveling to the coast, where New York advertising guys mixed easily with Hollywood's beautiful people, especially beautiful women.) The lady was so wild for this account man, whenever she came to town she called him from her hotel for a Manhattan matinee. As we were dressing for our big game with the Bank League champs, he told us that she had called him an hour before. That put him in a spot; he had to choose between performance on the court or in the sack—and she was checking out of her hotel in a few hours for a flight to Paris. Time was short and he decided he couldn't have it both ways. He told her he had an urgent appointment that could not be changed.

"Are you stuck with a client?" she asked.

"Well, no," he blurted, "I gotta play basketball."

She gasped in disbelief. Fearing she might think he was ending their delicious affair, he decided to tell her the whole truth. "Listen, sweetheart," he explained, "you gotta believe me. We have this team at the agency and we're the Advertising League champs. In an hour we have to play the *Bank* League champs because the winner gets to play the *Industrial* League champs."

"Let me get this straight," she said. "You're gonna pass up fucking *me* to play with some *boys?*"

If he hadn't told us that story we would definitely *not* have blown a nine-point lead in the last two minutes of the game.

Don't expect thanks for a big idea—
especially when a client believes it was his inspiration.

In 1964 I nagged Joe Baum, the Little Caesar of the restaurant business, to take over a fading restaurant in Rockefeller Center called Holland House, where six old ladies ate salad every day at lunch. Baum did nothing, but for two years he kept telling me it was a lousy location. Holland House was a block from the popular skating rink, and I was convinced it would make a great Irish bar that would pack 'em in. "Lois," Baum kept insisting, "you do great advertising, but you don't know a damn thing about the restaurant business. It's a *lousy* location."

Finally—to get me off his back—Baum took over the location and in two months flat we opened Charley O's Bar & Grill & Bar. From the moment we opened, the place was a smash. I even persuaded Bobby Kennedy to announce at this new watering hole that he would run for the Senate. The news reports gave the impression that "famous Charley O's" had been around for forty years!

A little while later I found myself fishing for a compliment from my client. "Charley O's is doing great, ain't it, Joe?" I said to Baum.

"Of course, George," he said. "It's a *great* location."

Always write down great quotes by great people.

A few weeks before Joe Baum opened Charley O's Bar & Grill & Bar, I was assembling photos with quotes for the new restaurant's walls. Our worshipful bon mots about booze, food, and the good life included these gems:

> *"I only drink to make other people interesting."*
> *—George Jean Nathan*

> *"Any man who has more than ten grand in the bank*
> *when he dies is a failure."*
> *—Errol Flynn*

> *"A gourmet who thinks of calories*
> *is like a tart who looks at her watch."*
> *—James Beard*

Additional pungent quotes were needed to cover a few bare spots on the restaurant's wall. One evening I spotted the playwright Marc Connally at The Four Seasons and worked up the nerve to ask the famous author of *Green Pastures* if he had ever said anything on the good life he would like to have quoted.

"I don't think so," he said, "However . . . this might be interesting: when a restaurant served me a particularly abominable wine, I told the sommelier: *'Break the bottle . . . smash the barrel . . . and uproot the vineyard!'* "That quote, with a photo of Marc Connally, is still on the wall at Charley O's.

That unforgettable quote was on my mind when I later visited the country estate in France of Baron Philippe de Rothschild with a group from my agency, where the baron served us a jeroboam of a great Mouton Rothschild. No smashing barrels or uprooting vineyards would ever occur in this wine-lover's heaven. The wine from that jeroboam defied any words that could be mustered—but I would try! A mere bottle of that year's vintage (1895) had just fetched $5,000 (in 1973) at New York's Sotheby Parke Bernet. As the baron beamed with pleasure at our enjoying a $20,000 bottle of wine, I leaned over and asked, "Baron, would you please pour me another $300 worth." (One of my fellow admen once tried to impress Rothschild, telling him of the purchase of "a '37." The baron looked down his substantial nose and observed with a bored expression, "Oh, a 19 or an 18?")

Humor and health: they must go together.

One of my closest colleagues suffered a heart attack. He was taken to the emergency ward of his suburban hospital, where they stabilized his condition and sent him for an angiogram to see the extent of his coronary damage. I was concerned about the possibility of bypass surgery (a less ominous-sounding procedure than "open heart surgery," but open heart surgery is what a bypass is all about).

I was traveling out west while he was having his angiogram and I told him to expect my call sometime over the weekend to find out how he was doing and whether or not he would need the bypass. I was en route to New York from Las Vegas, where I had been a guest of my client Seth Abraham of HBO Sports at the heavyweight doubleheader, the Tyson/Tillman fight that lasted slightly less than three minutes and the Foreman/Rodrigues fight that lasted a little less than six minutes. Flying to Las Vegas from New York to watch nine minutes of palooka bashing was a long way to go, and I was eager to get back to my beloved New

York, especially to be with my new grandson, Georgie. In Colorado, I had a two-hour layover and called my colleague from the airport.

"Well, George," he said in a resigned voice, "two of my main coronary arteries are 90% clogged with plaque. It's all that wonderful high-cholesterol food I've been eating with you for so many years. So I need bypass surgery, and it's scheduled for a week from Monday."

He sounded down, an understandable reaction to having one's chest opened and heart rearranged. I had to say something to cheer him up without sounding schmaltzy.

"Listen," I said with authority. "You think *you* got problems? It's Sunday and I'm in *Denver.*"

An important lesson for all.

Joe Baum was greeted ceremoniously by the director of The Four Seasons when we arrived there one day for lunch. Baum asked him peremptorily, with his usual growl as he flicked an enormous ash from an oversized Macanudo cigar onto the carpet, "What was wrong with the consommé today?"

"Well, Mr. Baum," said the director, "we had some difficulty with the vavava so we added some jajaja—and now it's just right."

"*Aha,*" said Baum.

As we strolled down Picasso Alley[2] toward the restaurant's pool room for dinner, I asked him, "Joe, how did you know? That was fantastic. You're a *genius.* How did you know they had trouble with the consommé?"

"Lois," he said, placing his hand on my shoulder, "let me teach you something about life I don't ever want you to forget: There's *always* something wrong with the consommé."

---

[2] The stately corridor that leads to the restaurant's famous Pool Room, named for its breathtaking centerpiece, the world's largest Picasso, a stage curtain that measures 20 by 22 feet. It was created by Picasso in 1919 for the Diaghilev and Massine ballet *Le Tricorne.*

A Communicator's Credo

The big idea will always be what great advertising is all about

85% of all advertising is invisible.

This wasted work may not be all bad, but it's not good enough to win your attention. Much of it could be thoughtful and well "positioned." A lot of it may even be visually appealing. But none of it is good enough to stop you in your tracks.

14% of all advertising is terrible—ugly, stupid, patronizing, demeaning. Paradoxically, that's better than being invisible; at least it might get your attention.

The remaining 1% is terrific advertising.

These percentages are the seasoned speculations of creative mavericks like me whose entire careers have been in pursuit of the magical

1%, who understand that we go about our lonely work on a rising sea of dreadful advertising.

There are many reasons for this dearth of brilliance and talent. Advertising, an art, is constantly besieged and compromised by logicians and technocrats, the scientists of our profession who wildly miss the main point about everything we do, that the product of advertising, after all, is *advertising*. Not a marketing study or a media analysis or a research report, vital as these may be—but all of zero value if what appears on the television screen is so bad it causes people to go for a beer or switch to another channel. Advertising is what you see on the television screen, period.

I'm always struck by the colossal naivete of those announcements that are reported every few years in *The New York Times* advertising column on momentous changes under way at some of our major agencies—like Young & Rubicam or Ogilvy & Mather—where major shifts of direction with a new focus on being more *creative* are revealed as big news. They are admitting that their advertising hasn't been so hot and therefore "an improved creative product" must be made the new focus of their efforts and resources. These giant shops are telling us that despite their formidable size and sophisticated technology, they must return to what advertising is all about: *advertising*.

Despite these periodic illuminations, creating great advertising in most big "marketing agencies" continues to be a lesser priority than getting more billings. The industry constantly fails to understand that its first priority should be to create big ideas for its clients—big creative ideas with extraordinary power to attract customers and build sales, so that one plus one can equal three. (Often we will be attracted by a single commercial, a "nice" spot. Every once in a while a new young agency does a "nice" spot and is hailed as the brilliant new innovator of our business—but one swallow does not make a spring and one commercial does not make a campaign that is based on a big idea.)

Often, when I read in the ad columns about new "campaigns" being unveiled, I look in vain for the big idea, for that one theme or slogan that says it all, that can be played back by the average consumer after one viewing. If you can't describe the big idea in one sentence or in three or four words, you don't have a big idea. But what can you expect when so much energy by so many intelligent people in our business is devoted to issues that have absolutely nothing to do with advertising itself, but are concerned first and foremost with *growth*.

The only thing that gets better when it gets bigger is a penis, but the ad agency world has been invaded and almost swallowed up by the British and the French, with an obsessive primary commitment to the bottom line and to exercise rigid control over their acquirees. Big agencies are thus getting bigger and agency conglomerates have become a sinister force in the industry. Takeovers, overall, have had a corrupting impact on the quality of advertising. Talent has been squeezed out and agency managers pay less attention to advertising than to organizational acrobatics. (In explaining his agency's loss of an estimated $120 million in billings, Scali, McCabe, Sloves chairman Marvin Sloves told *The New York Times* [November 14, 1990] his agency's troubles had resulted in part from having been "distracted" the last several years with negotiations to buy the agency back from its parent, Ogilvy & Mather.)

In an earlier chapter I said, "You gotta have a *slogan* . . . the *word* comes first, then the visual image." This may sound like an inversion, coming from an art director, but the best art directors communicate with a big idea, expressed in a few words, wed to powerful graphics. *"I want my MTV!"* is a big idea because it blends a powerful slogan with an image of physical action, an image of a young person demanding this new cable television concept. By contrast, there's a cosmetic commercial that runs now and then which shows an airplane casting a shadow over a glitzy pool. This is a graphic pirouette, not a big idea. Yet year in, year out, advertising pundits misread graphic tricks as significant trends. Every year these new techniques are trotted out by media reporters as the wave of the future—quick cuts à la MTV . . . computer graphics . . . cinema verité (see page 231) . . . black and white with color accents . . . bigger stars doing testimonials . . . big-name directors to shoot commercials . . . the return of animation. You get the idea. (There's also a new theory that a commercial or an ad should not be seen or experienced as a commercial or an ad. Wrong—a great commercial or a great print advertisement signals you that, yes, this *is* a commercial message, that an attempt *will* be made to sell you, but by charming your ass off, not by pounding on your head with a hammer. Americans enjoy being sold products and they fully understand that the act of selling is being done through the popular art form of advertising. In answering research questions, many people will insist that they *hate* advertising—but trust me, they eat it up with a spoon!)

Quick cuts and animation and computer graphics are *techniques,* and ephemeral techniques, at best. None of these devices is an *idea.*

Some might attract attention temporarily, but nothing will be communicated. Nobody ever bought a new car because of quick cuts and nobody will ever buy a six-pack of beer because of animation. A great verbal idea can survive even terrible graphics, but a lousy idea has no intrinsic strength and will go nowhere with the most famous celebrity or with Hollywood's hottest director.

The big idea is what great advertising is all about.

The big idea can change popular culture.

The big idea can transform our language.

The big idea can start a business—or save a business.

The big idea can turn the world upside down.

The big idea is what this book is all about.

Who really knows how far the big idea can go? If you believe in its power, the big idea can even save the world.

Despite the curse of bigness and the blight of acquisition for bottom line's sake, people who dream impossible dreams and think big ideas will always surface. They are like dandelions, defiant of weather and soil, always blooming toward the sunlight. It's immensely encouraging to see young, new agencies spring up. Unknown today, they will be much more important to our industry and to communications ten years from now than the European behemoths who are swallowing up and ruining agencies that once were wonderfully inventive and original.

Where you work also affects *how* you work. If it's possible, find the right ambience where people want and respect great work. If you have writing talent or graphic talent or both, always try to do work that makes you proud. If it's possible, find an agency where your talents will be encouraged rather than smothered by Pecksniffian business managers. Such agencies are always surfacing. Search hard.

I believe deeply that we have to create our own opportunities to do great work. I've done it by trying to control everything I've done, all my life. I have the power to decide my ambience—from the way coffee is brewed in the morning (always use a cinnamon stick), to the way our conference room is prepared for a client presentation the next day. It's not easy to balance the needs of an organization while preserving the kind of environment so precious to me—and while staying unswervingly loyal to those creative standards that have made our work memorable.

I regard this as a natural extension of the personal values and experiences that have shaped my life since childhood: the striving for achievement that I learned from my immigrant parents, the love and loyalty from my wife of forty years, the anguish of losing my first son at an early age, the joys of watching my younger son succeed as a photographer, the deep pleasure of seeing my new grandson grow before my very eyes, while hoping to leave behind for him that same legacy of values that has shaped my life. Yes, there has been a pattern to my years —a pattern of tenacious determination to make life purposeful and to direct its unfolding as creatively as one possibly can.

And for me, advertising has always been a glorious pursuit, as well as a tough business. Dealing effectively with clients summons up every talent at your fingertips. Dealing with your own staff may be even more complicated as you try to negotiate among strong individual egos to extract brilliant work in a shared, partnership-style ambience. But it's the only way I want to work.

When asked to define the problems of creativity in American advertising, some sensitive ad people say that young people entering the business are afraid to take chances, that they're as conservative as big agency bureaucrats. But that's the story of mankind. We live in fear of life, in fear of work, in fear of death. On a professional level, our kids are instructed to assemble a "professional" portfolio rather than one that explodes with imagination and inventiveness. Some of our best creative professionals protest loudly that they want young people to take chances, but when they see a portfolio that's somewhat off the wall, they say the kid lacks discipline or that he's a flake. Alas, our young people receive no clear signals from their elders, no brave direction. Perhaps this book will fill in some of the gaps.

I spent my entire life listening to people say, "George, be careful," but being careful in our business is synonymous with doing invisible advertising. "George, be reckless" has served me better. I can never say it too often: We are being paid by our corporate patrons to excite and arouse, not to sedate America.

I hope my adventures (and misadventures) will at least enable the reader, in or out of the business, to understand advertising more acutely —and to realize that the big idea, rich in human expressiveness, will *always* be what advertising is all about. The big idea inspires unforgettable *imagery*—the magical force of advertising that enables me to communicate with power. My continuing obsession will always be to create vivid human images that catch people's eyes, penetrate their minds, warm their hearts and cause them to act.

Index

Whitney, Jock, 96, 136–37
"Who says a good newspaper has to be dull?" ad campaign, 96
Wilkins, Dominique, 189
Wilson, Joe, 64, 262
Winick, Myron, 254
Wolf calls, recording of, 252
Wolfschmidt vodka, 48–49, 208
Women
  gender stereotypes and, 197–98, 209–11
  as targets of advertising, 60

Women's Wear Daily, 27, 115
World Chess Championship, 252–53
World Financial Center, 18–22, 36
WQXR-Radio, 147
Wright, Steven, 204

Xerox, 64–66, 134

Young & Rubicam agency, 172
"You're the king of the Castle" ad campaign, 174–75